# Exegetical Reflections on Galatians:
## A Text-Linguistic Analysis of the Greek Text

# Table of Contents

Preface
4

Galatians 1:1-5
8

Galatians 1.6-12
13

Galatians 1.13-2.2a
26

Galatians 2.2-10
42

Galatians 2.11-14
61

Galatians 2.15-21
67

Galatians 3.1-5
86

Galatians 3.6-9
100

Galatians 3.10-14
108

Galatians 3.15-18
122

Galatians 3.19-22
131

Galatians 3.23-29
145

Galatians 4.1-7
162

Galatians 4.8-11
177

Galatians 4.12-20
187

Galatians 4.21-31
199

Galatians 5.2-6
215

Galatians 5.7-12
229

Galatians 5.13-15
240

Galatians 5.16-26
246

Galatians 6.1-5
283

Galatians 6.6-10
292

Galatians 6.11-16
303

Bibliography
312

# Preface

The book you hold in your hands was not originally written for public consumption. It contains a rather unedited version of my personal study notes as I read reflectively through the Greek text of Galatians. (This is why you may find me making some conflicting statements at times. These notes are me working through the text and wrestling with the issues presented.) Because of that, be aware that I have not approached this material in any academic fashion. It is not a thoroughly footnoted document. I have included a bibliography at the end listing the tools I referenced. In many cases, those tools are credited within the body of the text. I decided to publish this material because I felt like it may provide a helpful supplement to the Christian life book I wrote about the major themes of Paul's epistle to the Galatians, *The Enchanting Gospel*. In that book, I did not think it was effective to give a detailed textual analysis at every turn. Instead, I attempted to make as little "textual commentary" as possible while still attempting to get the point across. After removing around 150k words from the original form of that book, I wondered if I had gone too far. What was I to do? I felt like it wouldn't be palatable to make that book any longer than it was, but I also wanted to provide some answers to the questions some of the interpretations I stated may have induced. And that's why I decided to provide the material in this study.

My approach to writing this commentary—if it can be called that—is my approach to studying a book of the Bible. Based on my training under John Sailhamer I approach Scripture from a "text-imminent" foundation. That means I am mainly concerned with the words of the text and not trying to deduce the historical situation that precipitated the occasion of the epistle. You can read about his hermeneutical philosophy in his work, *Introduction to Old Testament Theology: A Canonical Approach*. This hermeneutic leads to a "text-linguistic" (some might say structural) analysis of the given text. For me, that means I am chiefly concerned with the text as written in the original language. It also means that the structure of the text (the text grammar) helps define the meaning, the semantic landscape and the interpretive context above and beyond the historical situation. You will notice that I often refer to parallelisms, in-textual links, seams and other similar structural concepts. This emphasis reveals a belief that the meaning of the text is found *within* the text. Or to say it more simply, the author of the text will tell us what the text means.

I, no doubt, did not do a perfect job at sticking to this approach, but it does serve as my foundational hermeneutic. One area where I stretch these boundaries relates to lexicography, the study of the meaning of words. A text is made of words (text-signs). Those words have understood range of meanings in the mind of the intended audience, a native (or fluent) speaker in the language in which the letter was written. The semantic range (range of possible meanings) of a word includes mental concepts from the world of the audience. These words with their semantic ranges are a part of the text. Additionally, the text-grammar itself determines the semantic context and limitations of the words (and all the other parts of the text). The text-signs (including all the morphemes, words, phrases, clauses, etc.) in a text often contain a level of ambiguity. The structure of the text helps us limit the options included in that ambiguity down to the author's intended meaning.

As for me, as I read the Greek text, I like to build a list of all possible meanings for a lexeme. I start with the Greek Lexicon BDAG (*A Greek-English Lexicon of the New Testament and Other Early Christian Literature* by Walter Bauer, Frederick William Danker (revised and edited by Frederick William Danker.). I list all the possible glosses noting the option BDAG suggests for the particular verse. Next, I consult the *Louw-Nida Lexicon* filling in any gaps of understanding. I follow up this process by referring to Spicq's Greek Lexicon and then the *New International Dictionary of New Testament Theology and Exegesis*. After I have a good solid range of meaning based on these lexicons I look at all the uses of the root word in the Bible. I start with other examples from the same author noting how he may uniquely use the term *and* how he might build a biblical theology around the ideas related to the term. Next, I expand to the "Testament" wherein a term is used and then finally I look to other language resources, mainly the Septuagint (LXX) for Greek terms. I include this description here because I don't always articulate these details in the actual exegetical material below.

To understand the structure of the particular pericope I am working with at the moment, I then create a clausal analysis of the text. This allows me to note any "in-textual" structural organization. Next, I note where similar lexemes occur elsewhere in the book (similar lexemes, roots, synonyms, etc.). This helps me begin to build a text theory, an idea about the arrangement of the pieces of text that make up the whole. This text theory allows me to begin to understand the peak moments of the book and allow those peak moments to drive the notion of "context." (We hear a lot about the importance of context on the topic of accurate Bible study; it's the discovery of these semantic "peaks" that should most deeply influence our sense of the context of a given piece of literature, much more than simply the verses that immediately precede or follow a clause or other inductive elements like word-count.)

I also find it helpful to read the text in as many translations as I can and do so in one sitting. When I read a text in Greek or Hebrew I read rather slowly, sometimes this stage has to be spread out over a few days, but the more a reader can hold the global strategy of the book in their mind as they work through the parts the better one can see the structure.

My next stage of study is to turn to other resources. I like to hold off on hearing from other teachers as long as I can so that I can approach the text at face value, but I also know that other scholars can help me see elements in the text that I may have missed. So next I turn to Greek or Hebrew Grammars, as many critical commentaries as I can get my hands on, monographs and journals that address any theological or exegetical issues in the text and the plethora of translations available to the modern reader. I compile notes on every piece of research I find.

Finally, I write down comments on each verse, phrase by phrase. My general approach is to scribe all the possible ways a text can be read (all the linguistic choices available to the author) and then consider structural elements like those described above to help me determine what choice(s) the original author intended to convey in the text at hand. This process often leads to my attempt at a final wooden reading of the text using the theoretical meaning the author intended and then, after that, a paraphrastic and "filled-out" translation to help convey the nuances that a fluent reader would have likely picked up, consciously or subconsciously.

This latter stage is where the translations come from that begin each paragraph below. It may be helpful to remember that no translation is a perfect reflection of the original text and that all translations are interpretations and paraphrases even when they attempt to be as "word for word" as possible. But, let me be clear, my translations are not intended to be word for word. They are completely and transparently paraphrased interpretations. For that reason, you can consider them as much of a commentary on the original text as a "translation." The material that follows these paraphrases is typically the textual analysis that led to the translation itself.

This process created the study notes before you. I hope you find them helpful as you dig deeper into Paul's epistle to the Galatians. Because these notes weren't originally intended for public consumption they may often feel a little extemporaneous and no doubt I've missed some typos and other errors in preparing the material. I hope any such issues don't prevent anyone from engaging with my thoughts below. And that's what they are- my running thoughts, an internal dialogue (and sometimes debate) between me, myself and, in the best cases, the Spirit, some of which still remains unsettled in my own mind.

All Biblical quotations are, when in English, from the ESV and when in Greek from the 28th Edition of the Nestle-Aland Greek text as provided through Accordance Bible Software. See the Bibliography at the end for a list of other references used.

# Galatians 1:1-5

**Interpretive Translation:**

From: Paul, a super-delegate[1] not sent representing the authority of human beings but with the authority of Jesus Christ and God the Father who raised Him from among the dead, together with all the Christian family[2] that is with me.

To: the multitude of gatherings in[3] Galatia.

I want you to experience unmerited favor and a supernatural, internal calmness and confidence[4] flowing from God our Father and Lord Jesus Christ. As you begin this letter keep this thought front and center,[5] Jesus gave himself up to death because of our depraved hearts and degenerate actions contrary to the nature of God.[6] He sacrificed

---

[1] Preferred translation of apostle (apostolos). More literally it would be sent one. It would have been used when a person was sent as the representative of one person on behalf of another. This of course was a unique form of delegation because of the kind of authority that came with it.

[2] Literally "brothers" but may suggest more than male coworkers at this point. Brothers was a neutral term to describe brothers and sisters in many contexts similar to the Spanish *chicos* which literally means boys but also means children in many contexts.

[3] Literally "of Galatia" so maybe not just "from Galatia;" maybe characterized by Galatia and in the location of Galatia.

[4] Here we are trying to capture a few things. One, that there is intention behind Paul's greeting. "Grace and Peace to you" is more than trite words. It is an unveiling of Paul's ultimate will for the Galatians and therefore God's will too. Also, the words grace and peace have meaning beyond a surface welcome to his audience. Especially in Christian Scripture, these are supercharged concepts. The goal behind this translation is to bring that to life excavating some of the nuance of the words "χάρις ὑμῖν καὶ εἰρήνη ἀπὸ θεοῦ πατρὸς ἡμῶν."

[5] This portion of the text acts as a theme (or tone) for the letter (not a thesis, that comes later).

[6] Literally, "who gave himself for the sake of our sins." Here, trying to articulate the theological nuances presumed in these simple words.

Himself so that we could be set free from the reign of evil that has dominated the universe for millennia.[7] This is what God, our Father wanted. Glory to Him forever.

**Summary Commentary:**

As Paul opens his letter, he follows the common introductory elements of an epistle. He begins with a description of who it is from and who that author represents. This seemingly perfunctory beginning does take on some extra significance because it so closely serves one of his major purposes in writing the letter, namely to establish his authority as an apostle-level voice on matters related to clarifying the message of the gospel and its missional reach. He follows by noting its recipients, the assemblies that are in the area of Galatia.

Of more significant note is the description of Jesus Christ as "the one who gave Himself for our sins so that he might loose us from the evil dominion long since established" (my translation). This phrase establishes a thematic direction for the letter: Jesus gave himself over to death for a reason: to deliver us from the power of evil established at the fall.

Let's look at this sentence in a bit more detail.

**Galatians 1.4a** "who gave himself for our sins" (τοῦ δόντος ἑαυτὸν ὑπὲρ τῶν ἁμαρτιῶν ἡμῶν)

Jesus is the one who gave Himself for our sins. In this case, "gave" is left somewhat ambiguous. What does it mean that He gave Himself? Is it implied? Is it left open so that the author can then fill in the ambiguity as he unfolds his narrative? It is something to watch for as

---

[7] Literally, "that He might deliver us from the evil reign that has begun." The modifier "ἐνίστημι" in the perfect form which means "that which has begun and now is." In this context it speaks to the dominion of evil that creation is under sense the fall. A translation like "present evil age" may miss the perfective aspect of the participle.

we read through the text. The word "didōmi" (to give) can be coupled with "psychē" (life, person, soul) as its object and then means to die for, i.e. to give one's life for someone means to die for someone. The absence of "psychē" may imply that this is not what Paul intended for us to read. He could have easily added this term to provide that clarity. However, when *didomi* is used with "heauton" (himself) as it is here it typically means "to dedicate oneself." With that in mind, Paul was likely referring to Jesus's broader mission here versus just his death. (Though theologically we might argue it is hard to separate the two, it is important to read the text as it would have been intended by its author.) If that is the case it may be better to understand this description of Jesus *as the one who devoted Himself* to something. We might now want to requisition an answer to the question our minds naturally ask: What did Jesus devote Himself to? The text should elucidate the answer to that question. We do read, though, what He gave Himself *for*. What does "for" mean?

The word translated "for" can mean either that this was why He gave us Himself -He gave himself because of our sins- or, it can mean that He gave Himself "on behalf of" our sins, i.e. He died on behalf of our sins. Based on the understanding of "didomi" above it might be best to read it as the former not the latter. He devoted his life to his cause *because* of our sins instead of "dying on behalf of our sins." (I think it's important to wrestle with this ambiguity here in the same way that an original reader might have done so that we are drawn into the dramatic tension caused by it.) Later, though, Paul will make it clear that both ideas are true. Here the emphasis seems to be on the idea that Jesus devoted Himself to the mission of God because of our sins. Our sins motivated His dedication. Then, his dedication was to suffering and dying in our place on behalf of our sins which will become more and more clear as we read. (See Galatians 2:20-21; Galatians 3:6ff)

**Galatians 1.4b** "to deliver us from the present evil age" (ὅπως ἐξέληται ἡμᾶς ἐκ τοῦ αἰῶνος τοῦ ἐνεστῶτος πονηροῦ)

The description of Jesus as the one who devoted himself to his mission because of our sins is followed with a purpose statement. If our sins motivated the impulse of his mission, this is the direction of the mission: "to deliver us." We start to see the object of Christ's dedication as we read- *us*. "*Our* sins;" "To deliver *us*." Jesus Christ is the one who devoted Himself to us. The end of his dedication to us was that we might be delivered or freed from "the evil domain that now exists" - or now rules. The ESV says "this present evil age." Age is a literal translation of "aiōnos" and it generally does mean age. Here though it seems to be an emphasis not on a period of time per se but on a characterization of that period. One might think of the English phrase "the age of Queen Elizabeth" or the "Kennedy era." In these cases, more than time is signified. There is an influence during the period. One could easily read each of those English phrases as "the reign of Queen Elizabeth" or the "Kennedy administration" and they would essentially mean the same as the previous parallel phrase. With that in mind, the concept of age implies more than just a time period. It is a "ruling system" or administration, government or economy, spiritually speaking of course.

This understanding is reinforced by the use of such clear descriptors for this "age." It is an evil age. It is, in other words, a dominion of evil. The word translated simply as "present" in the ESV is also important. This is a translation of the participle "enestōtos" which means "to be or exist." The more significant element in this word is that it is in the perfect tense. The perfect tense in Greek should be understood as something like "having been previously established and still exists." This evil domain or age was established in the past and presently exists. What is this "evil" age? Paul leaves it a bit ambiguous but a few possibilities exist. 1) The "age" of sin and the fall. This makes sense theologically. 2) The dominion of the law. This makes sense (and maybe the most sense) in the context of the book (the literary meaning). See Galatians 4.1-11 where Paul describes the era (using "chronos" a similar word to "aiōnos" to designate a period) before and after one is "in Christ." (Also consider 2 Corinthians 4.13 and Ephesians 2.2. 3) 3) This could conceptually simply mean something akin to "the world" or culture that is permeated with evil and persecutes the church. This idea of a ruling dominion in the universe is a subtle thread throughout the entire epistle.

**Galatians 1.4c** "according to the will of our God and Father" (κατὰ τὸ θέλημα τοῦ θεοῦ καὶ πατρὸς ἡμῶν)

Paul expresses a Trinitarian view of the salvation mission. It was not the Son of God operating alone or of his unique desires. This was the plan of the Father with the Son. This phrase is structurally parallel to the description of the Father in Galatians 1.1 where He is the "one who raised Him out of death." This may denote two additional details. 1) This is how we know this was the Father's will. He raised Him from the dead and 2) This is how this mission is being accomplished, by the resurrection of Christ accomplished by the Father.

# Galatians 1.6-12

**Interpretive Translation:**

I cannot get past this feeling of confusion and bewilderment I have for you.[8] How could you abandon me so quickly? I am the one who invited you into the grace of Christ. How could you abandon me and believe another gospel message?[9] This so-called gospel message is not really just another possible option.[10] Some people, though, are confusing you by stirring up your emotions.[11] They do not stop altering the gospel message about Christ. But, let me be clear, if any of us or a mystical being descending from heaven presents a gospel message different from the one we have already taught you, that person must be unwaveringly banned from your gatherings.[12] This is so important I am going to say it again, if anyone presents a gospel message different from what you previously received from me, he must be banned from your gatherings.

---

[8] The verb "θαυμάζω" is a present tense verb that means to be astonished or bewildered. Being present tense it may be that Paul is calling attention to the fact that as he is writing he is writing in a state of bewilderment that has gripped him. That is being brought out in this translation.

[9] The dative form is used to describe the movement from Paul, "the one who called them into another gospel." Paul takes this personal. It is more than just the fact that they turned to another theology (though that is the biggest issue) Paul also suggests that their "turning" is a personal affront. They turned from him.

[10] "It is not another" - Paul seems to be making the point that this is not an option to be considered. "Everyone has a perspective on this." This is a (or even the) make it or break it issue.

[11] The word "ταράσσω" can mean to stir up, to confuse (Spicq) and in some contexts "to cause to riot." The interpretation here is that the word choice has the connotation of confusion that was caused by "a stirring up" similar to the one that might cause people to riot, i.e. by being emotionally enflamed.

[12] "ἀνάθεμα" could be a reference to God's destruction so that the understanding here is akin to a prayer "God destroy this person" or it could be referring to a ban from the community. Paul typically uses ἀνάθεμα in the same way as the LXX which typically follows the latter understanding. (See commentary above for more information.)

Why is the gospel message I presented "the right one?"

Consider, do you see me submitting to other people or God?[13] Do I obsess[14] over keeping other people happy with me? If I am focused on pleasing human beings, I am not focused on serving Christ. You have to see that the gospel message, dear family, the one I presented, is not an attempt to impress any man. Consider the fact that I did not receive it from men. No human taught it to me. I received it and was taught when Jesus the Messiah himself made it fully known to me.

**Summary Commentary:**

Paul moves from his introductory comments quickly and, as many have noted, without even perfunctory praise for their positive qualities. The emotional exclamation at the beginning of this section highlights the emotional urgency that moves him into his correction. He is amazed and shaken that they no longer believe the gospel that he had preached to them and that they had originally received and accepted. Others have started preaching a counterfeit version of the message of Jesus. Paul makes it clear that this perversion is not an option. There is one option: the gospel he originally preached. This *first gospel* is so essential that Paul himself cannot make adjustments to it. Even if a heavenly creature were to manifest and try to correct their understanding they were to deny it. The seriousness of believing the right gospel was so important that it defined the boundaries of the Christian community. If anyone preached a different version, they were to be removed from the Christian community. (Note the epistemological implications of Paul's statement.)

---

[13] The verb "πείθω" is used here. It has a very wide variety of nuances in meaning. Generally it means to "persuade." According to Spicq, it can take on the nuance of "obey" or submit. It is parallel to "please" which suggests a similar meaning. In the greater context of the book, Paul goes onto deny his need to convince other people of his validity multiple times.

[14] Present tense of "seek" and "to please" implies a continual action.

He then moves into a justification of his position and the particular gospel message he preached. He used the Greek conjunction *gar* (γάρ), typically translated "for" or "because," to organize the material that follows, each one introducing a justification for the previous. Verse 10 states why they should return to belief in the gospel he preached and reject others: because his approach was not to try to please other people in the content of the message he taught. Then, in verse 12, he explains why this is the case. He had not received the gospel he taught via the teachings of another person or community. It was revealed to him directly through a revelation of Jesus Christ. He will continue into the next verse with the final *gar* with a description of his interaction with the leaders of the church in Jerusalem further validating the authority of his message and elucidating for us his readers who he meant when he said he was not trying to please men. He will soon show that the "men" he was not trying to please included: Peter, James, the Apostolic leaders of the Jerusalem church and people who still followed legalistic practices of the Jewish religion that came to visit Galatians. Generally, the antagonists in this epistle are those who "preach another gospel" and those who would have the Galatians obey the law. Specifically, it is those who have come out of the circumcision party initiated by James and perpetuated by Peter and others in Antioch, the gateway church to "the ends of the earth" as seen in Gal 2:10-15. (i.e. this is no small unimportant discord.)


**Galatians 1:6** "I am astonished that you are so quickly deserting him who called you in the grace of Christ and are turning to a different gospel." (Θαυμάζω ὅτι οὕτως ταχέως μετατίθεσθε ἀπὸ τοῦ καλέσαντος ὑμᾶς ἐν χάριτι [Χριστοῦ] εἰς ἕτερον εὐαγγέλιον)

Paul begins the body of his letter making it clear just how distraught he is that churches in Galatia are starting to believe a different version of the gospel message from what he had originally preached to them. Here, he uses the Greek word *thaumazō* (θαυμάζω). In a general way, it means "to marvel or to be amazed." It is used by the Gospel writers to explain the emotion that people had as they watched Jesus do miracles like calm the sea or heal the blind and lame. It implies a sense of "I do not know what is happening here." This is only one of two instances where Paul uses this verb. He uses the present tense for the verb which may denote that Paul's amazement is both temporarily associated with the writing of the letter ("As I write this letter I am amazed by you") helping us as the reader understand the situation that drove the writing of the letter and also associated with the aspect of Paul's amazement. Also potentially, he is saying that he was in a state of continual amazement. He was not able to get past it. He was confused and bewildered at their heresy. It did not make sense how they could have gotten to such a position of misplaced belief so quickly. Paul will go on to note many reasons why he is astonished but he does point out here that one simple reason was that it had not been very long since they had strongly embraced the gospel message that he had presented. We will continue in verses 10, 11, and 12 with an enumeration of sorts where he begins to make his argument using the connector *gar* three times to build one idea upon the other. They are each an answer to the question implied in this statement: Why is Paul so astounded at the Galatians's quick reversal of faith?

Before he moves into the layers of explaining his bewilderment, Paul describes the seriousness of the issue. He starts by highlighting that they are abandoning *him* (the most common identification of "the one who called" the Galatians). This is a personal issue for Paul. This theme, akin to a personal offense, not just a theological error, comes up a few times in this epistle. He will soon describe his commitment to the Galatians church and later even describe their devotion to him when he was sick. He is surprised, after the closeness of their relationship with him, that they would abandon the message he preached. (See Galatians 4.15-20) The word used to describe the Galatians' movement away from Paul can be translated as "desert." It is used to refer to Dionysus who abandoned the philosophical community of the Stoics to join the Epicureans. He was thereafter labeled "Dionysus the Turncoat," i.e. deserter. This example is helpful here because it describes both the emotional/communal abandonment Paul feels and the philosophical/theological cause behind it. They are, Paul says in essence, turncoats.

One question that is raised in a reading of this text might be the identity of "the one who called you." So far, we have read this as Paul. An alternate understanding could be that it refers to God (or potentially more specifically Jesus or the Spirit). While it could mean either *Paul* or *God* and make grammatical and historical sense, the context and the flow of thoughts Paul uses may suggest that he is the one who called them. Consider that what follows is Paul's reference to his personal engagement with the Galatians.

On the other hand, if this is the case, it goes against almost all of the usages found in the Pauline corpus. Paul, with rare exception (Old Testament quotes or unique, isolated narrative references for example), clearly uses "to call" with God in mind. This is the case in the more immediate context of Galatians too. Soon after referencing "the one who called you," Paul describes his salvation and refers to God as the one who "called me by His grace" (Galatians 1:14) using almost the same language as what is found here. God is the subject or agent in Galatians 5:8 (This persuasion is not from Him who calls you.) and Galatians 5:13 (For you were called to freedom, brothers.)

It would appear that while most translators and commentators would associate "the one who called you" in verse six with Paul, there is just as much justification to understand it as a reference to God. If this is the case, the Galatians are not deserting Paul, they are turncoats against God Himself. The implications that will begin to be apparent are that believing the correct "version" of the gospel is pivotal to one's association with God Himself. To believe an erroneous gospel, in other words, is to abandon, in a personal, emotionally impactful way, not just Paul, but God.

As noted above, the one who called the Galatians did so "in the grace of Christ." Note that some Greek texts do not include "of Christ" but simply say "in grace." This prepositional phrase could be modifying "the one who called you" and speak to Paul's ministry to the Galatians. In this case, it might be something like, "Paul, who called you being empowered by grace." This would mean that Paul wanted to highlight the fact that his ministry flowed from *his* own calling by grace. Or, if the one who called is *God*, it more likely speaks to what God called the Galatians into, namely his grace. If this is the case, then "in grace" is in contrast to "into another gospel." (This contrast may be intended either way.) This is a way for Paul to highlight the nature of the gospel message he had presented to the Galatians. It was a gospel of grace as compared to the "other gospel." The Galatians, in other words, had turned from a gospel that was all about grace to a different gospel that contrasted grace.

What is the gospel? The word means a "good" or "positive" message, a message that would make those who heard it feel happy. It would have been used to describe a herald running back to the city from a battlefield declaring a message of victory. In the writings of Paul, it is the message or "informing" that Christ has taken away our sins by dying in our place. He notes simply in 1 Corinthians 15, "Christ died for our sins" and then expands on how this event impacts all things. While we noted above the possible meaning of "for our sins" as being the motivating factor, in other places (and maybe in Galatians 1:3 as well) Paul explains further that our sins were removed by Christ through his death. For Paul, this was a simple statement of the good news, Christ died for our sins.

As implied by some of the philosophically related terminology (see above) and as developed in this epistle, the gospel also led to an entire philosophical system that then impacted all of life (and even the universe). We see Paul articulate the "paradigm" of the gospel in almost all of his writings. He repeatedly shares the basic gospel message, shows its origin in the Hebrew Scriptures and then shows how we live out a life that is founded on the gospel, i.e. if the gospel is true and we believe it, we should live in alignment with how the gospel defines a new reality. He does the same in his epistle to the Galatians. It might be that the reason Paul uses language that has historically been used to describe abandoning a philosophical system (and the communities founded on those systems) is to help his readers see the gospel as a philosophy that builds a community and impacts one's ethics as it did with the Stoics and Epicureans - one universe pivoting idea affecting the trajectory of creation since its inception in the paradoxical eternity past. This is also implied in the language Paul uses at the beginning of the epistle, that Christ delivers from the evil dominating system, including the philosophical system at its foundation.

**Galatians 1:7** "not that there is another one, but there are some who trouble you and want to distort the gospel of Christ." (ὃ οὐκ ἔστιν ἄλλο, εἰ μή τινές εἰσιν οἱ ταράσσοντες ὑμᾶς καὶ θέλοντες μεταστρέψαι τὸ εὐαγγέλιον τοῦ Χριστοῦ. )

As he continues an explanation of his marveling, Paul clarifies that the other gospel is not really "another." He may add this clarifying remark to make sure the reader knows there are not several possible optional gospel systems to believe. There is one. This is the only message that *really is good news* at least at the level of the gospel of Paul. This is as if to say, "Their message is not really *good news.*" There really cannot be another message that is good news. As we uncover more about their message throughout the epistle we will discover that their message was burdensome and anything but actual good news. The genuine gospel is the only real solution to humanity's real problem. An "all grace" gospel is man's only hope, the only truly good news. Even though their message is not an optional paradigm to consider, Paul does want us to know there are personalities that are real. His emphasis semantically makes a switch from the content of their heretical teaching to the teachers themselves. There's no other gospel, but there is a group of people you need to watch out for. Paul uses two descriptors to help us identify the apostates. These descriptors are both present tense particles. This verb form is to be read as repeated or continual action. So as we look at the lexical meaning of these words consider that they are describing the action the contrarians as continually doing. They do not stop. They are relentless.

The first action Paul highlights is that they are *troubling* the Galatians from tarassō (ταράσσω). This word can range in meaning from "to stir" (as in water) to "incite a riot." The English colloquialism "stir the pot" comes to mind. The word carries with it the idea of stirring up emotions so that a person is disturbed, maybe confused and ready to riot. Think of the intensity of an incited crowd acting with minimal rationality. As we consider Paul's use of the term "traitor" or "turncoat" earlier a picture forms of Paul describing the Galatians as being manipulated emotionally into an uproar against Jesus and/or Paul.

The second concept is that they do so according to their will. This is the second participle used to describe their action. They are stirring up the people and they are repeatedly "choosing" to do so. There is intent. This is not a stumbling into heresy. This is a rebellion led by strategists.

These two actions describe the action of the main verb translated as "distort" in the ESV. Their strategy and manipulation are fully a distortion of the gospel of Christ. Distort assumes a negative change to the gospel and fits well in this context. The word itself (metastrephō) simply means to transform or alter an object as in the sun turning from light to darkness as in Acts 2:20. These agitators are altering the gospel. No doubt alterations do pervert the gospel, but it's the alterations themselves that Paul focuses on or the act of altering. They appear to have reflected on Paul's gospel with a "there has to be more required" mindset. They wanted to add their addendums, footnotes and legal small print to the simplicity of a gospel that singularly focused on grace.

One last note about this verse: this is the gospel *about* Christ as the sentence structure suggests. "Gospel of Christ" is parallel to "grace of Christ": two ways to say the same thing. Paul's gospel is Christ-oriented. It is about what *he* has done and what *he* does. Christ is the subject and the star of any real gospel, its only real active agent. The real gospel will always be a story about Jesus.

**Galatians 1:8-9** "But even if we or an angel from heaven should preach to you a gospel contrary to the one we preached to you, let him be accursed. As we have said before, so now I say again: If anyone is preaching to you a gospel contrary to the one you received, let him be accursed." (ἀλλὰ καὶ ἐὰν ἡμεῖς ἢ ἄγγελος ἐξ οὐρανοῦ εὐαγγελίζηται [ὑμῖν] παρ' ὃ εὐηγγελισάμεθα ὑμῖν, ἀνάθεμα ἔστω. 9 ὡς προειρήκαμεν καὶ ἄρτι πάλιν λέγω· εἴ τις ὑμᾶς εὐαγγελίζεται παρ' ὃ παρελάβετε, ἀνάθεμα ἔστω. )

There are few statements in Scripture as emphatically stated as what Paul writes when he condemns any alterations to the gospel of Christ's grace. First, he purposefully states the same basic idea twice to drive the point home. A clear and accurate understanding of the gospel and living on a solid foundation of the same may be the most important reality for a follower of Christ. Paul insinuates as much here with such clear emphasis through the double rebuke. Who has the authority to make adjustments to the message? No one. What about Paul himself? No. Paul cannot even correct it himself. Why? He will explain that later in the epistle (hint: it's been promised from antiquity as clearly taught in the Old Testament). Mainly, his point is that he did not invent the idea himself. What if a mystical heavenly creature appears? Still not good enough. No emendations at all, ever, by anyone.

If someone does make any edits or alterations they are to be "accursed." The word translated as "accursed" is the potentially familiar word *anathema*. It is a word that has been borrowed into English with a similar range of meanings. It is used frequently in the Greek translation of the Old Testament (known as the Septuagint, often abbreviated LXX). In most uses of anathema in the LXX, it describes a formal disassociation, a separation of a person from the community and its benefits. In that way, it can be a communal judgment. It is also used in many contexts as a spiritual judgment. A person can be accursed before God. In its extra-Biblical uses, it is used to describe the sacrifices one may make to a deity and in some cases the cultic consequences that come from failing to do so appropriately. (It means to "set or place up" as in setting up an idol.) It is mainly from this concept that the spiritual connotations are derived. Paul does return often to language culturally associated with the world of cultic religions and corresponding beliefs about magic throughout this letter. Paul's usage here could be either signifying the cultic cursing related to a worldview that would have been saturated with magic or the communal separation that results from abhorrent behavior as described in the LXX. There are contextual reasons to see both options as plausible. The book of Galatians is written polemically against those who would hold to a strict view of obeying the law. They would have immediately had in mind the cursing community rejection that would have been described in the law in the LXX. Also, Paul does go on to use specific terms related to cultic magical spells in chapter 3. It may be that the readers would have seen these as two aspects of the same curse. A cursing would have left one out of the community and under a cultic spiritual curse (in the eyes of the recipients of this letter).

**Galatians 1:10** "For am I now seeking the approval of man, or of God? Or am I trying to please man? If I were still trying to please man, I would not be a servant of Christ." (Ἄρτι γὰρ ἀνθρώπους πείθω ἢ τὸν θεόν; ἢ ζητῶ ἀνθρώποις ἀρέσκειν; εἰ ἔτι ἀνθρώποις ἤρεσκον, Χριστοῦ δοῦλος οὐκ ἂν ἤμην.)

Paul begins his movement into another section by explaining why he is astonished at the Galatians' swift abandonment of the truth he taught. He marks each reason with the conjunction *gar* which is translated "for" in the ESV. Each "for" is an argument for the previous thesis. Here he explains the cause of his astonishment at their quick abandonment of him (or Jesus). He argues first from what might be unexpected justification. The quick turn from Paul's gospel by the Galatians astonishes because of the motivation and source of Paul's message. It did not come from a motivation to please men. He was not trying to give people confidence in His message. He was only interested in God's buy-in. The term translated "seeking the approval" (peithō) is generally understood as closer to "persuade." Of course here that might be problematic considering that Paul would be trying to persuade man *and* God. Readers should maintain an open and objective mindset while reading a text that seems contrary to Paul's typical thinking about God. Instead, in this case, it is in parallel to "to please" and then "to serve" in the phrases that follow. "Seek or win approval" is then more fitting than "trying to win over." As we read on, we will see that Paul's authority to teach the gospel (and therefore the gospel message itself) does not gain its validity from the authority of men even those who are considered the most powerful within Christendom.

Consider that *peitho* may also be translated as "obey" or "submit" as was chosen in the paraphrase below. The connection to "a servant of" implies this concept.

Next, he says he is "not trying to please" man. It could be that Paul in using these two complementary phases to describe his approach ("not winning the approval of" and "trying to please") attempts to clarify two different aspects: namely, that he does not seek to please men intellectually or emotionally. If there is any nuance of meaning between the two phrases it is that "peitho" suggests, maybe slightly, to convince someone at the intellectual and volitional level while "to please" (areskō) leans more toward the emotional aspect of approval.

In the last thought, Paul gives in this sentence, he gives his imaginary unfaithful self a judgment. If he pleases people or submits to people instead of God, he is no longer a servant of Christ. Again, it is important to see that Paul argues for his doctrine by establishing that it is not derived from an intention to submit to, please, or serve any group of people.

We should also not fail to see the connection to the similar language used by Paul later in Galatians to describe justification by faith, (faith, *pistis*, comes from the same root as *peitho)*. Not only does Paul suggest two possible paths in this early reference, to please God or man, but he also hints through this literary linking to an upcoming thesis: God becomes pleased (justifies us) with us through faith. This paragraph sets the semantic tone for Paul's message about justification that dominates most of the epistle.

**Galatians 1:11** " For I would have you know, brothers, that the gospel that was preached by me is not man's gospel. " (Γνωρίζω γὰρ ὑμῖν, ἀδελφοί, τὸ εὐαγγέλιον τὸ εὐαγγελισθὲν ὑπ' ἐμοῦ ὅτι οὐκ ἔστιν κατὰ ἄνθρωπον·)

Paul is not concerned with the authority of others. Why? Because he does not preach the gospel or doctrine of humanity. The authority of his message does not come from a council. This is not a human idea. Of course, Paul implies that his gospel doctrine is God's gospel. The doctrinal implication for his readers is both the validity of his doctrine and how a doctrine is validated. Readers should watch closely how Paul justifies his position. He makes this more clear in the verses that follow.

**Galatians 1:12** "For I did not receive it from any man, nor was I taught it, but I received it through a revelation of Jesus Christ." (οὐδὲ γὰρ ἐγὼ παρὰ ἀνθρώπου παρέλαβον αὐτὸ οὔτε ἐδιδάχθην ἀλλὰ δι' ἀποκαλύψεως Ἰησοῦ Χριστοῦ.)

Paul moves on through the layers of his argument. The third "for" (gar) introduces the third step in his argument. Here he explains how it can be that his teaching is not from man. If not, how did he get it and where is it from? It is important to keep in mind the purpose Paul has in writing this material. Ultimately, he is challenging the Galatians' heresy and implying their need to believe his gospel. Paul's teaching arises not out of a place of submission to men because the message did not come from men. He directed the Galatians to condemn any teaching other than what they *received* from him originally because he did not *receive* it from human origins. He describes what he means by "did not receive it from man" by going on to say men did not teach him this message.

Again, he has put together three ideas to form one larger concept: this is not "man's doctrine." 1) He did not receive it from a man nor was 2) he taught it by a man. Where did it come from? 3) "Through a revelation of Jesus Christ." As modern readers, we have the context of Acts to help us build out Paul's meaning. This is both helpful and dangerous. While it may be obvious why this might be helpful, it is dangerous because we might be tempted to get ahead of Paul and *read into* the text what he means by a revelation of Christ. To discern what he wanted his original readers to understand look at the context (by looking at the structure) and the meaning of the word and grammatical choices. The main word that we need to understand well in this phase is "revelation" from *apokalypsis* (ἀποκάλυψις). A common definition for apokalypsis might be "a revelation, that which is made fully known or that disclosure itself." It is a compound word with the negation "a" and the root "kalypto" meaning "to cover" -as in cover with a cloth or to be covered by the sea. The real question for this text derives from the ambiguity of the phrase. Is the uncovering or revelation from Jesus or about Jesus or Jesus Himself? Is it specifically something Paul learned from Jesus or his Damascus road experience? Instead of jumping to a conclusion let us as readers simply take that it was something related to Jesus in some way and therefore "not of man or from man" but of and from God. (See commentary on Galatians 1.16 and 2.1.) That is all the information we have in this epistle at this point.

One structural note- in verses 8-9 above, he uses a structural juxtaposition of "a person preaches" to "you received." Here he reverses it. First, he says he did not "receive it from men" and then "nor was taught it by men." These markers may show that verses 6-9 are one thought and verses 10-12 are a second subsection with a similar structure (*preach/taught* and then *received*). This gives verses 6-12 cohesion. The parallel nature of this structure is further supported by the missing "received" in the last phrase of verse 12. The ESV adds it in for clarity but it is not in the original text. It also fits what is about to happen and puts the reader on alert for it, a major transition into the last "for" (gar) that then both justifies the previous *gar* clause and also moves the epistle into a major new section.

If we look at all the parts of his argument up to this point, his basic thesis is not as we might expect, "Listen to me" (i.e. a defense of his apostolic authority). Above he condemns himself if he potentially shows up preaching a different gospel. Instead, it is the content itself that is important. Here, Paul says the content is from God so believe it.

# Galatians 1.13-2.2a

**Interpretive Translation:**

Let me explain. You heard about my previous approach to religion (and all of life for that matter) when I practiced Judaism. You heard that I constantly[15] attacked the true community of God, the church,[16] and constantly tried to destroy it. I was so successful at my persecution that I became famous among my peers who had grown up in the religion of Judaism with me. I wanted to take the church down and I was good at my job. Everyone knew it.[17] My extreme passion for the religious practices my teachers had entrusted to me, the same ideas that our ancestors had taught for generations, motivated my actions.

Contrast that to what happened in the next stage of my life.[18] Behind the scenes, unbeknownst to me, God had assigned a mission to me the moment I was conceived. He commissioned me not because of any talent I possessed or performance he foresaw but simply because of his unearned kindness and favor. The mission he assigned me was the responsibility of announcing Jesus, his "good news,"[19] to non-Jewish people all over the known world. At the moment God wanted, he

---

[15] Imperfect verb denoting continual action.

[16] Simply in the text "the church of God." In this paraphrase, I hope to bring out something of the meaning of the word ekklesia (church) while also making sure the referent is clear. Ekklesia means assembly or gathering but here is a reference to more than a single, local group of people that has gathered. Paul could be using a term like "community of God" as a subtle knock against the followers of Judaism since they would have seen themselves as the sole group that fit that description.

[17] This is a repeat of the previous material to show the emphasis it appears Paul intends for this material.

[18] Paul makes a shift within this sub-section using the simple connection de.

[19] Literally it says, "to announce good news (one word in the text), Him." The verb "to announce good news" is difficult to translate into English because the verb is to action what we see as an object, good news." It is something like "to good news" which does not make sense to our ears. It may be something like "to good proclaim." The object of this verb is "him," Jesus, hence the translation above.

revealed his Son before[20] me. I did not then run to find a new set of teachers. I did not go up to Jerusalem to sit under the teaching of the first Apostles like I had done when I first started to learn to practice Judaism sitting under the rabbis.[21] Instead, I went the opposite direction[22] into the Arabian wilderness. After that, I came back to where it all started for me, Damascus.

After I had stayed in Damascus for around three years, I went up to Jerusalem to hear the details of the story of Jesus from Little Rock[23] (Peter) and did so for 15 days. I did not meet another single church leader from Jerusalem except for James, the Lord's biological brother. (Before God, this is not a lie!) After I spent this short time with Peter[24] I went on a missionary journey in the regions of Cilicia[25] where I grew up and then I also spent time in Syria helping lead the church in Antioch to expand its mission to the Gentiles.[26] At this point, the

---

[20] The preposition "en" can be near or within the range of. Here "before me" captures that idea Paul is most likely portraying, that Jesus was unhidden in his presence or within proximity of his senses. See commentary below for options.

[21] There may be an intended contrast here between Paul's earlier teaching under the "fathers" and his revelation here where he did not confer with "fathers."

[22] This is denoted by the prepositional prefix "apo" -from- affixed to the verb erchomai (to go) as opposed to the "ana" -up- that is affixed in the previous clause.

[23] Cephas mean rock. Petros is small rock.

[24] The term epeita is used to form sub-structure in this section. It simply means "Next or After" but has more strength than that based on its use as a significant structural element.

[25] Tarsus, hometown of Paul, is in Cilicia.

[26] In the text Ciliica comes second and Syria comes first. The chronology would have been in the order as noted in this translation. Why would Paul reverse the order? Maybe to show that his mission's authority came from Antioch and not Jerusalem. Something subtle may be implied here. Paul could be hinting at the authority of the Church being loosed from Jerusalem and moving to Antioch (or possibly to local churches generally). "I did not need to get authorized from Jerusalem. I was authorized from Antioch." While we should probably not take too much from something so subtle, we should read, as the context of ch.1-2 suggest, that Paul did not consider the authority of the church (or its leaders) in Jerusalem as final or supreme. The mission moved outward from Jerusalem but authority moved into each place the gospel was preached and a new Christian community was founded.

multitude of Christian communities meeting near Jerusalem still did not know me personally. They just kept hearing that the one who had previously been known for attacking the church now preaches the hope-giving message about what happens when you trust in Christ, the same message he previously had relentlessly tried to shut down. Because of this, they praised God for transforming me.

**Summary Commentary:**

Paul in verses 13-24 continues to highlight the elevated nature of the gospel message he had been preaching as compared to the message others had brought to the Galatians. His previous argument was that his message and ministry were not set toward the purpose of pleasing any group of humans. He did not edit his message to meet the approval of anyone. It was not a message that originated from any human person or board. His major thesis in this section is that the "version" of the gospel he preached to the Galatians did not have a human origin. These verses explicate that idea further picking up on the thesis as stated in verse 12.

He describes in vss 13-14 that he was strongly committed to destroying anything to do with Jesus, the gospel and the church for the first portion of his life. This creates part of his argument. What happened to him to transform him so? If he had been so zealously defiant against Christianity and then so strongly turned toward Christ in his life and ministry something supernatural must have occurred. That supernatural experience and the impact it had on Paul is a subtle indicator here of the veracity of Paul's version of the gospel.

The pivot of Paul's life was not something that happened at a specific moment in his life. God had pre-ordained the pivot even at conception. Every moment of Paul's life before Christ appeared to be against Christ. In actuality, God was forming Paul for the pivot. All of this was by God's grace. Paul was not chosen because of his talents, skills, or religious fervor. God chose him and equipped him out of grace. At the time God chose, He revealed Jesus before Paul on the road to Damascus. Paul gives the readers a reason why Paul had such a unique revelation. It was so that he would be equipped to take the message of Jesus to the Gentiles.

Paul's response to this revelation was not what we might expect. He went to the desert of Arabia. Instead of weighing his experience out at the feet of his teachers or by going to Jerusalem to discuss it with the Apostles, he went into the desert. Paul does not elucidate the exact nature of this journey into Arabia. In the text, the most important aspect of this statement is that he went away from Jerusalem. He followed the revelation of Jesus and not the guidance of the Jerusalem council. This is seen by his usage of the prefixes showing the direction of his journey. He did not go "up" to Jerusalem (prefix of ana (up) in verse 17a) but in contrast, he went "from" into Arabia (prefix of "apo" (from). The literary contrast creates the emphasis of the text: he did not get authority from the Apostles in Jerusalem. His gospel was not second-hand information.[27]

**Galatians 1:13** "For you have heard of my former life in Judaism, how I persecuted the church of God violently and tried to destroy it." (Ἠκούσατε γὰρ τὴν ἐμὴν ἀναστροφήν ποτε ἐν τῷ Ἰουδαϊσμῷ, ὅτι καθ' ὑπερβολὴν ἐδίωκον τὴν ἐκκλησίαν τοῦ θεοῦ καὶ ἐπόρθουν αὐτήν,)

---

[27] The text raises the question of Paul's biography. We do not have any information about a journey into Arabia in Acts or in other Pauline accounts of his conversion. From this text we know that this time period was around 3 years and included time in Damascus and in Arabia. It preceded any journeys to Jerusalem. REV. C. W. BRIGGS in the article "THE APOSTLE PAUL IN ARABIA" suggest that Arabia stands for the Hebrew dispersion in the East where Paul would have found Hebrews that claimed to the purist of the pure of Hebrew thought. (https://www.journals.uchicago.edu/doi/pdf/10.1086/474761). His point might be in this case that he went on mission immediately to the most Jewish part of the world. It could also infer that Paul's competition might also be out of this school of thought. And, so Paul could be defending his knowledge of Hebrew scriptures and traditions. I think we have to be careful reading this into the text. Paul would have included anything in the text that he would have wanted his readers to know. He includes here that it was simply that he went from Jerusalem. He wants the readers to know that he did not know of the gospel from the teaching of the apostles in Jerusalem but through revelation. His gospel was not tainted.

One way this would give his gospel message authority was that it was not "group-think." He was not just repeating what he was taught. In contrast, as one who was so thoroughly trained in the Scriptures (at the feet of Gamaliel and *maybe* the Hebrew teachers in Arabia) and having seen Jesus in a life changing revelation came to the conclusions of the gospel via his own personal experience and study. The gospel of the Paul was *text derived* and not tradition determined.

One concept that may be inferred in the text -though this reference is minimal at best- is a connection to Paul's visit to Arabia in Galatians 1.17 and then his reference to Arabia as being synonymous with Sinai and the Law Covenant in Galatians 4.25. "She corresponds to present Jerusalem" - may be a reference to the dominant theological paradigm in Jerusalem. Literarily that may simply be "of Sinai." Historically, the idea might be, if Briggs is right, under the influence of the strong Judaizer mindset that arises from Arabia.

Note also, that Paul states in 2 Cor 11.32 that the King Aretas, the King of Arabia, is the one who wanted him to be arrested in Damascus right before he was let out in a basket. This would be a small contextual clue to understand what was happening in the life of Paul during this time period.

What we should not do is try to make what Paul did in Arabia a part of the meaning he codified into the text. The simple fact he did not go to Jerusalem but went to Arabia is Paul's one and only point.

This is the fourth "for" or "gar" in a row. It is the last moment in this structure but it does not form the end of Paul's treatise. It forms a new step in his series of ideas. From here, Paul then describes his former life. He uses his former life and the events that followed as a way to validate the gospel he had taught the Galatians. This "for" introduces a more personal biographical element to help prove the veracity of the message.

Paul says that the Galatians had "heard" about his former life. They knew his story already. This was not new information. The word "life" translates the word "anastrophē." It signifies something a bit beyond simple "living" but instead has more to do with one's daily lifestyle and the habits that form that lifestyle. According to BDAG, it is a lifestyle that arises from principles or a belief system. It means "to return upside down." His life was in orbit around these ideas. This etymological structuring of the word's meaning reveals the nuance captured in the idea of a life and its actions having been significantly impacted by one's ideas and religious ideals. Paul, here is saying more than that he lived according to the principles of Judaism. He is saying that his life was completely oriented within Judaism.

Paul does not leave his audience in the dark about the focus of his obsession. It was not God Himself but a religious paradigm. Paul was obsessed with a religion, Judaism. The result of being "religion" oriented was an exceptional and relentless persecution of the church. He says he persecuted the church "with excess."

Here Paul layers three imperfect verbs to describe his former religion-oriented lifestyle. These imperfect verbs emphasize the continual and even relentless nature of Paul's actions. 1) He continually persecuted the "community of God." 2) He continually attacked it (with the intent to end it), and 3) He was continually advancing in Judaism (see commentary on verse 14 below).

This is most likely a chiastic structure something like the following simplification below:

Former lifestyle in Judaism
Continually persecuting the church
Continually attacking it
Advancing in Judaism

The center portions help us understand the main idea of the outer portions. Paul's commitment to his religion led to his prosecution and destruction of the church.

**Galatians 1:14** "And I was advancing in Judaism beyond many of my own age among my people, so extremely zealous was I for the traditions of my fathers." (καὶ προέκοπτον ἐν τῷ Ἰουδαϊσμῷ ὑπὲρ πολλοὺς συνηλικιώτας ἐν τῷ γένει μου, περισσοτέρως ζηλωτὴς ὑπάρχων τῶν πατρικῶν μου παραδόσεων. )

As noted above, this verse is a continuation of three imperfect verbs Paul uses to describe his story in Judaism. The verb translated here "advancing" is also in a parallel position to "life" (or lifestyle or daily religious practices) in verse thirteen. Paul is making sure we do not miss two things as he writes in this section. 1) That his commitment to Judaism led to his attacks on the church and 2) that he was more committed to Judaism than anyone else. In a letter that serves to deconstruct Judaistic ideals that had emerged in the faith of the Galatians, this is an important contextual element from Paul's biographical background. Paul in effect says, "Been there. Done that. Found it wanting." Later Paul will show that the gospel leads to loving the church (Chapter 5) whereas Judaism led him to try to end it.

He explains that he was progressing upwards in the ranks of the religious establishment faster than most of his contemporaries and he reveals the reason: he was more zealously committed to the traditions of his ancestors. He uses a present participle "being" to modify the previous phrase showing cause -this is why he was advancing- and showing duration -he was continually or constantly zealous for the traditions of his ancestors.

Note the language he uses to describe the object of his obsession. Traditions. Ancestral. Judaism. He is subtly showing that all of this was not "of God" but simply a human religion like any other. Paul uses this background to contrast the source of the gospel. The one, his former religion and the religious underpinnings of those who were deceiving the Galatians, were given to him via ancestral traditions. The other, the gospel, was given to Him by God Himself.

**Galatians 1:15** "But when he who had set me apart before I was born, and who called me by his grace" (Ὅτε δὲ εὐδόκησεν [ὁ θεὸς] ὁ ἀφορίσας με ἐκ κοιλίας μητρός μου καὶ καλέσας διὰ τῆς χάριτος αὐτοῦ )

Here, Paul describes how his story changed. Formerly, he was a professional practitioner of Judaism and was so committed that he tried to bring down the church itself. What happened to change that? To change Paul? This biographical shift begins with the description of the main actor in the story -God. Paul describes God as the one who "set me apart" in the abdomen of his mother, i.e. before he was born and called him, Paul, by His grace.

"set me apart" - Paul clarifies the timing of this biographical shift and it is not when we might suppose. While he begins the description with a time element pointing to the future "But, when he was pleased" -the first words of the sentence in the Greek text referring to his eventual salvation- he quickly gives his readers insight into other elements of the timeline. He does this to show that God was the initiator of his ministry and that it happened even before his time in Judaism. It may be that Paul is implying that even his time in Judaism was part of God's plan. Nonetheless, Paul wants his audience to know that God was the active agent in assigning him his ministry and that it happened before he was born.

Note here that Paul saw himself as having full personhood in the eyes of God before he was born. God separated Paul into his unique assignment in the womb.

"called me by his grace" - Not only did God separate Paul in the womb to a specific function but this was by God's grace. Paul connects two aspects together related to his calling: 1) The idea of calling is in parallel to "separated me" so that a calling is also a culling. He had a special assignment. This is similar to his description of himself as an apostle. An individualized component is included in calling. 2) He was called by grace. In other words, he was not chosen because of his own ability or skills. Post-conception but pre-birth, Paul was assigned to be a missionary focused on preaching the gospel to the Gentiles. God took Paul as he was in the womb, with his unique background, location and DNA and chose him for this role. But it was not because of any element Paul brought to the table via lineage or location, skill or strength. It was because of grace. He was called pre-birth. He had not done anything to earn his place. His scholarly ability. His experiences. His rearing. None of these things contributed to God's choice to use him. It was by grace.

**Galatians 1:16** "was pleased to reveal his Son to me, in order that I might preach him among the Gentiles, I did not immediately consult with anyone;" (ἀποκαλύψαι τὸν υἱὸν αὐτοῦ ἐν ἐμοί, ἵνα εὐαγγελίζωμαι αὐτὸν ἐν τοῖς ἔθνεσιν, εὐθέως οὐ προσανεθέμην σαρκὶ καὶ αἵματι)

In verse 15 Paul begins this thought with a temporal idea "when." In simple terms, he is describing the timing of an event. He then, still in verse 15, describes the active agent for his topic, God. Now, in verse 16, he completes the thought. "When it pleased God."

"was pleased to reveal His Son in me." - It may be easy to miss the sense of this phrase because of the common phrasing in the English text. Paul is speaking about the fact that this event gave God joy. That is the basic meaning of "to be pleased." Interestingly, the word is an active verb but often has a passive sense. A more active way to look at the verb might be to translate it as "When God took delight." The emphasis is both on God's will -"he chose this event" and the emotions that paralleled it -"He was happy." In English, we think of emotions as something that happens to us. In Greek emotions are something that we execute. A person executes their own happiness. While it can be dangerous to focus too much on the parts of a word while studying Greek because a word does not typically get its meaning from the total of its parts (morphemes), in this case, it may help us. The word is two Greek morphemes: *eu* meaning good or happiness and *dokeo* meaning to think. One could translate this word as "I think good" or more expansively "I create happiness by thinking about it." God determined an event that made him happy. The point here may simply be a subtle reminder that God does what gives him joy. Always. Happiness does not *happen* to God. He creates it.

And what did God do when he determined pleasure? He revealed his Son in Paul. The ESV translates this as "reveal his Son to me." The Greek text uses the preposition "en" so that some have translated the phrase "to reveal his Son in me." The unexpected preposition causes us to slow down and make sure we have the same event in mind as Paul. It could simply be that Paul is using the preposition to denote proximity: "God revealed his Son *near* me." That is a possible meaning of the word. In this case, Paul may have used *en* instead of *eis* (to) so that his audience got a sense of the intimacy in the moment of revelation. It is also possible that Paul is referring to a different experience.

The term *revelation* is a translation of the same root word used in verse 12 where Paul describes how he received his gospel message, i.e. he was not taught this gospel message it was given to him as a revelation. It is also used in Galatians 2:2 when Paul says that he "went up to Jerusalem according to a revelation." When taken as a whole, this could mean that Paul is referring not to his Damascus road experience but to a personal encounter with Christ through his Spirit.

He does use the same word in Ephesians when describing his hope for these believers. He prays that they would have a "Spirit of revelation." He described the same experience in Colossians as being filled with "all wisdom and spiritual understanding." If these verses are a part of the same idea Paul is teaching in Galatians then it might be that the experience Paul detailed in Galatians 1:16 (and 1:12) is what he prays into the life of the Ephesians and Colossians. If this is the case, it is not the Damascus road experience that Paul refers to here but a revelation of Jesus *inside* of him by the Father at some point later. In favor of this latter perspective, is the simple coordinated linking between the concepts in the three epistles. (See also Ephesians 3:2-4 where Paul speaks to the content of this revelation as the *mystery of Christ*.) This understanding seems to fit better, then, with the Pauline corpus and the basic message of the book of Galatians: trust in the Spirit. (It also seems to fit the timing of the event better. This is related to his ministry assignment and not his conversion.)

"in order that I might preach him among the Gentiles" - This next clause describes the purpose of God revealing Jesus in the heart of Paul. This revelation was in effect a call to Paul to proclaim the message of Christ to people who were not Jewish. The inclusion of this purpose statement may just show the effect of Paul experiencing this larger revelation or it may define a specific revelation. "As God revealed that his Son was in me this one time his Son showed me I was to be a missionary to the Gentiles." So, it is either the purpose of the revelation or the content of the revelation. The grammar of the text suggests that the former is more likely but the literary context *may* suggest the latter. To support the second option consider Paul's very next phrase and the main idea of this sentence.

"I did not immediately consult with anyone." - This is the main clause of the sentence. To simplify it we may say something like "When God chose to reveal his Son in me, I did not immediately consult with anyone." When we read Paul's conversion in Acts it suggests that he immediately consulted with Ananias. So, unless we have a contradiction in Scripture, again, Paul may not be referring to his conversion experience on the Damascus road but a different "revelation." This may be the "revelation" that happened not just to Paul but to the Elders of the church in Antioch when it says, "While they were worshipping the Lord and fasting, the Holy Spirit said, "Set apart Barnabas and Saul for the working to which I have called them."

(Acts 13:2). If this is the case, we can take this to mean that Paul upon having a revelation to go preach the gospel to the Gentiles did not consult with any human. He had heard from God and that was enough.

The word translated "consult" is the Greek word "prosanatithemi" (προσανατίθημι). Consult is a good translation. It could also be translated as "to present for consideration or approval." It only occurs in the New Testament in two places, here and in 2:5. This is significant to the structure between 1.13 and 2.14. Note that this is almost the same word that Paul uses in 2:2 for "to set before": "anatithemai" (ἀνατίθεμαι) . So, eventually, Paul does "consult" with others (the ones who would "consider" his position) but not "immediately." See below on comments on 2:5 for more. Paul does expect the readers of his letter to think back to this statement when he writes in Galatians 2 that he "set up to before them" the gospel message as he understood it. Notice the use of the term "revelation" in Galatians 2:2 also, providing another lexical link between these two sections.

In summary, when God gave Paul a clear understanding of the gospel via revelation and the Gentile's place in it, he did not consult with anyone or get approval from Jerusalem. That is his point. That was not step one. As Paul seeks to prove his authority and verify the gospel message he teaches, he considers it essential that his readers know that it started via revelation. This could be to showcase that it is in contrast to a contemporary movement coming out of Jerusalem that focused on practicing the law. Better than guessing though, the reader should identify that there is still ambiguity in the unfolding of Paul's thinking and watch carefully for Paul to clarify. Presently, Paul has emphasized his deep knowledge of "Judaism" (and following the law as a result) and, in contrast, that his gospel came by revelation from God around the nature of Jesus. In the case of the latter, he did not get approval from any authority to move out on mission to the Gentiles.

**Galatians 1:17** "nor did I go up to Jerusalem to those who were apostles before me, but I went away into Arabia, and returned again to Damascus." (οὐδὲ ἀνῆλθον εἰς Ἱεροσόλυμα πρὸς τοὺς πρὸ ἐμοῦ ἀποστόλους, ἀλλὰ ἀπῆλθον εἰς Ἀραβίαν καὶ πάλιν ὑπέστρεψα εἰς Δαμασκόν. )

Starting in verse 16 Paul puts together four aorist tense verbs. These four verbs give cohesion to this subsection making it a sub-unit with the text.

The four verbs:
I consulted (Negated)
I went up (Negated)
I went from
I returned

Then, as we will see below, Paul puts together 3 more aorist verbs with a directional focus (1:18 -I went up; 1:21 - I went; 2:1 - I went up) each preceded by "Then" (*Epeita* in Greek). The result seems to be that 1:16-1:17 form a sub-unit and 1:18-2:1 form a second sub-unit with 2:2 starting an elaboration of his "going up to Jerusalem as a result of revelation to put the gospel in conference before the council."

Paul's point is that instead of going up to Jerusalem, his revelation led him away from Jerusalem into Arabia and then into Damascus. Some see here a season where Paul spent time alone in the desert preparing for ministry. While this may very well be the case there is nothing in this text that suggests (at least clearly) that this is the best reading. The point Paul seems to be emphasizing is not where he went (Arabia and Damascus) or what he did when he went there (though he does imply he preached the gospel to the Gentiles there), but Paul emphasizes here that he did not go toward Jerusalem but away from it. Paul could be trying to help his readers find release from the authority that Jerusalem might have over their thinking. Christianity is not, Paul could be emphasizing, a "Jerusalem" religion. This idea is somewhat paralleled later in Galatians 4 where Paul compares "Spiritual Jerusalem" to earthly Jerusalem. We, too, should go away from earthly Jerusalem (the law) and instead go into Spiritual Jerusalem, which he defines here as "by revelation."

**Galatians 1:18** "Then after three years I went up to Jerusalem to visit Cephas and remained with him fifteen days." ( Ἔπειτα μετὰ ἔτη τρία ἀνῆλθον εἰς Ἱεροσόλυμα ἱστορῆσαι Κηφᾶν καὶ ἐπέμεινα πρὸς αὐτὸν ἡμέρας δεκαπέντε, )

The first "Then" coupled with a directional verb occurs here starting a new subunit. It is contrasted with the statement "I did not go up to Jerusalem" in verse 17. The journey to Jerusalem happens, Paul makes clear, only after the three years he spent in Arabia and Damascus. (This three-year time period appears to be between Acts 9:25 and Acts 9:26.) During this visit, Paul's main task was to spend time seeking information from Peter. Paul uses the word "historeō" (ἱστορέω) to describe his purpose. It most likely means in this context "to visit to obtain information." We get our modern word *history* from it. It appears Paul wanted to hear firsthand about the life of Jesus.

**Galatians 1:19-20** "But I saw none of the other apostles except James the Lord's brother. 20 (In what I am writing to you, before God, I do not lie!)" ( ἕτερον δὲ τῶν ἀποστόλων οὐκ εἶδον εἰ μὴ Ἰάκωβον τὸν ἀδελφὸν τοῦ κυρίου. 20 ἃ δὲ γράφω ὑμῖν, ἰδοὺ ἐνώπιον τοῦ θεοῦ ὅτι οὐ ψεύδομα )

Paul then makes clear he did not spend any time with any other apostles except for Peter and James, the Lord's brother. Interestingly, Paul implies here that James was considered an apostle at this time. This portion of the text is aligned structurally with 2:9 and shows that the contents of 2:2-10 are to be read in parallel with 1:10-2:1. This "stitching" may be the main reason Paul mentions James here, but we should ask ourselves if is there any other reason he might mention James, the Lord's brother? One possibility is that he wants to make the connection stronger back to Jesus himself. Another possibility comes from a canonical perspective. David Trobisch has suggested that there was possibly a final form of the 27 NT books published as a single unit at some point in the forming of the canon. If so, this could be a note to help readers see that James, the epistle is to be in some way compared and contrasted to this material, i.e. this material (Galatians) is in a parallel position to that epistle. In Trobisch's theory, the New Testament as a whole focuses on resolving a tension between two versions of the gospel, one most clearly represented by Paul and the other by James (And maybe Peter). While this position is untenable for someone who believes in inerrancy in the way that I do, it still may be helpful. If a "whole" New Testament literary unit or canon existed in this way, it could still be helpful to see Galatians and James (And maybe 1-2 Peter) forming two major structural units that are to be read in parallel.

The final comment by Paul in these verses (v. 20) may feel surprising and unnecessary. A literal translation might be: *Now the things I am writing, Listen! Before God, I do not lie.* Again, why did Paul add this comment? Maybe, it was simply to emphasize the nature of his letter. "You can trust me!" There are some similarities to 2:11-14 where Paul describes a confrontation with Peter. This could simply be another way for Paul to add structure so that we read not just 2:2-10 in connection with 1:10-2:1 but instead, 2:2-2:14. Notice again the mention of James, Peter, Judea/Jews, I saw, only, and even the geographical references (Antioch; Syria, the region where Antioch was located; Cilicia). It simply could be that 1:18-2:1 (or maybe 2) includes multiple lexemes that are then again found in 2:9 (or even 7)-2:14 forming a clear parallel structure so that 1:10-2:1 is in parallel to 2:2-2:14 with 2:9-2:14 being specifically structurally connected to 1:18-2:1.

For now, it is only important to know these verbal links so that as we read we remember to compare by reading them together.

**Galatians 1:21-24** "Then I went into the regions of Syria and Cilicia. 22 And I was still unknown in person to the churches of Judea that are in Christ. They only were hearing it said, "He who used to persecute us is now preaching the faith he once tried to destroy." 24 And they glorified God because of me." (Ἔπειτα ἦλθον εἰς τὰ κλίματα τῆς Συρίας καὶ τῆς Κιλικίας· 22 ἤμην δὲ ἀγνοούμενος τῷ προσώπῳ ταῖς ἐκκλησίαις τῆς Ἰουδαίας ταῖς ἐν Χριστῷ. μόνον δὲ ἀκούοντες ἦσαν ὅτι ὁ διώκων ἡμᾶς ποτε νῦν εὐαγγελίζεται τὴν πίστιν ἥν ποτε ἐπόρθει, 24 καὶ ἐδόξαζον ἐν ἐμοὶ τὸν θεόν.)

As noted above, Paul uses many elements that give structure here. This is the second "Then" statement of the subunit which begins in verse 18 and ends in 2:1. Syria is the region where Antioch is located possibly linking verse 2:1 to 2:11 and the section that follows. It also shows a connection to the end of the subunit in 1:16-17 and 1:18-2:1. Paul wants his readers to know that he left Jerusalem after a short stay and went right back on mission preaching "his" gospel. The churches that were in Judea, in contrast to the ones in Antioch and Cilicia, did not know who he was. They only knew that Paul who had persecuted the church and its faith, now preached the gospel. Paul connects "gospel" to the term "the faith" here. This helps determine what Paul means when he says "the gospel" which for him is then strongly connected to "faith" here and "grace" and "Jesus" previously. It may even be more helpful to have in mind that when Paul mentions "the faith" he could just as easily have used the term "gospel" and meant the same thing. He appears, in other words, to use the terms interchangeably.

Paul here declares that the churches are "in Christ." This subtle reference to their position and identity saturates Paul's thinking and therefore his gospel. To be a Christian means to be "in Christ." We are in Christ and Christ is in us. (v.17)

Paul adds a bracket to his statement in Galatians 1:13 "I persecuted the church of God violently and tried to destroy it" when he says here "He who used to persecute us is now preaching the faith he once tried to destroy" forming a unit of thought within. He also uses the same root in Galatians 1:15 "pleased" (eudokēsen) as he does here "glorify" (edoxazon). Also, as a reader, keep this text in mind when we read 2:9-14. Paul describes here his relationship to Peter, James and the churches of Judea. He will do so again in chapter two. See commentary on 2:9-14 for more details.

# Galatians 2.2-10

**Interpretive Translation:**

Then[28] I went back up to Jerusalem with Barnabas. It was our first visit in fourteen years. We took Titus with us this time, too. I went back because Jesus revealed in me that it was his will to do so.[29] *When I got there*, I presented in detail to each individual church leader[30] the Gospel[31] message I had been announcing to the non-Jews for the leaders to evaluate.[32] This process was in place to make sure I was not

---

[28] The last "then" in the text showing a closing out of the previous structure as Paul moves toward an epexegetical section describing his experience before the "thinkers" in Jerusalem.

[29] This is the last iteration of "revelation" language too as he ends the previous section and then moves toward describing his experience in Jerusalem. You summarize the previous section as being about "Revelation" and *not* prioritizing a visit to Jerusalem. This Jerusalem theme may intentionally come up again in Galatians 4 where "spiritual Jerusalem" is set in victory over earthly Jerusalem.

[30] Lit. "According to privacy or each's own" Could mean that it was done so in a private venue to a group or maybe individually, one on one.

[31] Capitalized Gospel here to show that it would appear that the term had possibly taken on a technical meaning at this point to refer to "the message about the work of Jesus." Of such there were many different iterations.

[32] The word translated "set before them" is the word *anatithēmi* (ἀνατίθημι) and means "present or explain very clearly" and "lay before someone for consideration." LN/BDAG. Also consider the word "dokeo" "to think, decide, choose" that is usually translated similar to the ESV in most texts: those who seemed influential." Another possible way to translate this word would be "those who evaluate." This may fit better considering the preceding concept of Paul "presenting for evaluation" in the same sentence. Against this understanding is the use of the same word in 6 and 9. Especially in verse 9 where Paul says that they were "thought to be pillars."

running or had not run a meaningless race.[33] But,[34] they did not require[35] Titus, who was with me and also a Greek, to be circumcised. Now,[36] during all of this, traitorous and pretend friends were snuck[37] into our presentations to investigate the freedom we demonstrate as we live with Jesus the Messiah. They kept trying to find a reason to condemn us and bring us back into slavery. We did not give them even an inch[38] because we wanted to keep the true Gospel message standing strong and clear for you. Now, from the ones who thought themselves to be something important ([39]whatever quality they had possessed before I didn't really care because God does not prefer one person over another because of their personality, experiences or special qualifications.)[40] -The so-called "Special Apostles" who evaluated my

---

[33] It seems here Paul is describing the evaluation process rather honestly. The subject is possibly the evaluators. They were making sure he had not run in vain. (Versus Paul trying to find out if he had run in vain.) This could also be translated as "that I had not run vainly," i.e. it is not in question from Paul's perspective.

[34] Hard to translate what is in the next. "all' oude" which is literally "But, and not" This a strong contrast to what has preceded. It is difficult why there is a strong conjunction here. It may be to show that this was the issue at hand.

[35] This is actually a passive verb in the original text leaving quite a bit of ambiguity. The translation here is that the Jerusalem council are the implied subject of the passive verb. They did not compel or force Titus's circumcision. This seems to fit the strong contrast noted above.

[36] This is noted by many as a difficult contrition. Is it "because of" these traitors? Is it (as above) during or throughout? the presentation? Could also be "We did not submit for the sake of." And maybe an interrogative "Why?" Why did we not submit? (unlikely)

[37] The word was used to describe spies or traitors who infiltrate an opposing camp.

[38] Literally "did not submit to for an hour"

[39] Alternate translation- "Now from the ones who thought to something, whatever they ever where, it makes no different to me"

[40] Most translations say "God does not show partiality." Literally it says, "God does not the face of man." The idea is that your unique qualities do not make you more special to God or preferred by God.

message did not ask that I change it at all.[41] But, on the contrary, they perceived that God had handed me a unique responsibility to announce the gospel to the uncircumcised just like Peter was given the same responsibility to the circumcised because the one who worked through Peter in his assignment to the circumcised worked also in me to the non-Jews. They also knew the grace God gave to me. So,[42] James, Cephas and John, the ones who were considered the main leaders of the Church[43], endorsed me and brought me into their community.[44] They assigned the non-Jews to Barnabas and me and themselves to the circumcised. They only asked that we would find a way to support the poor in Jerusalem, which I was already invested in doing.

**Summary Commentary:**

Paul continues a description of his personal story, one that he believes should give his version of the gospel authority over others. It is a continuation of an answer to the question "Am I trying to please man or God?" and is an elaboration to the first part of the answer: "Because the gospel I preached to you is not an invention of a man. it was taught to me through a revelation from Jesus Christ." He starts this text and ends the previous one by describing his eventual trip to Jerusalem. Just in

---

[41] Literally "Did not add anything to me." Most likely refers to not adding or amending his message at all.

[42] The previous 3 sentences in this translations are actually modifiers of the verb coming in the next verse each in the original being built off of participle. (three different participles)

[43] Maybe, Paul is here acknowledging that at least these three have a meaningless place of authority as his tone towards them seems to change. Maybe they were even distinct from the earlier "perceived as influential" groups. Before Paul is only seen presenting to "those who are taught to be influential" or "considered." Could this be simply a group of other leaders? As opposed to the those who are actually considered pillars? To support this interpretation is the strong contrast from "tounantion" "on the contrary." This could be brought out by translating, "Contrary to these, James, Cephas, and John…"

[44] Literally "gave me the right hand of fellowship or partnership."

case his readers mistake his intent as being contrary to his previous statements about his message not being "from man," he makes sure to share that the only reason he is going to Jerusalem is because Jesus told him to via another revelation. This paragraph begins with several clauses that begin with the preposition "de" in Greek, usually translated as *but*, and or *then*. He goes through each one and then at the end, he uses three participles to describe why James, Cephas (Peter) and John took him on as a partner. He begins with a reference to "those who are influential." He does so again right in the middle in verse 6 (twice). Then, he finishes this section with one last reference to the last group. Overall the message of this paragraph is that Paul's version of the gospel was validated by James, Cephas, and John and nothing was added to it.

**Galatians 2.2** "I went up because of a revelation and set before them (though privately before those who seemed influential) the gospel that I proclaim among the Gentiles, in order to make sure I was not running or had not run in vain." (ἀνέβην δὲ κατὰ ἀποκάλυψιν· καὶ ἀνεθέμην αὐτοῖς τὸ εὐαγγέλιον ὃ κηρύσσω ἐν τοῖς ἔθνεσιν, κατ᾽ ἰδίαν δὲ τοῖς δοκοῦσιν, μή πως εἰς κενὸν τρέχω ἢ ἔδραμον. )

"I went up because of a revelation" - Now for a third time, Paul references a revelation. He does so for three possible reasons. 1) To give clear structure to the text. He uses the same term throughout the previous paragraph. This is the transition to his next idea. 2) It appears to be important to Paul to describe his spiritual life in terms of "revelations." This may become a contextual clue to his meaning later in the epistle when he says we should "walk with the Spirit." 3) It may seem odd that, after he gives so much fuss to explaining that he did not need to go to Jerusalem he now goes there. This statement explains why. He did so because he was told to.

"set before them (though privately before those who seemed influential) the gospel that I proclaim among the Gentiles" - What did Paul do in Jerusalem? He presented the gospel to a group there. The word for "present" is anethemēn (ἀνατίθημι). It means to present for evaluation, or literally "to hold up." It is the same word used when Festus presents Paul's cause before the king in Acts 25:13. It pictures a lawyer arguing for the defense of a position. Who did he present it to? Well, at the beginning of the paragraph we only know that it was 1) to people in Jerusalem and 2) to "those who consider." From the previous paragraph, it may assumed that this might include Peter and James but it could also be a more ambiguous group of leaders. Some translations say "those who are influential" and that is possible. It could be a more typical use of the participle form of "dokeo"(δοκέω) which means "to consider, to think." So here it could be "Those who considered or evaluated the gospel" instead. Either is a possible understanding of what Paul intended. It may be best to simply translate it as "leaders." The exact group is ambiguous this word refers to. Most translators see it as referring to the Apostles and Elders as we see in Acts 15. Even in this case though, who would that be? It is more clear what an apostle is but what is an Elder and who is included? Though James seems to be referred to as an apostle earlier he might have also been an Elder leading to a conflation of the two. The group may include many more than just the twelve. It may include many different parts of the church and different leaders. While verse 9 does designate James, Peter and John as "those who were considered," there are reasons to see them as being in contrast to the original group or at least as a subsection of it. In other words, it may be that Paul presented his message to many "evaluators" but the subsection of James, Peter, and John gave him the right hand of fellowship. It does appear a heresy had formed in Jerusalem as described in Acts 15 and it is this heresy that Paul is addressing in this letter to churches throughout the province of Galatia.

"Privately" comes from the Greek word "idios" and typically means "one's own" or "of one." It can mean privately so that Paul is giving his teaching in a private place versus a public one, i.e. not at the Temple court or the synagogue but in a house-type setting. It may also mean "individually" so that Paul is describing going from person to person presenting his *version* of the gospel. If the latter is the case, then it could help us picture correctly the entire set of events. Paul goes from house to house explaining the gospel he had been preaching. Many groups did not accept his teaching, but James, Peter and John -the ones who were pillars did. (See verse 9)

"in order to make sure I was not running or had not run in vain." - Because much of the situation Paul is describing is a bit unclear and ambiguous, Paul might have intended two potential opposite, optional meanings for this phrase. If he is presenting to the Jerusalem leadership that later confirms his ministry (James, Peter and John) then we should take it literally and straightforwardly. "I presented my gospel to James, Peter and Paul to make sure that I did not run (go forward) in vain." If this is the case, he was stating a genuine and simple purpose for his visit. He wanted the endorsement of the Apostles and Elders in Jerusalem.

Paul, though, appears to speak of his audience in less positive terms for most of this paragraph. He also has stated rather clearly up to this point that it was not important for him to get this kind of approval or endorsement from Jerusalem. He might be speaking rather "tongue in cheek." He may also want us to understand that his journey to Jerusalem might be in vain if they did not accept his gospel. The ambiguity should pull us in and make us pay attention.

The word translated "run" (trechō) is used two times in this phrase and could be understood more as "to take action" or "to attempt to do something." In its most general usage, it speaks to exertion and sometimes progress. Paul simply says that he desires to not act or exert himself in vain. He may simply be saying that his presentation was to show that he did not act in vain. Paul could be saying one of three things in this text:

That he was defending his mission as "not being in vain." - "I made a presentation *showing* that it was not in vain."
That he was defending his mission so that his endeavors would not be wasted - "I made a presentation *so that* my endeavors would not be worthless."

That his presentation was done in the best way and therefore not wasted - "I made my presentation privately to the group who has authority over such matters therefore the presentation was not in vain."

While all three are possible, I lean toward the first option. The *purpose* of his presentation was to prove that his actions made a real and theological sound impact. They were not in vain. "I am not acting nor did I act in vain" -i.e. without purpose and true impact.

The word translated as "vain" in the ESV can also be read as "not true" (See LN). This most likely and more accurately fits the context. "I did not progress into falsehood."

**Galatians 2.3** "But even Titus, who was with me, was not forced to be circumcised, though he was a Greek." (ἀλλ' οὐδὲ Τίτος ὁ σὺν ἐμοί, Ἕλλην ὤν, ἠναγκάσθη περιτμηθῆναι·)

"But even Titus, who was with me, was not forced to be circumcised, though he was a Greek." - This sentence rather simply makes a statement about Titus. We will look at some of the details together in a moment but before we get to that, let's not miss the position of this sentence as denoted by the conjunction *but*. Paul says he made his presentation showing that his actions were not without purpose or impact *but* Titus was not compelled to be circumcised. Again, Paul could mean at least a couple of different things. The most common understanding of this clause is that it simply states that Titus, even after this church conference, did not feel an inner compulsion to be circumcised. Another option relates more to the understanding I am presenting above. If Paul is saying that his presentation showed his actions were impactful then the transition to this sentence with the conjunction "but" could be a way to show what his ministerial actions (the ones that were not in vain) looked like. "I have proven that my ministerial actions were *valid* and, even with this being the case, Titus, because he is a Greek, had no compulsion to get circumcised."

If Paul intends for us to read a more positive view into the audience of his presentation -or maybe at least a neutral one, then the meaning of this sentence might read more as "I presented a defense of my gospel message to the church leaders in Jerusalem and they did not obligate Titus to be circumcised." If Paul intended this idea, then he is probably presenting Titus's non-circumcision as an argument against "law following" in the gospel. In other words, the church leadership in Jerusalem did not obligate Titus to be circumcised so no one should obligate anyone to do so or be constrained to follow the law in any way. I believe Paul intends this direction for his text. Notice that this statement about Titus occurs at the beginning of this paragraph and then at the end, starting in verse seven, Paul begins to make his main point, that the Jerusalem leaders didn't add anything to the gospel he presented. As he does he repeatedly refers to Jews and non-Jews as circumcised and uncircumcised. He does this to show that what happens here, in 2.2, concludes with what happens in 2.7-10 -they added nothing to his gospel message. Verse 2 illustrates biographically verses 7-10.

Let's focus on one word in this sentence. The Greek word, anagkazō, is translated as "forced" in the ESV. It can mean *compel, force, urge* or *press upon*. It can refer to internal and external forces. A person's heart can compel them. Another person can press upon or urge another person to an act, thought or feeling. Paul uses the same word again in 2:13 where Paul describes that Peter "forced the Gentiles to live like Jews." Notably, Paul also ends the entire epistle with a similar statement: "It is those who want to make a good showing in the flesh who would *force* you to be circumcised." This verse serves as an ending "thesis" statement or summary of the book. (See Galatians 6:12-16) So, while Peter tried to press upon the Gentiles the need to live like a Jew when he visited Antioch, this council did not do so to Titus. And, as Paul closes the letter he gives a scathing review of anyone who compels others to get circumcised:

> "It is those who want to make a good showing in the flesh who would force you to be circumcised, and only in order that they may not be persecuted for the cross of Christ. For even those

who are circumcised do not themselves keep the law, but they desire to have you circumcised that they may boast in your flesh. But far be it from me to boast except in the cross of our Lord Jesus Christ"
(Galatians 6:12–14 ESV)

We will look at Paul's commentary on his experience with Peter when we get to 2:11-14. For now, though, don't miss the similarity in language between his rebuke of Peter in 2:14 and his rebuke of anyone who adds the law to the gospel in 6:12. He strongly intends us as readers to make a connection between these three sentences. With this in mind, he sets up Titus as the "counterpoint" against any compulsion or obligation to follow the law.

**Galatians 2.4** "Yet because of false brothers secretly brought in—who slipped in to spy out our freedom that we have in Christ Jesus, so that they might bring us into slavery—" (διὰ δὲ τοὺς παρεισάκτους ψευδαδέλφους, οἵτινες παρεισῆλθον κατασκοπῆσαι τὴν ἐλευθερίαν ἡμῶν ἣν ἔχομεν ἐν Χριστῷ Ἰησοῦ, ἵνα ἡμᾶς καταδουλώσουσιν, )

"Yet because of false brothers secretly brought in" - The fourth "de" clause begins here in verse 4. The main reason this is helpful is to track how Paul is building his argument and explaining his thoughts. As we see clearly how he is progressing from one idea to the other we can better understand what he means in each part. Each of these "de" statements except the first one, has also included a preposition that helps us understand the relationship to the first "de" statement. The first one, in verse 2, says "Now (de) privately or individually I presented to the leadership." Literally, it says something more like "Now, *according* to each individual" with the "according to" representing the first preposition. Then in verse 4, "Now, but Titus did not" where "but" is fulfilling a similar position. Next, in verse 4, "Now, *because of*." The point is that each "de" statement explains something new about Paul's "going up" to Jerusalem. 1) He presented *privately* to the leadership. 2) *Contrary* to what one might expect and to what happens in Peter's visit, Titus was not asked to be circumcised. And 3) *Because* false brothers have been stuck in. The way this is structured might suggest that this phrase should be read as an additional description or modifier for the previous two statements versus introducing what comes next. In other words, Paul may be saying "I went up to Jerusalem and because false brothers were snuck in I presented privately to the leadership."

The word translated as "secretly brought in" comes from a word that at times describes spies who sneak into the camp of an enemy army. The clear picture Paul gives his readers is one of nefarious enemies. He explains their nefarious purpose in the next phrase.

"—who slipped in to spy out our freedom that we have in Christ Jesus so that they might bring us into slavery—" - Paul repeats a similar sounding word to "snuck in" above. These false brothers came to spy out just how far Paul took "freedom in Christ." Freedom in Christ becomes the issue at hand during Paul's visit to Jerusalem and also a shorthand for the issue addressed in the book of Galatians. One could re-word the concern as "Just how free are we according to Paul?" He doesn't use the same word again until he makes a major transition in the book towards "limitations" on freedom in 5:1 where he will describe how we use our freedom. In other words, we are completely free in every way, but we should use our freedom for a certain purpose. He will also use the same root from the word behind "spy out" again in 6:1 where he says "Keep watch over yourselves." In contrast to those who inspect Paul (others), inspect yourself.

The wording "who slipped in" comes from a verb in the middle voice. This voice reveals a unique level of personal agency in this process. "They snuck themselves in" could be another way to say it. They found a way to sneak in and did so with the necessary care to be successful. This endeavor was not purely academic either. These spies did not simply hope to get information about Paul's approach to freedom. They wanted to use what they learned to bring Paul and his team back into slavery. Paul will soon clarify that the slavery he speaks about comes from being under the law, i.e. responsible before God to follow the rules and requirements written in the law.

**Galatians 2.5** "to them we did not yield in submission even for a moment, so that the truth of the gospel might be preserved for you." (οἷς οὐδὲ πρὸς ὥραν εἴξαμεν τῇ ὑποταγῇ, ἵνα ἡ ἀλήθεια τοῦ εὐαγγελίου διαμείνῃ πρὸς ὑμᾶς.)

"to them we did not yield in submission even for a moment" - So how did Paul respond to those who snuck in to bring him into slavery under the law? What compromises did he make? He did not yield for even a moment to obey them or respond to them -which is another way to understand the word translated *submission* above. Paul did not give them an inch. That is the point. This is the fifth "de" statement further developing the narrative and expanding what happened when he went up to Jerusalem. Literally, "Now, who, we did not give up to then obey for even an hour."

And why was he so resolute? What motivated him?

"so that the truth of the gospel might be preserved for you." - The faith of the Galatians motivated him. The truth of the gospel was at stake. And, so, Paul did not budge. Compromises can be made but not with the message of the gospel. The word translated *preserved* derives from the Greek word "diamenō" a compounded word from "meno" meaning to remain or stay. The compounded form most likely simply gives "meno" a more emphatic nuance. Paul wants the message -as he taught it- to remain just as it is with them. Other writers used the word *meno* at the time to describe a soldier who refuses to leave a battlefield or a pillar that can be described as "unmovable." Paul defended "his gospel" against all assaults so that it stood strong like an unrelenting soldier or unmovable pillar for the Galatians.

**Galatians 2.6** "And from those who seemed to be influential (what they were makes no difference to me; God shows no partiality)—those, I say, who seemed influential added nothing to me. " (Ἀπὸ δὲ τῶν δοκούντων εἶναί τι, _ ὁποῖοί ποτε ἦσαν οὐδέν μοι διαφέρει· πρόσωπον [ὁ] θεὸς ἀνθρώπου οὐ λαμβάνει _ ἐμοὶ γὰρ οἱ δοκοῦντες οὐδὲν προσανέθεντο)

"And from those who seemed to be influential" - Paul continues with the sixth "de" statement but returns to a previous concept as he ends what might be read as part one of the paragraph. He uses the idea of "those who seem to be influential" (from *dokeō*) in verses 2 and now again in verse 6 as a bracket around the content in the middle. The conjunction "de" will occur again 2 more times in this one verse forming an end to the series of statements that begin with "de" that Paul started in verse 2. So, verses 2-6 form a sub-unit.

As we discussed when we went through verse 2. The identity of the group Paul describes as "those who are considered influential" remains somewhat ambiguous. In verse 2 they were the "considered important" or "ones who think through things" but nothing beyond that defined them. Here the picture gets a bit clearer as if Paul focuses his lens. They are described as "those who seemed to be something" here at first, as opposed to simply those who "seemed" (or had a reputation) or "considered" and maybe "evaluated." Interestingly, Paul still, even in this advance, only says that they seemed to be something. It is as if he is avoiding describing this group as anything special. First, they seemed or considered. Now they seemed to be something. (The Lexicon BDAG adds the possible meanings "had the appearance of" and "recognized as" to our range of possible meanings from Paul.) This exact phrasing occurs in Plato where it means "those who are reputable" according to most translators.

Either way, we know only at this point in the narrative that 1) they were recognized to be something, 2) They were in Jerusalem and 3) They were Paul's audience when he presented a defense of his gospel message.

"what they were makes no difference to me" - This text literally translates as something like: "Of what sort at some point they were, not one thing to me is different." If we were to smooth that up a bit it may be: "It makes no difference to me what sort of people they ever were" or "It does not make them better in my eyes because of what they have done or experienced in the past." Paul's point is clear either way. The ambiguous undefined group, whoever they were and whatever they had done did not cause them to be elevated in his mind.

"God shows no partiality" - And why did Paul not consider this group to be elevated in any way? Because God does not show partiality. A literal translation of what Paul says is "The face of man, God does not prefer or accept." Paul means that God does not accept a person based on surface issues or their "personal identity." Think of the face as the unique identifier of a person, the part we recognize. God does not prefer one person over another based on anything unique about them.

"those, I say, who seemed influential added nothing to me." - Paul temporality pauses what he was going to say about "those who seem to be something" to add a note that "They were not special to him because of what they were" and explains why "God does not prefer one individual over another." Then, he picks up the thread again regarding the role of "those who seem to be something." Here he returns to the simplified form, "those who seemed" not adding "to be something," but it should assumed. What did this group do? They added nothing to Paul. In the wording above it might appear that they did not add anything of value to Paul. "They weren't special to me." But, while that is a possible understanding, context might suggest that they did not add anything to his message. Paul presented his version of the gospel and they did not amend it in any way. This phrase may have a connection to the previous statement that after presenting to "those who seemed to be something" Titus was not compelled to be circumcised. They are in a similar position semantically.

The phrase "added nothing to me" comes from the same Greek word that the ESV translates as "consulted" in 1:15. Notice the many other shared terms between the texts. See the commentary on 2:9 for further discussion.

**Galatians 2.7** "On the contrary, when they saw that I had been entrusted with the gospel to the uncircumcised, just as Peter had been entrusted with the gospel to the circumcised" (ἀλλὰ τοὐναντίον ἰδόντες ὅτι πεπίστευμαι τὸ εὐαγγέλιον τῆς ἀκροβυστίας καθὼς Πέτρος τῆς περιτομῆς,)

Just like the statement about Titus earlier, "but" gives contrast to what was stated. (Translated "on the contrary" in the ESV.) They did not add anything to the message of Paul and then, "instead." Paul follows up the contrast with what they did (as opposed to adding anything to his message). This contrasting conjunction helps us determine that the previous phrase "they added nothing to me" is to be read as "they added nothing to the gospel message I preached."

Previously, Paul used a series of the conjunction "de" to form his thoughts. Now that he has closed out the last one in verse 6 (when he also returned to the idea of "those who seemed to be something" to close out that sub-section), he uses a series of participles to build out his next thought: "they saw" in verse 7, "who worked" in verse 8 and "perceived" in verse 9. These three participles all modify the main verb "they gave" in verse 9. In other words, the Apostles endorsed Paul and his partners when they "saw," because God "worked," and they "perceived" different aspects of his ministry. You could read these three particles as an explanation of Paul's earlier phrase: "showing them that I did not labor without impact (in vain)" from verse 2. He showed them. They observed.

The first participle states that they gave Paul the right hand of partnership (verse 9) because they saw he was entrusted with the gospel of the uncircumcision just like Peter was entrusted with the gospel of the circumcision. This sentence, the first of the three participle phrases, i.e. phrases based on a participle, starts with a simple idea but leaves much to be explained. The simple point is that the Apostles observed something about the ministry of Paul via his presentation: his ministry had similarities to Peter's, but one was to Jews and one to non-Jews. Here, Paul, for the first time in Galatians, uses the terms "circumcised" and "uncircumcised" to describe these two different groups (Jews and

Gentiles), most likely to connect this sentence back to the statement about Titus not being compelled to be circumcised above. (Paul clusters the words relating to circumcision here in this paragraph, the one following, then at the beginning of chapter 5 and again at the end of chapter 6 to show the structure of his letter.)

In this paragraph, we do see a hint about the intention of the law. It was written as laws, rules and regulations for the Jewish community and for living within the Jewish community. The legal code was not written for all people to obey. Note though that the law does not equal the Old Testament nor the first five books of the Bible (The Torah or Pentateuch). These books of the Bible *include* the laws but are not synonymous with them in the same way that the book of Acts includes the story of Paul's conversion but it would be inaccurate to conflate the two as one and the same.

**Galatians 2.8** "for he who worked through Peter for his apostolic ministry to the circumcised worked also through me for mine to the Gentiles" ( ὁ γὰρ ἐνεργήσας Πέτρῳ εἰς ἀποστολὴν τῆς περιτομῆς ἐνήργησεν καὶ ἐμοὶ εἰς τὰ ἔθνη, )

In the ESV translation, this text is in parenthesis though there are no parenthesis in Greek text. Paul does put this phrase in the middle of the three participle phrases giving it emphasis. One could say that the main reason that church leaders in Jerusalem "gave Paul the right hand of fellowship" is because of what he expresses in this phrase. In this phrase, Paul says that God worked for an apostleship in him toward the nations in the same way that he worked in Peter towards the Jews. What does he mean by this statement? Consider that "apostleship" represents Paul's term for his assignment and mission. He operated as an agent sent by God and on behalf of God. Paul, by using this kind of language, claims a position of authority. God himself validated this authority by working supernaturally through Paul. He sets up Peter as the example and purports that the movement that started under Peter's authority possessed similar characteristics to his work and the resulting movement. What God had done through Peter, he also did through Paul.

**Galatians 2.9** "and when James and Cephas and John, who seemed to be pillars, perceived the grace that was given to me, they gave the right hand of fellowship to Barnabas and me, that we should go to the Gentiles and they to the circumcised" (καὶ γνόντες τὴν χάριν τὴν δοθεῖσάν μοι, Ἰάκωβος καὶ Κηφᾶς καὶ Ἰωάννης, οἱ δοκοῦντες στῦλοι εἶναι, δεξιὰς ἔδωκαν ἐμοὶ καὶ Βαρναβᾷ κοινωνίας, ἵνα ἡμεῖς εἰς τὰ ἔθνη, αὐτοὶ δὲ εἰς τὴν περιτομήν·)

Paul, in the Greek text, immediately follows up verses 7-8 with the next participle phrase: "And knowing [perceiving]" giving the reader of the letter in its original form a better picture of the structure. This phrase parallels the phrase we read in verse 7, "Seeing I was entrusted with the gospel." It says something similar: "Knowing or perceiving the grace given to me." Notice how each phrase connects with the others and helps us define each part more fully.

v.7 - Seeing I was entrusted with the gospel for the uncircumcision
v.8 - God worked through me as an agent assigned to Gentiles
v.9 - Perceiving I was given grace (a gift) that we are assigned to the Gentiles

Breaking the text into parts like this can help us see how the pieces line up with each other and also how one part can define the other. This gives insight into two particular pieces of the phrase at hand. The first is the Greek word "ginōskō" translated *perceived*. It is usually translated as "to know" but perceived gives a more clear understanding here as it is in a parallel position to "seeing" in verse 7. This parallel connection suggests the concept of insight and not just "knowledge" and that this insight resulted from observable information not just conceptual. Second, notice how Paul defines "apostleship" in this structure. It is "being entrusted with the gospel" in verse 7, "apostleship (an assignment as an authorized agent)" in verse 8, and then, in verse 9, "a grace or gift" God gave Paul. The idea of a calling being synonymous with "grace" or gifting occurs frequently for Paul. Paul did not see his assignment as a result of his skill or ability, but only an unearned gift of grace. Think, too, how this idea of calling might change our understanding. Our calling does not result from our skills or ability either but God packages it within his kindness and favor towards us. This, of course, repeats what Paul said in 1.15. There Paul did not consult with anyone but operated out of the revelation of Jesus. Here he gains the endorsement of the church leaders after going up to Jerusalem as a a result of a revelation. Paul intends a contrast between what we read in 1.15 and what we read here in this cluster of verses. This also gives us a sense of bracketing so that 1:12 through 2:6-12 (and maybe 14) form a unit. The point of this contrasting structure appears to be to have the reader compare his original posture: did not go up to Jerusalem to his secondary posture: I did go up and was endorsed. What do we take of this? We should potentially gain a sense that Paul wants us to understand the authority of his ministry (and therefore his gospel) primarily comes from God himself and a revelation within from God and then secondarily from the "pillars" in Jerusalem. Both points of authority, though, are recognized.

"James and Cephas and John[45]- Now, after the three participle phrases that support the main sentence, we get to the main sentence. James, Peter and John form that subject. This is the second time Paul has referred to Peter and James. In 1.18-19, Paul says he spent time with Peter and that he saw James. In 2.11-12, he will speak to a time when Peter visited Antioch and when a cohort was sent from James. He will go on to describe that he stood against Peter and this cohort because they did not represent the gospel accurately. In some ways, he deconstructs what he describes here in 2.9 and may be referring back to the context he established in 1.6-9 where he says that some have troubled the Galatians and that if they preach another gospel, even if they are an angel in the flesh, should be condemned. In other words, Peter and the cohort from James represent "those who are anathema."

---

[45] Interesting that John is mentioned here. This is the only place he is mentioned and could serve to highlight his "sanctity" in an otherwise condemning story. This could also reveal a "Johannine" perspective in this text.

Paul will go on to validate a more accurate view of the gospel by showing its scriptural foundation. Here though, he wants his audience to know that he had gained the approval and authority of the church leaders in Jerusalem even though he would soon be standing up against them.

"who seemed to be pillars" - As we have seen above, Paul uses the phrasing "thought to be" or "thought to be something" to describe the group to whom he presented his defense. Each time he gives a little bit more information. First, they "seemed to be" or are "ones who consider." (2.2) Second, using the same Greek word, he describes those who "seemed to be something" but clarifies that this means little to him. Then, the "ones who seem to be" did not add anything to his message. Finally, here, again using the same Greek root (*dokeo*), Paul says that James, Peter and John seemed to be pillars giving them the most detailed description yet. Is this a final positive description of his group of leaders? Or is it still negative? *They only seemed to be pillars.* It is still difficult to asses but as we said in the previous paragraph, Paul does seem to both use this endorsement as part of the validation of his ministry and devalue it when he previously states that he did not immediately confer with this group of people because he supposedly did not need to and when he, in the following verses, describes his rebuke of Peter and James's cohort.

"they gave the right hand of fellowship to Barnabas and me, that we should go to the Gentiles and they to the circumcised" - After the three participle phrases that support the main clause and the subject of the main causes being described, Paul makes his statement. The result of the "influencers" seeing and perceiving God's work in Paul is that he was given "the right hand of fellowship." Fellowship most likely speaks more to partnership than what we might read as "community" but both are seen as part of the same basic concept. Paul makes the point that James, Peter and John approved of his ministry work and his gospel message. They identified their work should focus on Jews (the circumcised) and that Paul and Barnabas should go to the "nations" or non-Jews.

**Galatians 2.10** "Only, they asked us to remember the poor, the very thing I was eager to do." (μόνον τῶν πτωχῶν ἵνα μνημονεύωμεν, ὃ καὶ ἐσπούδασα αὐτὸ τοῦτο ποιῆσαι.)

Paul makes clear in 2.6 that the Apostles did not add anything to the gospel message he preached. They did, though, ask that he and his ministry team remember the poor. Paul makes it clear he intended to do so anyway. As the ESV states, Paul had a strong eagerness or desire to help the poor. Canonically, this may connect to statements James later makes in his epistle that true religion takes care of the poor and that faith is demonstrated and made meaningful to others via this type of work.

# Galatians 2.11-14

**Interpretive Translation:**

Then, when Cephas came to Antioch, I spoke directly to him pushing back against his behavior. I told him that his actions showed that he was in the wrong[46] because, before James sent over a group of Jews from Jerusalem he typically[47] ate with non-Jews, but, after they came, he stopped eating with the Gentiles and began separating himself from them because he was afraid of the circumcised, the Jews.[48] The rest of the Jews displayed the same pretentious illusion of spiritual superiority.[49] Their behavior even convinced Barnabas to walk away from the gospel and into the same heretical hypocrisy. But, when I saw that they teetered and stumbled into and out of the truth of the gospel like a toddler who hasn't learned how to walk correctly I told Peter, in front of everyone, "Why do you demand that the non-Jews live according to the rules and customs of Jews found in the Torah, when you actually are a Jew but live like a pagan and do not practice those same rules and customs?"

**Summary Commentary:**

---

[46] The text says that Paul confronted Peter "hoti" which most translators explain as "because." It can also be explaining what he said to Peter in this confrontation. (It can be understood as either *because* or *that*.)

[47] Imperfect verb showing past continual action disgniied here by "always."

[48] "The circumcised" - Could be simply a short hand for the Jews as in 2.7,9. This contextual connection suggests that. Other translators refer to this as an isolated group who were proponents of circumcision.

[49] "Played the hypocrite together with" - The word speaks to "putting on a show" and in this case to elevate themselves spiritually. This connects thematically to what Paul says about James and Peter in 2.7. "They seemed to be something but whatever they were, it didn't make them better to me because God doesn't evaluate based on the surface" i.e. based on titles or religious performance.

As Paul ends the first major "biographical" or narrative introduction section of the text, he shares an experience with Peter (and James by extension) where he had to oppose them because they did not live up to a mature commitment to the gospel. In many ways, this operates as the crescendo of this section. After many statements and reflections about the gospel and his lack of need for endorsement, Paul begrudgingly admits to finally going to Jerusalem for an endorsement and then, in the section that falls immediately after, describes the Peter and James cohort as "condemned." Where previously they "perceived" (*kai gnontes*) the grace given to Him, He identified them as "wrong" (*katagnontes*) here. We also see a clear theme developing that spiritual strength and life comes in the "truth of the gospel" (2.14 and 2.5). In the previous paragraph, Paul fought to preserve this truth. Here he opposed Peter and James because they did not walk with maturity and stability within the truth of the gospel. Throughout this text, Paul appears to identify Peter and James as being part of the problem that he had identified in the first few verses of Galatians, those who preach another gospel. Those who preach another gospel, even if they are an angel from heaven, are anathema. Paul "set before" (from the same Greek word for *anathema*) the gospel. (He gave a presentation about his message.) In this text, 2.11, *Peter* is the one who stands condemned.

**Galatians 2.11** "But when Cephas came to Antioch, I opposed him to his face, because he stood condemned. " (Ὅτε δὲ ἦλθεν Κηφᾶς εἰς Ἀντιόχειαν, κατὰ πρόσωπον αὐτῷ ἀντέστην, ὅτι κατεγνωσμένος ἦν. )

Paul states his main idea in this paragraph: "I stood against him to his face." He had just stated that he did not see Peter and James as "better" in any way because God does not evaluate based on one's "face." Now, he opposes Peter to his face. He pushed against Peter's error of belief and corresponding behavior. Most translators suggest that Paul opposed Peter and James because they were already condemned. Another optional understanding of this phrase is that it serves as the content of his opposition. Paul stood against Peter by stating he was already judged to be in the wrong. The word translated "stood condemned" is the Greek word "kataginōskō." Notice the same root word that Paul just used in 2.9, "kai ginosko." This may be to provide a contrast. While Peter and James *identified* Paul as having grace from God as the apostle to the Gentiles, Paul *identified* Peter as "guilty" or condemned. This term "condemned" is often used in the context of a court as "shown to be guilty." The choice could be relevant to the fact that in 2.2 Paul presented his case (like a lawyer from the Greek word "anatithemai").[50]

**Galatians 2.12** "For before certain men came from James, he was eating with the Gentiles; but when they came he drew back and separated himself, fearing the circumcision party." (πρὸ τοῦ γὰρ ἐλθεῖν τινας ἀπὸ Ἰακώβου μετὰ τῶν ἐθνῶν συνήσθιεν· ὅτε δὲ ἦλθον, ὑπέστελλεν καὶ ἀφώριζεν ἑαυτὸν φοβούμενος τοὺς ἐκ περιτομῆς. )

Paul begins to describe the experience in Antioch that led him to oppose Peter. Peter had made it his habit to eat with Gentiles. The verb "to eat" is an imperfect verb signifying continual or repeated action. Peter practiced this approach to eating. These meals could either occur regularly as normal daily meals or as a part of communion which would have been celebrated as a full meal possibly like a Passover feast. They also would have had these communion meals every time they gathered as the church in Antioch. When they did so, Peter shared the meal with Gentiles. This expands the issue at hand concerning the law beyond circumcision and into any possible rule one might apply from the Torah for following Jesus and living according to the truth of the gospel.

At some point after Paul left the Jerusalem council he described above and in the writing of this letter Peter spent time in Antioch and at some point while he stayed there, James sent a group of people to visit with them too. Paul makes it clear that the error he rebukes comes from Peter and James. In so doing, he shows his willingness to stand against the pillars of the church for the sake of the gospel and reveals that the true church has been de-tethered from the authority in Jerusalem. No

---

[50] Additionally while the root word Paul uses for "to oppose" comes from different main root word it is similar phonetically to "anathema" - "antestan"

hierarchy existed or should be respected. This subtly implies the autonomy of the local community. Peter and James did not hold a position above the Galatian churches nor did they define an accurate or acceptable position in the gospel.

In the same way that he made it his habit to eat with the Gentiles, Peter then, after James's cohort arrived, stopped eating with them and made it his new habit to eat only with the Jews. "He pulled back and he departed himself" both reflect two more imperfect verbs and continual action. Paul uses the same word he used when God "separated" him into a calling by grace. Notice again the connection to 2.9; "Peter, James, fellowship." So, a thread links 1.15-16 to 2.6b-9 and now to 2.14-15.[51] Paul seems to draw our attention to three facts 1) God separated him by grace as an Apostle to the Gentiles and he did not seek approval or counsel from anyone 2) when he did eventually consult with others they did not add anything to him or his message but recognized God's grace and work in Him and then 3) He stood against these same "pillars" as they *separated* themselves based on a weak faith in impure gospel.

The emotion of fear motivated Peter's action, fear was the cause. He feared the Jews or "the circumcision." Some identify this as a special group within Jewish believers and that may be the case. Paul had just used the same term though to describe the Jews as a whole. Either way, he may intend to emphasize the requirement of circumcision or other legal issues from the Torah as part of their identity. Peter allowed their emphasis on following the legal requirements of the law to create a fear of acceptance that then motivated anti-gospel behavior.

**Galatians 2:13** "And the rest of the Jews acted hypocritically along with him, so that even Barnabas was led astray by their hypocrisy." (καὶ συνυπεκρίθησαν αὐτῷ [καὶ] οἱ λοιποὶ Ἰουδαῖοι, ὥστε καὶ Βαρναβᾶς συναπήχθη αὐτῶν τῇ ὑποκρίσει.)

---

[51] Called by grace, Separated, "Consulted/added to me"

Peter's behavior had a ripple effect. He withdrew and then so did the other Jews. Paul characterizes this behavior as "synypokrinomai" -"to pretend together or to join in hypocrisy." (Louw Nida) The idea paints a picture of pretense and illusion. They put on a show of being superior spiritually though no authentic superiority existed. In other words, their actions had no connection to reality. Reality: all are what they are before God because of the grace of Jesus given freely to all. The act: some Christians are elevated because they practice Jewish rules and customs. As a result of this groundswell of hypocrisy and snobbery, Barnabas himself stopped believing the gospel and began to believe in the law. The Louw Nida lexicon defines the word translated "led astray" above as "to cause someone else in addition to change from belief in what is true to belief in what is false." The issue here, then, relates to a change in belief amongst Peter first, then the Jews in Antioch, and then Barnabas. A movement against the gospel gained momentum.

**Galatians 2:14** "But when I saw that their conduct was not in step with the truth of the gospel, I said to Cephas before them all, "If you, though a Jew, live like a Gentile and not like a Jew, how can you force the Gentiles to live like Jews?"" (ἀλλ' ὅτε εἶδον ὅτι οὐκ ὀρθοποδοῦσιν πρὸς τὴν ἀλήθειαν τοῦ εὐαγγελίου, εἶπον τῷ Κηφᾷ ἔμπροσθεν πάντων· εἰ σὺ Ἰουδαῖος ὑπάρχων ἐθνικῶς καὶ οὐχὶ Ἰουδαϊκῶς ζῇς, πῶς τὰ ἔθνη ἀναγκάζεις ἰουδαΐζειν; )

Barnabas joined their heretical hypocrisy. Paul saw their actions and spoke up against them. Paul stood up and spoke against Peter, the de facto leader of Christianity, Barnabas, his partner in gospel ministry and the Jews, his own people group and community. He describes their behavior as "not in step with the truth of the gospel." The word translated as "not in step" comes from the word "orthopodeō." It can mean, as translated here, "to be out of step." It can also mean "to live in moral correctness" so here it might mean they did not make moral choices and take the corresponding actions that reflect the gospel. Most commonly from other Greek documents at this time it was used to describe teetering in one's walk. The Lexicon Spicq explains, "The word refers to children who are beginning to get around on their own two legs without having to hold the nurse's hand to keep from falling. Thus our verb would be the opposite of *choleuein*, 'walk unsteadily, limp.'"

This word paints a picture of the challenge Paul addresses here in this immediate historical context and in many ways throughout the book of Galatians. Paul identifies that at times believers walk like toddlers as it relates to the gospel. They teeter and totter. They fall down. They wobble. This reveals what it looks like as we mature in the gospel. In our immaturity, we wobble back and forth between believing the gospel and living out a life that corresponds to that truth. Maturity here is growing stronger and firmer in our constant belief in the gospel.

Next, Paul describes the decisions and actions that are "anti-gospel." Simply put, Peter tried to force the Gentiles in Antioch to live under the rules and customs of Jews. He uses the same word here to describe Peter's *forceful* compulsion of these Christians to live under the law as he did earlier to describe the fact that Titus did not experience any compulsion or direction to receive circumcision in verse 3. Paul may have created this contrast to show that soon after Titus did not experience such a compulsion from Peter and James, Peter, along with James's cohort visited Antioch and did require similar stipulations. They displayed a toddler-like waddle, back and forth, and ultimately that is Paul's rebuke.

# Galatians 2.15-21

**Interpretive Translation:**

Those of us who are biologically Jewish and not of Gentile stock, even we are sinners. We also know that God does not consider any person righteous because they follow the rules and customs written in the Torah. We know that a person is only labeled righteous when they trust in Christ himself. Because we know that, we ourselves trusted in Jesus Christ so that we would be labeled righteous as a result of the trustworthiness of Christ and not out of obeying the commandments in the Torah. This is because God has never considered any human being as righteous because they obeyed the collection of commandments listed in the Torah. Have I made my point? But what happens when find ourselves characterized by sinning -as we will!- even though we continually look to Christ to make us righteous before God? Does this mean Christ succumbs to sin? That's impossible! Here's what it does mean: I only continue to exist as a transgressor of the law if I re-establish the law that I had formerly annulled.[52] Sin no longer exists in Christ because the law that defines sin no longer stands. The law caused my death, but then I was dead to its power and authority so that I could live under the power, authority and life of God himself. Follow me here. I was crucified when Christ was crucified because I am unified to Christ. Now, I do not live my own life. Christ lives in me and through me. This life that looks like my life is actually the life of Jesus. I live out what Christ lives in me as I trust in Him to do all my living for me. He is the Son of God. He loves me. He really loves me.[53] And, He gave himself up to suffer and die in my place. I do not disdain

---

[52] This may be one of the more important and more difficult sentences in this text. This translation ultimately leans heavily on context. Paul says basically that Christ is not empowering people to sin by justifying them apart from works because that would mean that the category of "sinner" is still in effect. But, Paul says, basically that Christ can't succumb to sin because no such thing exists in the new paradigm. The Law established sin. Sin established death. Remove the law and the entire system falls.

[53] Repeated here to show emphasis of an aorist form.

God's free unearned favor. If I try to get God to consider me righteous because I obey the rules, customs, and commands written in the Torah then Christ died needlessly.)

**Summary Commentary:**

Paul makes a significant shift as he moves from historical narrative to exhortation. After telling the story of his ministerial development and endorsement, concluding with the identification of Peter and James as sources of anti-gospel behavior, Paul explains the content of the gospel he preached. He does so within the context of the tendency of some Jews to suggest following the rules of the law remains a requirement for those who would be considered righteous. He begins by simply stating that the Jews -even though they are not Gentiles- are still sinners. He then says three different times in only slightly different ways that no one is justified by doing the commandments found written in the law. Only those who trust in Christ are justified. After this emphatic description, he comes back to the first statement that began the section. What does it mean that we are still sinners after pursuing justification through Christ? Does this mean that Christ has no authority over sin? He answers this question emphatically. No! He then explains his answer by suggesting that the category of "sin" no longer exists because the law, which gives identity to sin, has been disempowered. He is dead to the law because the law makes him dead he says. If he is dead though, how does he live? This is the deeper and more detailed dive into the experience of "being dead to the law."

Paul moves into a description of his spiritual life once he explains that he is dead to the law. He makes five coordinated statements:

1) He lives by God (or is alive to God)
2) He was crucified with Christ
3) He no longer lives his life
4) Christ lives inside of Him
5) The life he now appears to live in his body he lives by faith in the son of God

As he ends this sentence he comes back to a thought that he began the section with: Christ, the one who loved us, gave himself on behalf of us. Then, to bring final closure he summarizes this sub-section and in many ways the first two chapters of the book: If a person is justified by works of the law then Christ died needlessly.

**Galatians 2.15** "We ourselves are Jews by birth and not Gentile sinners" (Ἡμεῖς φύσει Ἰουδαῖοι καὶ οὐκ ἐξ ἐθνῶν ἁμαρτωλοί)

Paul here makes a significant transition from historical narrative to explaining why the events he has described have an impact. This begins his exhortation to the Gentiles. We can read this sentence in two ways. The first appears in the ESV translation where Paul says in what most would read as a "tongue in cheek" way that the Jews differ in spiritual quality above and beyond the sinful Gentiles. "We are not Gentile sinners." While most translations and commentaries agree with that option I prefer a different but equally possible reading. We can read Paul's statement oppositely so that Paul lines up two modifiers of his subject, "we:" 1) By nature Jews and 2) not out of the Gentiles. Then, and this is his main point, he says that this group, those that are by nature Jews and not the Gentiles, are sinners. In other words, he says, "We, too, are sinners." This understanding fits the context of the previous section where Paul describes Peter and the Jews showing off their superior spiritual pedigrees as Jews. It makes sense then that he would then make a statement about their status as sinners. It also fits with the parallel statement in 2.17, "We are found, even ourselves, sinners." Paul, with this transitional sentence, introduces a key idea: what to do with the fact that people are sinners ever after they have "sought to be justified by Christ" including the supposedly (but not really) superior Jews.

**Galatians 2.16** "yet we know that a person is not justified by works of the law but through faith in Jesus Christ, so we also have believed in Christ Jesus, in order to be justified by faith in Christ and not by works

of the law, because by works of the law no one will be justified."
(εἰδότες [δὲ] ὅτι οὐ δικαιοῦται ἄνθρωπος ἐξ ἔργων νόμου ἐὰν μὴ διὰ πίστεως Ἰησοῦ Χριστοῦ, καὶ ἡμεῖς εἰς Χριστὸν Ἰησοῦν ἐπιστεύσαμεν, ἵνα δικαιωθῶμεν ἐκ πίστεως Χριστοῦ καὶ οὐκ ἐξ ἔργων νόμου, ὅτι ἐξ ἔργων νόμου οὐ δικαιωθήσεται πᾶσα σάρξ. )

The emphatic nature of this next verse shows the weightiness of its content. Paul says basically the same thing three times in a row. A version of: "No one is justified by the works of the law but through faith in Jesus." If we see this text (2.15-21) as a transition into the primary exhortation of the text, this may imply that this portion serves as a "thesis" or launching pad for the next major section even as it ends this, the first major section. In other words, at least at some level, the book of Galatians expands on the ideas found here: God justified sinners based on faith in Christ alone and not based on doing works in the law at all.

The main clause of this verse occurs in the middle and is translated as "so we also have believed in Christ Jesus." Two dependent clauses above and below this sentence support the idea of the main clause showing the purpose and context for this "belief." The Jews also believed, Paul explains, a) *because* they knew (verse 17a) that no human is justified by works of the law but because of "the faith of Christ" and b) *because* no flesh is justified out of the works of the law. This verse follows a chiastic structure:

A1 - Knowing that no person is justified out of the works of the law but instead through the faith of Jesus Christ
B - We also trusted in Christ Jesus so that we might be justified out of faith in Christ and not out of the works of the law
A2 - Because of the works of the law no flesh is justified

This structure highlights a few key elements. First, the central idea emphasizes Paul's main point: The Jews *also* trusted Christ for justification. They needed his work of justification as much as anyone. (Why? Because of the second idea.) Verse 17a, translated in a woodenly literal way might read: knowing that not justified is a man out of works of law, and 17c might be: because out of works of law not is justified, any flesh. So, because a person is not justified nor any "flesh" is justified by "works of law," Paul and the other Jewish Christians trust in Christ *too* for salvation. Paul will go on to show that this concept of justification comes from the Torah as we move into Chapters 3-4.

Notice from the literal translation above that Paul says "out of works of law" and not "out of *the* works of *the* law." The term "law" can mean several things in Scripture. It can mean "The Torah" of the Pentateuch, i.e. the first five books of the Bible -which were originally written as one five-part book.[54] It can refer specifically to the rules, commands, and ordinances listed in the Torah, some 613 legal requirements that reflect an idea of what a holy lifestyle looks like. And, it can refer to a way of living, i.e. living by rule-following. Which idea is represented here?

Here, it appears that Paul intends for us to read the term "law" in the broadest way possible: as a life lived based on human performance and obedience (as opposed to simply obeying the laws of the Torah or the Torah itself.) I derive this conclusion based on three elements of this text (2.15-21) and the uses of "law" that follows. First, here in our immediate text, Paul repeatedly uses the term "law" without an article. He does not refer to *the* law but to "law." This might imply a broader understanding of law in the thinking of Paul. Second, elsewhere, when Paul does want to refer to the "law written in the Torah" he refers to it as "the law." In verse 19 he, for the first time in this text, shifts to using the the article with law:

Verse 19 - Why then *the* law?
Verse 21 - Is *the* law contrary to the promises of God?

He then refers to "the law" as the writings (verse 22 "Scripture"). It would make sense for Paul to narrow his reference to "the law" versus

---

[54] Sailhamer

the idea of "performance-based living" as he switches to an explanation for why God gave the laws written in the Torah specifically.

Third, as Paul transitions into his main thought for section two in 3.1-6, he repeats some of the same phrasing and verbiage here in this present text. He also adds a description of what he means by "living by the works of the law." He says in verse 3 that living out of the works of the law is the same as (or at least similar to) "being perfect by human flesh." While we will get into that in more detail once we get into chapter 3, note for now that this implies that "living according to the works of the law" means living a religious life of any kind out of the flesh.

Also of importance for this discussion is Paul's reference to *"the* law" in Romans 7 where he also clearly describes the commandments in the Torah (Romans 7.8) as a defining element of *the* law but then later describes law as a broader concept and does not include the article. You also see an interplay between *the* law and law in Romans 2:12-18. Also in this text, Paul provides a logical argument for considering the law (Commandments written in the Torah) as having the same place theologically as any other approach to living according to works and obedience to a set of rules or a moral code of any type. (v. 14) Also of importance in Romans 2-3 is Paul's description of the Scripture -as the oracles of God in this case- as something different than the "commandments" of the law.

In other words, when we read "law" in Galatians, we should read the choice a person has to live according to any moral code or set of rules or commandments. When we read *the* Law we most likely should understand this to be the commandments listed in the Torah. When we read Scripture or oracles of God it most likely refers to the Torah as a book itself. As always, we should allow our minds to be changed by the text as we read.

Another important concept introduced here comes from the idea of justification. Paul uses the term and the concept for the first time here in his letter to the Galatians. The word "dikaioō" means "to be declared righteous" and is generally used in relation to the kind of decision made in a court of law. Paul continues to develop what he means by this word as he writes the rest of the book. We will stop short of defining the term completely here. Instead, we will continue to carefully look at how Paul colors in the details of *justification* as we read.

Paul also introduces the idea of justification by *faith* for the first time in the book of Galatians. His explanation of this concept here includes some controversy. Some scholars have used this text to suggest that justification is not by our faith but by the faithfulness of Christ. They use this verse and verse 20 to help prove this idea. The reason they believe these verses say this is because of what is written in the Greek text that may not be apparent in many English translations. In the Greek texts, this verse may say something like (emphasis mine), "We know that a person is not justified by works of the law but through *Jesus Christ's faithfulness* and we believed into Christ Jesus so that we might be justified out of *Christ's faithfulness.*" The portions I emphasized with italics are the source of debate. Many modern Greek scholars point out that the faith in these phrases is the faith *of* Christ. It is not faith in Christ. This is called a "genitive of possession" construction.

While there may be elements of this concept found in these texts, it appears to me that this emphasis should not be considered primary. Three reasons: 1) This text says both ideas together. It says a person is justified by Christ's faith and by placing faith in Christ. 2) This text's chiastic structure positions the two "Christ's faith" phases around a central idea of "we had faith in Christ." So, the emphasis of this text is the fact that Paul and other Christians had faith in Christ. 3) Many scholars suggest that "Christ's faith" can be read as "faith in Christ" in many cases and should be here. We will not answer these issues in a few paragraphs here. Multiple volumes have been written from many perspectives. Consider investigating the research more thoroughly for a deeper understanding of the issues. Consider, though, that we can keep three options open as we read:

Option 1: God justifies those who trust in Christ
Option 2: God justifies because of Christ's obedience

Option 3: Both options are intended by Paul

Let us look at one more important element of this text: the definition of faith. What does Paul mean by "faith in Christ?" Or more particularly, what does he mean by *faith*? Paul uses both a verb and a noun to describe faith here: *pistuo* and *pisitis* respectively. As you can tell, they come from the same root and have the same basic meaning: "that which is completely believable, reliable or trustworthy" or in the verbal form, "to believe to the extent of complete trust and reliance."[55] *Pistuo* is derived from the word *peitho* meaning "to persuade." So, with that in mind, it means to be completely persuaded that something or someone is trustworthy or believable. So, the word can mean a range of possibilities:

- to believe what a person or thing says
- to believe that a person or thing is trustworthy or reliable
- to trust in or rely on a person or thing
- to give yourself or devote yourself to a person
- to obey a person

As you can tell the word's semantic range follows a logical course from simply believing what a person says to believing in their reliability so much that you might obey them. A word of caution: the word will not mean all of the meanings at one time in one context. We must consider the context carefully where we find the word "faith" to understand how Paul intended us to read it at that particular place. This is essential because of how different one understanding of faith can be from another. It is quite different to simply believe a fact than it is to obey someone. It is as different as salvation by "faith" and salvation by works.

To further elucidate the meaning of *pistis* consider some uses of the word in other contemporary literature. One helpful use comes from the financial world. A *pistis* is a written guarantee of payment, like an IOU or a check. So, it is the thing a person might write up to assure another

---

[55] LN

person that they would do what they said a note of good faith or a promissory note. It was also used as the term for a title showing ownership of land. These concepts can be helpful because in each case we see a "stand-in" for the actual substance coming from a person or entity that we can either deem trustworthy or not. If someone writes an IOU, we can choose to trust it (and that person) or not.

We find another helpful usage in early Greek writings related to military actions where some armies "*relied* on their archers" and in another place where some armies retreated because they did not "*trust* in themselves." We also read of armies "cutting *trustable* oaths" between each other to initiate a pause in battle.[56]

It is important for us as readers to continue to hold this broad range of possible meanings in our minds as we continue to read Paul's understanding of justification by faith. Here, though, the first clue comes through the contrast provided by "works of the law." Whatever faith is, it is not works. Paul says something similar in Romans 4 where he says that faith itself is the opposite of works which is how that salvation can be by grace. "To the one who does not work but *believes* in him who justifies the ungodly, his *faith* is counted as righteousness" (Romans 4:5 ESV) This text reveals two ideas that help us read Galatians more effectively by clarifying Paul's thinking: 1) The concept of works extends beyond simply obeying the Torah specifically since Abraham's option to do works was before the law was given and, 2) Faith is not the same as "works" so that "doing good actions" of any type should not be considered a part of whom Paul means by faith. Paul will use the Torah's teaching about Abraham again in the next major section of his letter. For now, consider that he contrasts faith and "moral actions." Faith is not "obedience" in this sense. Faith is the opposite of works.

Another element that helps us define what Paul means by faith comes from Paul's hint in the next verse where what he says implies a similarity to "seeking to be justified by Christ." In this case "seeking

---

[56] NIDNTTE

for Christ to justify" and "trusting Christ to justify" would contain parallel ideas, one helping define the other. So, trusting Christ to justify places the emphasis on Christ himself making a person righteous as opposed to someone or something else making a person righteous including themselves and their own works of moral actions.

As you can tell from the amount of content written above about Galatians 2:16, it contains somewhat of a watershed concept in both the thinking of Paul and the book of Galatians. With that in mind let's continue into the next verse.

**Galatians 2.17** "But if, in our endeavor to be justified in Christ, we too were found to be sinners, is Christ then a servant of sin? Certainly not!" (εἰ δὲ ζητοῦντες δικαιωθῆναι ἐν Χριστῷ εὑρέθημεν καὶ αὐτοὶ ἁμαρτωλοί, ἆρα Χριστὸς ἁμαρτίας διάκονος; μὴ γένοιτο.)

As a reminder, verse 17 provides the second parallel line in the chiastic structure so that it connects to verse 15. Whereas verse 15 says, "We being by nature Jews and not Gentiles are sinners" and verse 17 says, "What if we are found also ourselves to be sinners while seeking to be declared righteous by Christ…?" Paul begins (in v. 15) by stating clearly that the Jewish Christians *are* sinners. He then describes how they seek justification: not by working works of righteousness but by trusting Christ to justify. His conclusion idea raises and answers a question: Doesn't it devalue "justification by faith" if a person continues to sin -which he has already established as the case for him and all others- while trusting in Christ? Doesn't it then turn Christ into the servant of sin? (Sin has authority over Christ; Christ has no power over sin.) Paul's answer: It cannot be; it is impossible.

**Galatians 2.18-19** "For if I rebuild what I tore down, I prove myself to be a transgressor. For through the law I died to the law, so that I might live to God." (εἰ γὰρ ἃ κατέλυσα ταῦτα πάλιν οἰκοδομῶ, παραβάτην ἐμαυτὸν συνιστάνω. ἐγὼ γὰρ διὰ νόμου νόμῳ ἀπέθανον, ἵνα θεῷ ζήσω. Χριστῷ συνεσταύρωμαι· )

Paul follows up his emphatic statement that Christ does not serve beneath the authority of sin, even when those of us he justifies sins, with two statements that both begin with "For." (*Gar* in the Greek text.) Here we find another highly debated text. The question the wording of this text raises comes from the phrase "If I rebuild what I tore down." What does Paul refer to here? He might refer to "returning to a life of sin." Many commentators lean toward a version of this understanding. Another possible meaning fits both the immediate context and Paul's theology of the law. I believe Paul refers to the law itself as the thing he rebuilds. The term "torn down" may cause our minds to see this as more destructive and therefore less open to this being the law. A better translation of this word (katalyō) might be "to invalidate" or "annul." Another parallel structure exists between the two verses helping us define the terms between the two. "The things which I annulled (or put to an end)" connects to "I through the law died to the law." Paul suggests that Jesus only becomes "subordinate to sin" in the gospel system he teaches if the law is not annulled.

How does this work? Paul uses a new word to describe "sinner" here that helps us. He says that he makes himself a "transgressor" when he reestablishes the law. This makes sense because one can only be a "transgressor of the law" when the law maintains its authority. Transgression is a technical term reflecting not simply "evil" or "bad" behavior but actions that conflict with the law. (Compare Galatians 3:19) A comparison to Romans 7 suggests more clearly what Paul says implicitly here: a person no longer should categorize themselves as a sinner or transgressor when Christ has annulled the law. Another way to put what I believe Paul is saying is that if sin is the transgression of the law and the law has been annulled or put to an end then we can no longer consider ourselves sinners.

Additionally, Paul uses the term *oikodomw* again in 4.1 where he clearly refers to the law. Later, in 6.0 he contrasts this to being in the "household" faith which suggests a similar "economy of law" concept here. One can either be in the economy of law or faith.

Another support to this understanding comes from Paul's use of the word translated "I prove" above. He basically says that the law itself provides a source of evidence against him, like a lawyer, that proves a person has transgressed the law. One does this to themselves when they choose to reestablish the law that has already been annulled.

Paul could have simply said: Don't reestablish the law that has been annulled. When you do that you present evidence against yourself that you are a transgressor, a sinner. Then, and only then, Christ could be seen as subordinate to sin because only in this paradigm does sin exist. Instead, the law does not exist in power in any way and therefore neither does sin, and Christ, then, cannot be subordinate to sin in a system where the law does not exist. If the law has no power neither does sin and those who are seeking to be justified by him are no longer sinners.

In the parallel verse, we see the disempowerment of the law in a different way. Paul says that he died to the law through the law. This again becomes a thesis statement that he attempts to prove in the next section. He shows successfully that the law itself teaches that he (and us) can expect to be dead to the law. (See commentary on Galatians 3:10-14) Paul being dead to the law, which condemns and separates from God, can now find reconnection to the life of God (which he defines as "the Spirit" and"the blessing and inheritance of Abraham" in chapter 3).

At the end of this paragraph, Paul launches into an elevated almost poetic description of the theme of his entire book. What he has said rather logically so far in these verses he says more artistically. He also returns to personal pronouns closing out this major section (1.1-2:21) with his personal experience. I am alive in, with and by God. The rest of chapter 2 fleshes this concept out some and then chapter 3-4 fully develops what this means to be "alive by God." As we saw above, too, this statement, "alive by God" imitates a structure of five coordinated statements, where one leads to the other. In some ways, we could simply call this book: "alive to/by God." As you may have noticed I have used several different prepositions to describe Paul's description of his new relationship toward God. Because of the form of the word (a dative noun), we can read this phrase in different ways. The context will have to tell us what Paul intended. He may have used a more ambiguous structure though to cast a wider net, so to speak, intending a broader meaning for what it means to be alive with God. It can mean alive to, alive with, alive by, alive in amongst other options. The point is that a new connection has been made to God and it has made Paul alive in a way that he had not been previously. The law had made him dead but then now he lived.

The parallelism between 2.19-20 is especially helpful to consider:

A1 - Through the law "In the law" (under?) I died. (death)
B1 - That "in/by God" I can live
A2 - In Christ (same dative form as A1 and B1) I was crucified (death)
B2 - Now, I live no more. Christ lives in me.

This parallel helps us understand each section: A1 and A2 refer to the same theological concepts as do B1 and B2. Paul will flesh out this logic more in the following section. Here consider the internal explanation of "being dead to the law because of the law or through the law." It follows and explains: If I re-build these things (the law and its spiritual economy) that I destroyed, then, and only then, am I in conflict with them. Paul will address this concept again in 3.19 when he says the law was added to "cause transgressions" i.e. to make transgressions an entity. No law. No transgressions.

**Galatians 2.20** "I have been crucified with Christ. It is no longer I who live, but Christ who lives in me. And the life I now live in the flesh I live by faith in the Son of God, who loved me and gave himself for me." (ζῶ δὲ οὐκέτι ἐγώ, ζῇ δὲ ἐν ἐμοὶ Χριστός· ὃ δὲ νῦν ζῶ ἐν σαρκί, ἐν πίστει ζῶ τῇ τοῦ υἱοῦ τοῦ θεοῦ τοῦ ἀγαπήσαντός με καὶ παραδόντος ἑαυτὸν ὑπὲρ ἐμοῦ.)

In the previous verse, Paul says "I died to the law that I might live to God." Now he walks through what this experience of "being alive to God" looks like. The first big point he makes corresponds to his death, the death that he just described as being "through the law." Beyond being "through the law" his death came as a result of co-crucifixion. "I am alive to God but I no longer live." Paul uses the Greek word "de" three times here to elaborate on what his life in God looks like. The first is that he no longer lives. The second statement he uses to describe his life in God with the "de" is simply Christ lives in me. So, we are crucified with Christ is the first statement he makes (without a de). (de) We no longer live. (de) Christ lives in us. (de) The thing I now live in the flesh I live in faith in the son of God.

Notice that the translation of "the thing" in the previous sentence. The word "life" does not appear in the Greek text. Most translators see it as an assumed part of the reading. Paul could intend this reading but, because he uses a neuter form of the article here, it appears to me that he is referring to his current *living* with more ambiguity. He intentionally wants us to read it as a broader concept than we might expect when referring to the existence of a dead person being lived by another person. So, "the thing I am presently living" or maybe "the life-like existence I currently experience occurs via the activation of Christ as I have faith in him." The wording here is admittedly awkward but Paul's use of the neuter article here may imply something like this.

Above he described his justification as being by faith. Here he lives "the thing" he lives in his physical body (*flesh* in ESV) by the same faith. The wording of this clause is somewhat unusual. "By faith" again could be "the faithfulness" of Jesus as noted in the debate about this text above. Or it could be by one's faith in Jesus. It appears to me that the most natural reading of the grammar and syntax suggests that faith is meant to be read as the instrument with which we apprehend the life of Christ but, again, this is a thoroughly debated topic beyond the scope of this commentary. It may be most helpful in both this text and the one above it to read both as the intended reading. Good reasons exist to read this text either way.[57] As we keep reading we may see other indicators suggesting to read it one way or the other. A couple of thoughts though on this subject: 1) in the case of ambiguity we should lean toward the clearer portion of the text. In the central, main clause of 2.16 Paul clearly says "We trusted in Christ Jesus" using the same root word behind faith elsewhere including the other dependent clauses in this text. 2) Paul defines "faith towards Christ" as "seeking to be justified by Christ" in verse 18 so that Christ is the "justifier" and our faith is synonymous with seeking something from Him, in this case justification. Then, when we get to 2.20 we should read the clauses there in parallel to the material in verse 16 so that "faith" in Christ is the same as "we trusted in Christ" and "seeking to be justified by Christ."

The sum of Galatians 2.20 is that Paul explains how he "lives." He lives by God having been crucified with Christ. He does not live his own physical life himself. He experiences the life of Christ living through him as he trusts in Christ. In other words, he lives by faith or rather Christ lives in and through him as he has faith, the same faith that "justifies" and the faith here that is synonymous with "seeking to be justified by Christ." This latter connection is especially helpful. Faith is the same as seeking Christ to take action. As I seek Christ to live in me he does. Seeking in this case is a simple desire for Christ to, first justify and second live his life in and through me. Simple "desire to obtain something" is the word most likely means in this context. If you want it you get it, as you want it you get it. (Seeking is a present tense particle.)

Paul ends this sentence with two parallel identifiers of Christ. He loves us and gave himself for us. Paul infers by this parallelism that the love of Christ is displayed in his "giving of himself." Paul repeats almost the same wording here that he began with in this letter. In 1.4, he says

---

[57] If I had to choose, I would choose to read the text as implying both at the same time. Paul intends both readings to be available to his audience intentionally leaving them in ambiguity.

Christ is "the one who gave himself for our sins." These two clauses share the same preposition "huper" describing the object of Christ's death. In the first case, Christ gave himself for (huper) our sins. Here Christ gave himself for (huper) us. This preposition can mean "because of" denoting the reason Christ gave himself. In this case, we (and specifically our sinful condition as the connected passage suggests) motivated Christ to die on the cross. It may also mean that he died "on our behalf" so that his death provided. In the verses that follow, Paul will articulate a substitutionary theology of the cross that suggests his main idea here is related to Christ dying on behalf of our sins. He took the punishment for our rebellious acts.

**Galatians 2.21** "I do not nullify the grace of God, for if righteousness were through the law, then Christ died for no purpose." (Οὐκ ἀθετῶ τὴν χάριν τοῦ θεοῦ· εἰ γὰρ διὰ νόμου δικαιοσύνη, ἄρα Χριστὸς δωρεὰν ἀπέθανεν.)

Paul ends section 1 of his epistle with the statement: I do not nullify (or annul) the grace of God. If justification was through the law then Christ died needlessly. Notice that he repeats similar wording to that he used in verses 17-19. He speaks in both of a negative position for Christ. In verse 17: Then Christ is the servant of sin and verse 21: Then Christ died needlessly. Also, in verse 18, the law is annulled and in verse 21 grace is nullified. These are different Greek words but have similar meanings. This is a semantic parallel. Lastly, in verse 19, Paul died to the law and through the law. In verse 21, Christ died. Also note the similar structure whereas in 19, Paul died to the law and then he was crucified with Christ. In 20 and 21, Christ gave himself over for Paul and then Christ died.

There may also be parallel connections to Galatians 1:3 where Paul starts with his common greeting: "Grace to you" which is paralleled here with "I do not nullify grace." And then additionally, he says in 1:3 that Christ gave himself over for us in very much the same way he does here in 2:20. He uses different words that are similar in meaning. These markers help us as readers keep Paul's materials organized the way he intended and they help us compare different parallel texts to each other; interpreting one by comparing it to the other.

In this case, one of the most important parallels happens between Paul's statement here: "I do not nullify God's grace" and his statement in verse 18, "I do rebuild what I annulled"(referring to the law). The words, again, used for *annulled* and *nullify* respectively are not the same Greek words, but since they share a similar position and a similar meaning, most likely are intended to be connected, contrasted and compared as we read. The word translated *nullify* in verse 21 means "to regard as invalid." or "to reject." The word translated "invalidate" above is similar but with more agency implied on the part of the subject. in the former, "I make invalid," in the latter, "I regard as invalid." Since these are English words that we are using to capture the meaning of Greek words, we should be careful to make too much of the similarities but, interestingly, Paul chooses a word in the first instance where the thing at hand, the law, actually becomes "invalid" whereas, in the second instance, he only *regards or rejects* the thing, grace, as invalid, not affecting its actual validity. So, the law, he made it invalid, he *annulled it.* Grace? He does not reject it as invalid. It would be rejected as invalid if righteousness could exist through obeying a set of rules. And, Christ died with no effect. The ESV says that Christ died for no purpose. The word translated *no purpose* here could be that or no cause, no reason. Simply put Christ's death accomplished nothing if righteousness comes from doing the law.

One note about this last verse. Paul uses the term "athetō" to describe the rejection of grace under the paradigm of the law. It has the root: "tithemi" meaning to set up or to stand up. It occurs most recently in 2.2 where Paul says he will set up before the council in Jerusalem the gospel he preached to be evaluated. Notice the connection between "gospel" and "Christ died." This is the same word that Paul used in 1.15 when he said he did not "set up his gospel" before anyone, or "consult" with anyone. Also, Paul used almost exactly the formation as 1.15 and 2.2 when he says that anyone who preaches another gospel should be "accursed." (ana+tithemi=anathema). Paul does this to tie these pieces and parts of the text together so that we see structure as we compare and contrast.

Another connection occurs both semantically and lexically across 2.20-21 connecting to 1.4. In 2.20, as we highlighted above, Jesus handed himself over on behalf of us from "para+didomi" and his death was not a meaningless, causeless "gift" from *dorean*, a noun form of *didomi*. In 1.4 Christ is the one who "didomi" (gave) himself on behalf of our sins.

"Giving" is a key concept for Paul in this first section. Christ gave himself for us, Paul states at the beginning and the end. Paul was *given* the traditions of his fathers, a shorthand for his version of Judaism. (1.14) Grace was given to Paul and then the right hand of fellowship in 2.9.

## A Summary of Section One (1.1-2.21)

Paul builds the first section on the backbone of the most important idea in the world: Christ gave himself on behalf of our sins. He says so at the beginning (1.4 "Christ gave himself") and the end (2.21 "the one who gave himself," did not die "in vain."). Everything is wrapped within this gospel. His narrative builds from statements about the importance of getting the gospel right; You will be anathema if not. And then jumps into Paul's biographical narrative. With each section, he ends with an idea that he then expands on in the next section, as if he were "double-clicking" on the last idea presented in each section and then developing that idea in more detail. He does this right up to the end and then finishes with a bit of an elevated pericope describing the way we live in God. He ends the section with a reflection on Christ's death for us and states that he does not "reject" (a+tithemi) God's grace using a Greek word that is closely associated phonologically with anathema (ana+tithemi).[58] His thesis is defined most clearly as he builds into hortatory material, material intended for teaching. He says three times that no one is justified by the works of the law. They are justified by trusting in Christ. He then crescendos into a statement about us being "alive in God" which ultimately is the essence of our justification. Additionally, our life in God is explained as Christ himself living our lives as we trust and desire him to do so, as we are "seeking" him to do so. The entire section is summarized as "not disdaining the grace of Jesus" by not living in the works of the law.

---

[58] Meta-tithemi in 1.6 - you *deserted* him who called. Ana+tithemi in verse 1.8-9 - Let him be accursed; pro+ana+tithemi in 16 - I did not consult with anyone; 2.2 - ana+tithemi "I presented before them the gospel I had preached" 2.21 - a+tithemi - "I did not disdain God's grace.

# Galatians 3.1-5

**Interpretive Translation:**

Galatian believers, wow![59] You are so unwilling to think.[60] Did witches deceive you with witchcraft holding you under the spell of their gaze?[61] Who are these magicians? Previously were *your* eyes[62] not captured instead with the whole gospel story of our crucified[63] messiah, Jesus, as explained clearly in the Hebrew Scriptures?[64] One question keeps coming[65] to my mind, though,[66] that I need answered about you. Did you begin to experience[67] the Holy Spirit as a result of doing enough good things or because you responded to the gospel message you read

---

[59] This is an attempt to show Paul's elevate language and exasperated tone.

[60] An attempt to capture the idea of foolishness as more than lacking mental faculty but an act of the will, or lack thereof, to engage from it.

[61] The word means to "put under a spell" or "give the evil eye" most literally but semantically may be more "deceive."

[62] There may be a word play on "give the evil eye" in contrast to the literal Greek: "To y'all, according to the eyes, Christ was written about as being crucified."

[63] Perfective, stative form showing a completed event.

[64] Most translations have "publicly pronounced" and this is a likely translation. Could also be "old writings." This seems more likely since Paul then goes on to describe the gospel from the "writings." both sharing the lexeme: graphe.

[65] Present tense

[66] Interesting that Paul asks other questions but this says "This is the one thing I want you to know?" He had just asked "Was Christ not shown in the old Scriptures as crucified?"

[67] A little tough for me to translate. The word means to "take or receive." The semantic context of "give life/live through" and "make righteous" in the previous chapter and then here in v. 5 with God's supplying of the Spirit and miracle working of the Spirit. There is both a passivity in this action and an activeness. So more than "experience" but less than take hold of... maybe. Also... [maybe better "take in" or "take hold of" or "take into possession of" - Did you take possession of the work of the Spirit by / Or Did you accept God's gift of the Spirit when you earned it with... or simply by responding...]

and heard with faith?[68] How are you so unwilling to use your brains?[69] You started by living in the strength of the Spirit. Why do you think you can grow out of your need for Him and start performing in your human strength? Are your previous experiences of God nothing to you now? Is it possible for such amazing encounters to be truly nothing?[70] Again, did God, then, cause the Spirit to flow[71] through you and create miraculous experiences in you because you did enough good things or because you responded to the message you read and heard by relying on Christ?

**Summary Commentary:**

At the center of this text stands Paul's main thesis: "Having begun by the Spirit, are you now being perfected by the flesh?" the Galatians started with Jesus by trusting what the Spirit revealed about Christ's crucifixion in the Scriptures. They had shifted though to trying to grow in godliness by doing the religious works and moral actions that come from the natural man. Wrapped around this thesis, we find two parallel clauses. 1) Did you receive the Spirit by the works of the law or by hearing with faith and then 2) Does he who supply the Spirit and works miracles among you do so by the words of the law or by hearing with faith? Through this parallelism we see that to "receive the Spirit" or "initially experience the Spirit" and God's "supply of the Spirit and working of miracles in you" all refer to the same kind of experience. This experience reflects how the Galatians started with God. It should also reflect how their daily lives are lived with God. The second part of this parallelism also defines how the Galatians participate in this kind

---

[68] Again doing what I can to show that the "prographo" refers to Scripture and, then in this case, now Paul refers to the Galatians hearing the gospel in these Scripture and responding with faith.

[69] Foolish again but trying create some parallel with "unwilling" but variation between brain and think.

[70] A lot of interpretive liberality here. Lit. "Did you experience so much meaninglessly? if truly/indeed/ also/even it was meaningless."

[71] Supply, provide. Used to describe how one part of the body via the connection from part to the other channels life throughout, like blood passing into and through.

of experience: by responding with faith and not by performing moral actions through natural, human strength. Note here that the flesh can act as a "moral performer" or "religious practitioner" and not just a part of humanity that simply displays human lusts as we might typically think. We learn a subtle truth from this: the quality of a thought or deed comes from its cause, not its effect. A thought or deed is holy when God does it. It is unholy when humans do it, or the flesh.

The way Paul has structured this portion of the text, he appears to want us to read this paragraph (3:1-5) beside his description of justification in 2:15-18.

**Galatians 3:1** "O foolish Galatians! Who has bewitched you? It was before your eyes that Jesus Christ was publicly portrayed as crucified." (Ὦ ἀνόητοι Γαλάται, τίς ὑμᾶς ἐβάσκανεν, οἷς κατ' ὀφθαλμοὺς Ἰησοῦς Χριστὸς προεγράφη ἐσταυρωμένος;)

Paul shifts the direction of his letter towards the Galatians as he had done at the beginning. Here he says "Oh, foolish Galatians! Who had bewitched you? or cursed you" In Galatians 1:6, 8-9 he says, "I am astonished that you are deserting the one who called you" and then at the end, "If someone preaches another gospel he must be put under a curse." Here, he also uses a similar structure as to what he uses in Galatians 2:15 where he lines up multiple nominatives, "We, sinners." He will go on in 2:15-18 to repeatedly state in a triad form that justification does not result from "works of the law but from faith." He will continue in 3.1-5 with the same language repeating another triad, this one focusing on "experiencing the Spirit."

His original rebuke of the Galatians here, "Oh, foolish Galatians" does not speak to their natural cognitive ability. Instead, "foolish" means "to be unwilling to think." The Galatians here do not pursue information and validate its accuracy via the mind by thinking. They refuse to think. Paul then gives us a hint as to where this inaccurate information comes from: "Who has bewitched you?" or this could be translated as "clouded or cursed your minds." In a similar way that those who preached another gospel would be "cursed," the Galatians were under a curse. We need to take on the first-century mindset as we read these words. Paul most likely uses metaphysical language because he sees metaphysical entities behind their heresy. Demonic forces work through the false teachers to impact the Galatians' thinking.[72] The result is a cursed and clouded mind. Note here that Nyland says that this, too, is a term related to witchcraft or cursing.[73]

Paul then describes the Galatians, the ones who refuse to think and who are under a curse: before whose eyes Christ was clearly shown as being crucified. When he writes "before whose eyes" he may be connecting the idea of "cursed" to what they experienced. The word translated bewitched in the ESV can be used to mean "to give an evil eye." This is the way this should be understood at times in the Septuagint, the Greek translation of the Old Testament. It is another way to say "bewitch" or curse as a witch might do by staring at a person and muttering a curse. Paul may be using the term "eye" in the second half of this clause ("before your eyes") to contrast "being under the bewitching gaze" of these demonic false teachers with their eyes or gaze being captivated by the crucifixion.

Most translators present Paul's phrase about the crucifixion something like the ESV above: "Christ was publicly portrayed as crucified." The word translated "publicly portrayed" can mean "described in detail" as one might do in a play or performance. It can mean "a publicly displayed document" as we might see on a public bulletin board. The word itself is created from two parts *pro* meaning "before" and *grapho* meaning "to write." A final possible definition appears to follow this construction: "written before." This appears to fit the context as Paul will show throughout the rest of the chapter that we are justified by

---

[72] Could this mean that Paul says "They are cursed" in 1.8 instead of they should be?

[73] Anoetos, senseless, foolish. A rare word. See 1DefixAudollent 52.16 (Attica, III-II BC), curse, "I bind him and his slave girls and his skill, his assets, his work, his words and his actions.

Nyland, A.. GALATIANS: The Source New Testament With Extensive Notes On Greek Word Meaning (Kindle Locations 732-733). . Kindle Edition.

faith *according to the Scriptures* (graphe). Nine of eleven uses of the root *grapho* will occur in this section. With that in mind, as Paul uses the root here, he must mean something related to "the Scriptures from before" i.e. the Old Testament. A translation of the phrase here might be "The story of Christ being crucified is in the Scriptures from a long time ago. You have seen it."

The last point about this verse shows up in the translation above, too. Paul uses a perfect tense verb when he says "crucified." The perfect tense refers to a completed event or a state of a thing because of the completed event(s). Here Paul may choose this tense to speak to the ontological reality and effect of the crucified Christ. Also, he does imply something here by referring to Christ's crucifixion. The gospel is the story of the cross; the story of the cross is the gospel. We also see this in the previous paragraph ending chapter two where Christ was crucified (another perfect tense). Also of importance as we consider this phrase is the fact that Paul has just described the cross above as "Christ giving himself on our behalf." We see in that an internal self-exposition: the story of Christ's crucifixion is one of him loving us enough to die on our behalf.

**Galatians 3:2** "Let me ask you only this: Did you receive the Spirit by works of the law or by hearing with faith? " (τοῦτο μόνον θέλω μαθεῖν ἀφ' ὑμῶν· ἐξ ἔργων νόμου τὸ πνεῦμα ἐλάβετε ἢ ἐξ ἀκοῆς πίστεως;)

While Paul ends up asking the question in multiple ways, the phrasing here shows the priority of the Galatians answering the question(s) he asks in this text. The translation "ask only this" may make the sentence seem contradictory since Paul asks multiple questions. We could render it more accurately as "I only want to learn this from you." So the repetition of many questions serves Paul's emphasis by turning to the same *kind* of question over and over. Also, the point of the questions seems to show that the Galatians need to reflect on these concepts. He does not expect an answer, per se. With that in mind we too should consider how we might reflect on these questions as if they were written to us. They will allow us to wrestle with the gospel's impact on us and our ongoing dependency on the Spirit through the gospel.

"Did you receive the Spirit." - Paul here describes in rather simple terms the focus of the experience Paul wants the Galatians to evaluate, "What was it like when you received the Spirit?" He repeats a similar idea three times below. We will look at each as we get to the verses where they are written in more detail. For now, though, we need to see that Paul connects the following ideas:

Receiving the Spirit. (v2)
Beginning in the Spirit. (v.3)
Growing in the Spirit (v.3) - As an implied direction from Paul (i.e. you should not grow through the flesh you should grow in the Spirit.)
God supplies the Spirit (v. 5)
God supplies supernatural actions (v.5)

Each of these phrases influences the other so that we should read each informed by the other. As noted above, this section sits structurally in parallel to Galatians 2:15-19 where Paul says three times that no one receives justification by works of the law. Instead, they are justified by faith. With this structure Paul connects the idea clearly stated in Chapter 2 -justification is by faith not works- with the statements here that we receive the Spirit by faith and not by works. So, when he says "you received the Spirit" it is parallel to "be justified." We can take two implications from this connection. One, receiving the Spirit and justification are two different ways to refer to the same event. Two, this fills in the idea of justification with life. The concept of justification describes a courtroom and speaks to how Jesus made us legally acceptable to God. Because we are legally acceptable to God, God, through His Spirit takes possession of us. As Paul also says in Romans 8: if we are justified we have the Spirit. These two descriptions help us understand salvation more clearly -specifically the beginning of salvation. This connection implies that the salvation experience occurs not simply "in the courtroom of God." It also initiates our tangible experience of God's presence and life through the Spirit. (Below Paul will describe the Galatians "feeling" of the Spirit.) This is a "warm handoff" from Galatians 2.15-19 to Galatians 3:1ff where he shifts from "justification" and "receiving the Spirit" to maturing in the Spirit (sanctification) as he has already suggested in the story of Peter above.

The word "receive" supports the idea Paul will introduce next, that their experience of the Spirit comes from the work of God, they just receive Him or accept Him. The gospel means that God is always the giver and we are always the receiver.

"by the works of the law or by hearing with faith" - With similar phrasing to how he challenged erroneous thinking when it comes to justification, here Paul asks the Galatians to reflect on the cause of their first experience of the Spirit. He wants them (and us) to consider again the cause of their salvation. Previously he focused on their salvation as a legal event. Here he focuses on the experiential aspect. In both aspects of the result, the cause is faith not works. He repeats himself exactly when he says salvation does not result from the cause of "works of the law." He uses a nuanced phrase to describe "faith" as a cause. The phrase he uses transliterated in Greek is *ex akoēs pisteōs* -"hearing with faith" in the ESV. Both of these words can be read in multiple different ways. *Akoes* signifies either what the Galatians heard, the act of hearing it or the response to what they heard (i.e. obedience, response). *Piseos* modifies *akoes or* tells how they heard, responded, etc. A review of several translations shows several different ways this text can be read. Because Paul has just desired the experience when the Galatians heard the gospel taught in the Hebrew Bible, I read the first word, *akoes*, as "the content heard" or message, and what did they do in response to that message? They believed it. They experience the gift of the Spirit (effect) when they believe (cause) that the message of the cross is true: Christ loved them so much he died to justify them or make them right with God.

Paul begins to pile up several different ways to understand the faith that saves. He uses the simple noun "faith in Christ" in Galatians 2.15-6 which can mean "believe in, rely upon, and/or trust in." He also uses the verb form in this verse. Paul and Peter trusted in Christ which implies that this faith was more "rely upon" than "believed in the existence of" or believed the facts. (That Paul believed Christ existed or believed the facts about Christ's life or identity seems too obvious to write.) He then restates his trust in Christ as "seeking to be justified by Christ" in Galatians 2:17. So "trusts Christ to justify him" gains the clarifying nuance of "looking to Christ to do this specific thing" or wanting or asking Christ to take this action so that this faith becomes two parts: Christ's action (make us right with God) and our response, we seek him to act this out for us. I think this latter idea is important as we try to break down salvation into its essential elements. Christ can justify us because he took away our sins on the cross. He does justify as we look for him to do so, or, most simply want Him to. The gospel can be simply stated. Believe that Christ can make you acceptable to God because he erased anything you have ever done or will do that offends God or makes you guilty before God. Then, want him to make that true for you. Maybe even more simply. If you believe Jesus can justify you, and want him to, you are. Here, he adds the idea of "responding to the message of the cross with faith" to this cluster of faith, seeking, wanting, etc. Maybe the most accurate summary of these too many words: faith is simply wanting Jesus to do what you believe he can and desires to do.

Paul leaves no doubt in this text or the ones that precede that salvation is 100% given to a person when they have faith in Christ. Works have nothing to do with it. Maybe, most surprisingly, here he says that our sanctification progresses the same way.

**Galatians 3:3** "Are you so foolish? Having begun by the Spirit, are you now being perfected by the flesh?" (οὕτως ἀνόητοί ἐστε, ἐναρξάμενοι πνεύματι νῦν σαρκὶ ἐπιτελεῖσθε;)

In verse three, Paul states, as the center of the chiastic structure, the thesis of this paragraph. "Are you so foolish? Having begun by the Spirit, are you now being perfected by the flesh?" As we look at the structure of the book, noted regularly above, it most likely stands as the thesis ruling over the next two chapters. This set of clauses starts with a repetition of the earlier rebuke: the Galatians are "foolish," unwilling to think. Or their minds are cursed as Nyland suggests within the similar word grouping. This repetition gives structure and shows that this set of clauses (verse 3) parallels the previous set (verses 1-2). This also suggests that the main content "after beginning in the Spirit are you now made perfect in the flesh?" has a similar meaning conceptually to "receiving the Spirit by the works of the law." In some ways, these clauses of verse 3 define the main gist of the paragraph and provide a conceptual transition from the content in the first set of clauses (vss. 1-2) and the second set (vss.3-5). The first set focuses on the initiation of salvation: "you received the Spirit." The second set focuses on the experience of the Spirit thereafter that should be continued by faith: "God continually provided the Spirit to you by faith." The verb (received) in the first stanza communicates a simple past action. The verbs in the last stanza signify a continual, present action (perfected, supplies, etc.).

With these structural elements helping us define context more accurately, we can understand Paul's meaning more accurately as we look at the main clause of this stanza. Referring back to the statement "received the Spirit" in verse 2 he says, "After you began in the Spirit." These two phrases refer to the same experience. Then he makes his transition to his topic for chapters 3-4. "Do you grow by the flesh?" Notice a few details about this clause.

First, as stated above, this is the main clause of this paragraph and the thesis for the next two chapters. For a couple of reasons, it may be the thesis of the entire letter. 1) The concept of "growing" or maturing comes up at an essential moment in chapter two also when Paul rebukes the Hebrew Christians in Galatia for "toddling" back and forth, waddling in their faith in the gospel like a child. His rebuke is in essence, "You are not mature in your faith in the gospel. Sometimes you believe the gospel. Sometimes you don't." 2) This text follows the central text of the book: Galatians 2:20-21 where Christ living out his life through us presently as a result of our justification takes center stage. While this stating of the thesis (in 2.20) takes on more prominence in its central position, this text restates the issue and identifies the thesis most clearly.

Second, what does "being perfected" mean? The Greek word behind this translation comes from the root *epiteleō*. It can mean "to finish the job or the duties of the job." Paul uses it elsewhere to describe completing "holiness" which he defines as "being cleansed from every defilement of body and spirit." He also uses it to describe finishing an assignment or fulfilling a commitment. For example, the Corinthians promised to raise funds for Paul to bring back to the church in Jerusalem. He challenges them with this word to *do what they started and promised.* In many cases, the root word, *teleo*, means "to perfect" as in the sense of maturation or growth. This latter meaning most likely fits the context in comparison to the elements above and because of the two thoughts below.

Third, Paul will later, near the pivot of his section on what we might call application, use this root again when he says, "Walk in the Spirit and you will not fulfill or complete the desires of the natural man." We notice immediately the semantic and lexical repetition between the two clauses. It is as if Paul wrote both of these sentences in the same bright red. In so doing he connects the idea of "growing in the Spirit" to "walking in the Spirit." A possible paraphrase of either might be "You started in the Spirit, now keep going in the Spirit."[74]

Fourth, to further establish this connection and clarify what Paul says here we need to highlight the use of the present tense verb which he most likely used to establish a perpetual or continual kind of action. He does not say "Now you grow in the flesh." He says *you continually grow in the flesh.* This, by the way, parallels what he says in Gal 5.16 when he says that we should *continually walk in the Spirit.*

In summary, in what may be the main clause of the entire book Paul says we should not continually seek maturity and growth -any of the

---

[74] Essential to notice this connection between this highly prominent clause and what will most likely be another highly prominent phrase near the end of the book. When he says in essence here, "Are you now completing the assignment of holiness though the flesh" and then later in 5:16 "You will not complete the assignment of holiness though *through* the flesh." In other words he could be repeating this statement more directly.

post-justification part of the Christian life- through our natural man. We should continually seek the Spirit to give us what we need.

**Galatians 3:4** "Did you suffer so many things in vain—if indeed it was in vain?" (τοσαῦτα ἐπάθετε εἰκῇ; εἴ γε καὶ εἰκῇ.)

Now, Paul transitions to the final stanza of this chiastic triplet. This sentence does not have a strong parallel to verses 1 or 3a but it does use the word *pathos* to describe the experience of the Galatians. *Pathos* is possibly an allusion to Christ's crucifixion. Positionally though, when you look at the structure of the other two stanzas, it stands in the same position as verse 1 compared to verse 2 and verse 3a compared to verse 3b. Some also see a phonetic connection between "mathos" (to learn) in 3.2 and "pathos" (to suffer) in verse 4.

Most translations share the approach of the ESV listed above and use "suffer" as the gloss for *pathos* or *paschō* as a verb. Many commentators prefer another optional meaning: to experience. The word itself does not mean "to experience something negative." It simply means to feel something or experience something with some suggestion of the emotional aspect of the experience. While the connection to the crucifixion might imply a move toward a negative experience like the cross, the rest of the paragraph repeatedly suggests a positive experience for the Galatians as they experienced the Spirit. If Paul did intend a connection to "mathos" or the crucifixion, it might be for other reasons such as a contrast of experience and/or the Christ on the cross defines the experience of justification and the Spirit defines the experience of the sanctification -with a possibly very subtle connection to the resurrection simply in the structure. (Cross/Jesus/Justification and Resurrection/Spirit/Sanctification.)

Paul's challenge here, then, probably targeted the experiences they had with the Spirit and not needless suffering. And, while "vain" stands in the object position, it still becomes a sort of marker of content for their experience. It operates somewhat like an object. Did you experience so much *emptiness*? Or more freely, are you saying your powerful experiences were meaningless and nothing? We as the secondary audience of Paul's letter, might notice a challenge. Do we give appropriate weight to the experiential side of Christianity? Not doing so may be a sign that we are moving towards heresy.

Paul can hardly bring himself to say that their experience was nothing. He immediately caveats with "if it was actually nothing."

**Galatians 3:5** "Does he who supplies the Spirit to you and works miracles among you do so by works of the law, or by hearing with faith?" (ὁ οὖν ἐπιχορηγῶν ὑμῖν τὸ πνεῦμα καὶ ἐνεργῶν δυνάμεις ἐν ὑμῖν, ἐξ ἔργων νόμου ἢ ἐξ ἀκοῆς πίστεως;)

After the quick introductory challenge of verse 4 which we might see emphatically as "You did not experience nothing!" Paul writes the last clause of this stanza and the paragraph. We notice immediately that Paul says something similar to what he has already said twice. In verse two he asks "Did you receive the Spirit by the works of the flesh or by the hearing of faith." In verse four he says a different statement but one that helps us define the others: After you began in the Spirit are you now growing each day through the natural man? Now, in verse five, he says a parallel statement, "Does the one who continually gives you the Spirit and works miracles in you do so because you do enough good deeds or because you respond to the message of the gospel with faith?" Again, we notice the similarities between the three stanzas, especially the first and the third.

This stanza can be broken down into three parts: God's supply of the Spirit, God's working of miracles and the cause of this work. Let's look at each one separately.

First, "The one who supplies the Spirit." Paul uses the present tense again to signify the action of this verb. So the action God (implied here) does toward the Galatians has a continual or repeating aspect to it. We might say that God does not stop but always supplies the Spirit over and over. We can also understand the word "supplies" from two other common uses, one in Pauline writings and the other in the literature of the day. A specially helpful usage of the word in Paul's writings comes from Ephesians 4:16 where he says one part of the body *supplies* what the other parts need. While it may be impossible to completely reconstruct the understanding of anatomy of the day, this basic word picture helps us grasp the concept Paul intended. In the same way that oxygen and nutrients travel from one part to another through a person's blood, God pours out the Spirit on each of us. Paul uses similar ideas and concepts in Ephesians 4 that he does here: spiritual maturity, growth, Spirit pouring out of gifts, the "filling of all things" which he will later say in Ephesians is the filling of the Spirit.[75]

The next usage of this term comes from writings from the same era Paul wrote. Consider the insights from Nyland's word study: This term cannot be translated as "provides" or "supplies", two words which are a gross over-simplification of the actual meaning. The verb *khoregeo* (see following footnote) refers to the paying of all the expenses, every single one of them, and the *epi* signifies that even additional expenses are paid – no stone is left unturned. *Khoregeo*, "to pay for all the expenses," and "to provide income," (see above note) are well attested in the papyri. See, for example, P.Oxy.Hels. 26.10, (13 June, 296) "...and since the death of my parents he has been providing us with income."

So, in this latter example, God supplies all that is needed of the Spirit and even more, bearing the costs himself. In the same way that a parent might provide a stipend for their child away in college and often include a bonus, God gives us what we need of the Spirit and then more and more.

---

[75] This is important because this means that when Paul says here "to grow by the Spirit" and "receive the flowing supply of the Spirit by faith" and then in ch.5 "walk in the Spirit." It is thematically connected back to being filled with the Spirit or Christ's "filling all things" of Eph. 1 and 3, 4. See also Romans 15.13. God fills you with all joy and peace in believing so that by the power of the Spirit you may abound in hope." "Peak of Ephesians: "to know the love of Christ that surpasses knowing that you may be filled with the fullness of God."

Second, "And works miracles among you." This serves as a good translation. The word *works* as you might expect again comes from a present tense verb denoting continual action. God does not stop working miracles among you. Notice, too, the parallelism between "supplying the Spirit" and "working miracles." The supply of the Spirit looks like working miracles and the miracles are the abundant outpouring of the Spirit. We might restate the two phases as one: God abundantly supplies the supernatural and miraculous working of his Spirit in our lives. Paul includes this second phase to make sure we get a sense of the action or "works" (same root in both uses of works in this verse) that result from the Spirit. It is supernatural and miraculous as the word *dunameis* means.

Third, "By the works of the law or the hearing of faith." Paul repeats himself verbatim. We pause here to see that God's continual work of sanctification (described as an extravagant supply of the miraculous working of the Spirit) does not come from trying to do good works as prescribed in the law. He works in us post-salvation in the same way as he does for justification -as we respond to the message of the gospel by faith. So, when he says "Keep growing in the Spirit" we might ask how? Here he says we keep growing by the Spirit as we have faith, or, as we saw with the idea of faith above, as we simply want Jesus to do for us what we believe he can and desires to do. Then, as the shared roots imply, we will not have the words from our flesh, i.e. the natural man, but the miraculous working of the Spirit. Hallelujah.

# Galatians 3.6-9

**Interpretive Translation:**

You're aware that those who are convinced that God accepts them because they trust his promise to do so, alone are in the lineage of Abraham. You've already read it in the ancient Scriptures, "Abraham trusted in God, and then, because of his trust, God considered him righteous even though he wasn't really." Remember? These Scriptures, aware of a future when God, himself, would make all kinds of people righteous simply because they trusted him to do so, previously recorded the good news all the way back in Genesis. Abraham was told, "God will transfer his magic-like power into all kinds of people of every ethnicity, even the unclean Gentiles." In summary, in the same way, Abraham trusted God, people who trust God to make them righteous are blessed with his magic-like power.

**Summary Commentary:**

Paul continues his dialogue on faith as the single responsibility of a person who hopes to be justified by God. This text most likely should be read in coordination with the previous text as if it were one unit. The central statement of this text comes at the center of the chiastic structure: The gospel was previously taught to Abraham: All the nations in you will be blessed. By connecting "justification" with "blessing" Paul expands on the message of the previous section. He tells the Galatians they are justified by faith just like Abraham and this justification includes "blessing." By using the term "blessing" Paul continues to work in the language of magic as he has through the last verses. Blessing reflects a transfer of beneficial magic, power or a spiritual force similar to what Paul has just said in verse 5: God infused you with his Spirit working supernatural miracles among you. Here it is: you were justified by faith which means you are "blessed" by that same faith.

**Galatians 3.6** "just as Abraham "believed God, and it was counted to him as righteousness" (Καθὼς Ἀβραὰμ ἐπίστευσεν τῷ θεῷ, καὶ ἐλογίσθη αὐτῷ εἰς δικαιοσύνην·)

Some translations and commentators suggest that this phrase should be seen as the end of the previous unit. This is reflected in the ESV. I take it to be complementary to the following verb phrase in verse 7, "You know." In the same way that a biography of Paul precedes Paul's jump into an overt teaching about justification and experiencing the life of Jesus tangibly day to day in Galatians 2:15 -3:5 here Paul moves into a biography of Abraham to further elucidate what he as just taught in the central section of the book. He uses familiar language "Abraham trusted God" (see previous section for further discussion on the meaning of "trust" or "faith.") His God-directed trust led Him to be "counted as righteous." The word "counted" can mean "credited to be righteous," or his faith was credited to be righteous. It can also mean that he was considered righteous though he was not. This usage is also found in the story of Judah and Dinah when Judah "counted" Dinah as a prostitute even though she was not.

What was Abraham's faith? John Sailhamer in "The Meaning of the Pentateuch" has shown that the major strategy of the author of the Torah/Pentateuch, the same "Scriptures" in reference here, was to show that a messianic king would come on the scene in the future and undo the curse of the fall. A person who trusted God's provision of the coming savior, the "seed," would be treated as if he were righteous as was Abraham.

**Galatians 3.7** " Know then that it is those of faith who are the sons of Abraham." (γινώσκετε ἄρα ὅτι οἱ ἐκ πίστεως, οὗτοι υἱοί εἰσιν Ἀβραάμ.)

This is the main clause operating in Galatians 3.6-7. Verse 6 supports this main clause. The main verb of the first idea of the paragraph then means "to know." It can be read as either an imperative and therefore a command or as an indicative and therefore a statement of fact. Either way, it appears that the author wants his readers to respond to the statement as a directive. His main admonition then is to "know" or "be aware of something." Paul used a present tense verb too so the audience would probably understand it as "keep knowing or keep maintaining your awareness of" the thing. We might say "Keep remembering."

What should the readers of this epistle keep remembering? That "the ones out of faith, these are the sons of Abraham," if we render it rather literally. He will elaborate on what it means to be a son of Abraham in the next few verses. In some ways, it becomes a sub-theme. He elaborates on the "Seed of Abraham" and the inheritance due to them and him in verses 3.15-20. He continues in the same kind of language in chapter 4 as reflects on the believer's status as an heir both before and after maturity contrasting slavery and sonship. Then, in Galatians 4.21-31 he ends the first half of the book with a reference to Abraham's two different sons contrasting Hagar/Ishmael with Sarah/Isaac. Here he hints at much that is to come and connects the justification of Abraham by faith to "true" Abrahamic sonship.

The phrase "out of faith" translates the Greek phrase "ek pisteou." It is not how we might typically speak about these concepts in English so it can be hard to translate in the way that Paul most likely intended. One can probably sense this sense in the literal translation, "those out of faith." It implies that faith is a source of a quality these individuals possess. We might say that they are characterized by faith, that their origin is faith, or that all that they are comes from the source of faith vs something else. Paul most likely meant something of both so a good translation might be, "Keep thinking about the fact those who depend 100% on what faith brings them are the sons of Abraham." It challenges the reader to think: what am I out of? What am I banking on? What contributes to my spiritual state? Faith in grace or works of the law/flesh?

**Galatians 3.8** "And the Scripture, foreseeing[76] that God would justify the Gentiles by faith, preached the gospel beforehand to Abraham, saying, "In you shall all the nations be blessed." " (προϊδοῦσα δὲ ἡ γραφὴ ὅτι ἐκ πίστεως δικαιοῖ τὰ ἔθνη ὁ θεός, προευηγγελίσατο τῷ Ἀβραὰμ ὅτι ἐνευλογηθήσονται ἐν σοὶ πάντα τὰ ἔθνη·)

The main verb of verse 8 occurs towards the end with the word translated with the phrase "preached the gospel beforehand." The beginning of verse 8 explains more of what's behind that event. Most commentators and translators understand this modifying phrase to suggest that the Scriptures "foresaw" a future time, Paul's present, when God justifies those who have faith. This reflects the most common usage of this word. It could also mean either that the Scriptures "had seen before, previously" or that they had seen clearly, as seeing something right in front of or before you. Because it modifies another "future" focused word, translated as "preached the gospel before" it should be read in the same way, the Scriptures "saw previously" and "proclaimed the gospel previously." This way of seeing the two concepts simply says that the record of Scripture was before the present and yet taught the same gospel. It does not imply that justification itself changed from one part of history to another. Conceptually the wording might have similarities to "already-" *the Scriptures already seeing.*

The Scriptures saw what previously or already? They saw that God justifies those who only have faith or receive only what is procured by faith (versus works of the law).[77] Paul uses a present tense form for "justify" which probably has both a temporal function "currently justifies" and an aspectual function "continually justifies." A simple way to convey this might be "always justifies" or always makes

---

[76] Could be "foresaw" so that the Scriptures were aware of a future where God would justify those leaned on faith alone. It could also that the Scriptures "had seen previously" that God justifies those who have faith. Or it could be "seen" clearly.

[77] Paul connects "works of the law" with "works of the flesh" which helps us understand a broader meaning of "works of the law" than simply "trying to follow the law code (or a part of it) written in the Torah." This connection reorients and clarifies *works of the law* as any paradigm where a person seeks to be considered righteous before God by doing good deeds of any type.

righteous. By connecting what happened to Abraham when he was "counted as if he were righteous" in verse 6 to the word "to make righteous" he further defines the theological concept of justification for both occurrences.

Because justification arises for those who are "out of faith" it doesn't have to be for those who are "out of the Jews." The nations in this case refer simply to anyone who has faith regardless of ethnicity, citizenship, etc.

The point of this dependent, participial clause is that the Scriptures already see that God justifies those who have faith. In the main clause, Paul explains what this looks like God has already or previously preached the gospel to Abraham. The Scriptures (personified here) reflect the spiritual conceptual and eternal "thinking" of God and in so doing already know that God justifies the nations from faith. They state as much when they preach the gospel to Abraham. The phrase translated as "they preached the gospel beforehand" is one word in Greek. It breaks down similarly to the phrasing here. The main part of the verb is "to give a message." So the Scriptures gave a message. This lexeme has the prefix "eu" which means "good." So the Scriptures gave a good message. One more prefix precedes "eu" -"pro" which means previously or before. So the message is good and previously shared.

The message was preached "to Abraham" and he responded with faith. The content of the message preached to Abraham was "All the nations are going to be blessed in you."

"All the nations" refers to the extent of the gospel promise. It wasn't just for the biological descendants of Abraham. The scope had no limits genetically or culturally. That represents the "bottom floor" of the gospel's scope. The promise has a ceiling element, too. The gospel would impact every nation culture or people group. We see the meaning of "nations" best by looking at how it is used to describe the people of God. They are a nation. Even when they are under the government of Egypt they are still a "nation." With that in mind, they are a group of people bound by a commitment to each other, racial and genetics, and cultural practices (like religion but not limited to it). "Shared heritage and background" also comes to mind. So the gospel will impact every group of people on the earth. Every sub-culture will experience the blessing of the gospel.

When God speaks to Abraham, as recorded here, he makes what appears to be a strange statement. He doesn't say "the nations are justified" but that they are "blessed" because of their faith. The parallel position of the two concepts suggests that one relates to the other and therefore helps us define each one. The nations are justified in v.7 is similar to "the nations are blessed" in verse 8. One connection between the idea of justification above and blessing here that may go unnoticed to the English reader is that they are almost the same word: In v. 6 "logizomai" and "eulogeō" in v. 8. They share a root. While we may not know everything this means, Paul, at the least, wants his readers to connect the two ideas.

The blessing goes further than justification. The simple meaning of the word is "to confer favor" or "to speak favor" over someone. If the basic root means "to consider or to credit" then here something similar is implied only the subject confers something good to the object." The word "bless" also has a connection to the "magic" word grouping we see through this text. It was the opposite of a "curse." It could mean to "transfer magic" or a supernatural force towards a person for their benefit."

Genesis also uses the word at the creation of animals and man when it says "And God blessed them by saying "be fruitful and multiply."

In the case of man the "blessing" contained several elements:

1) It was a designation of their created, pre-fall state.
2) It represented the image of God, a life that they possessed, which later we will discover is the Spirit/breath of God, which they would then share with others via reproduction. (Fertility, a common focus of religion, plays a part here. "I will make you fertile." And then later in the text agriculture, another common

focus of religion, comes up, "I will make the crops bountiful for you." So that the blessing is a promise of the supernatural work of God on behalf of man.)
3) It is connected to man's ability to commune with God as the same "kind."
4) Sex and the enjoyment of it becomes a part of the blessing probably more as a picture than simply just sex.
5) They were to fill the earth and have authority over everything there.
6) God's provision.
7) "Sabbath" was blessed and made holy, and special.

Throughout the Torah, a blessing is typically a statement of good towards a person, a promise or a prayer. One could say it reflected faith in that the speaker had to believe that the words would come to pass. In the worldview of the original ancient community, it would reflect something like a magic spell wherein the words had power. Those who followed Yahweh would see that they, as blessed by him, could then share a blessing from him.

In summary, blessing is shorthand for "to treat as Abraham who was to be treated as if he was righteous" and in the favor and blessing of Abraham was connected to the originally created state of man in the garden, God's magic-like outpouring of favor towards man.

In the immediate context, the magic-like element of the blessing is emphasized. The Galatians had been "put under a spell" by the heretics. Their minds were "bewitched by the evil eye." Paul had stated already that they were "under a curse" at the beginning of the letter. Then, he shifts to the positive contrast, those who have faith are magically supplied with the Spirit and experience supernal workings. Then, here, by faith, they are considered righteous and partake in the "magic-like spell over Abraham for his good."

We may pull back with such magic-like language but remember the audience. This made sense to them. We, too, can learn from the concepts by seeing God's work as magic-like.

*We hear the "spell" i.e. blessing from the Spirit, believe it and then experience it.

**Galatians 3.8** "So then, those who are of faith are blessed along with Abraham, the man of faith." (ὥστε οἱ ἐκ πίστεως εὐλογοῦνται σὺν τῷ πιστῷ Ἀβραάμ.)

Paul closes out this section with the final major clause, each being introduced by a conjunction (*kathos*, *de*, and here, *hoste*). This last clause returns to the faith of Abraham and those who are of faith. It parallels and closes out the chiastic structure of this triad (3.6-8) and summarizes it too, reminding the reader that in the same way that those who are "of faith" (are what they are because of their faith) are not only justified, they are "blessed."

The last phrase adds one subtle detail to this section. In the ESV it says "along with Abraham, the man of faith." Another possible way to read this phrase might be "in the same way Abraham trusted God, people who trust God to make them righteous are blessed" or as literal of a translation as possible: together with the faith of Abraham. Either we are justified by Abraham's faith or we are justified by faith like Abraham had. The alternate translation above reflects the latter option, the point being we are now in the spiritual lineage of Abraham -experiencing the justification and blessing promised him and his seed- when we have faith as he did together with him -"together with the trusting Abraham."

# Galatians 3.10-14

**Interpretive Translation:**

How can this happen like this? Anyone who seeks to gain acceptance with God by following the commands of the law will find themselves under the influence of the dark magic of a cursing spell. We know this because of what's written in the Torah, "Everyone who fails to continually obey everything that is written in the Laws of the Torah, any of the commands, is under an evil curse." Consider too, just how clearly the law shows that no one is ever righteous enough to be accepted by God through obeying rules, commands or laws. It's clearly stated, "The righteous live by faith." In contrast, the law is not compatible with faith, "The person who does these things will live because of them." So, when we think about the cursed state of those trying to gain acceptance by doing the rules in the Torah we should also remember that Christ bought our freedom from this dark curse conjured by the law by becoming cursed himself on our behalf. We see this in the Torah when it says, "The criminal that hangs on a wood pole for his crime is bound by a divine evil curse." When Christ took our curse for us it was so that the supernatural blessing of Abraham might be we shared the people regardless of their ethnicity or cultural background or, to say it another way, so that we could begin to experience the promise of the Spirit's presence and empowerment simply because of this faith we've been describing.

**Summary Commentary:**

Paul continues in Galatians 3.10-14 to elaborate on how the Galatians are to move out of the spell the false prophets have them under and "grow into maturity" through faith in the gospel to provide the Spirit's action and work. He returns to the language of cursing and blessing as he identifies those who look to the works of the law as a way to become righteous before God. Paul makes it clear though this path leads to being cursed because the law itself requires its adherents to "continually keep doing every rule that is written in the book about the law." If one fails in the smallest way, then they are bound under a curse.

In the middle of this section, he describes from Scripture how that life comes from one of two paths. Either a person has faith and then lives or they attempt to live by continually doing the "things to do" in the law. Here he implies that there is only one real choice. A person who has faith in another to take on the "doing" in his or her place has hope. A person who goes the way of the law has no hope because no one will ever be able to constantly do everything written therein.

He ends this section by returning to the curse mentioned in the first verse and describes how Christ freed us from the bondage of the curse becoming a curse for us. Though Christ had lived a sinless life, when he was crucified on the cross (here, pole or tree) he took on the curse of the law in the same way that one who did not obey it completely. Paul closes this paragraph and the major section of 3.1-14 by recapitulating the material of the previous section first, Christ's substitutionary death provided that blessing of Abraham for all people "in Christ" or "by Christ." Notice here that "of faith" and "by Christ" have been placed in equivalent grammatical positions so that faith shifts us from our doing to Christ's. Paul's last (second here) purpose statement for the cross returns to his first major premise when he says here, Christ died to give us the blessing of Abraham and then describes in the parallel sentence this blessing as "the promise of the Spirit" echoing what he wrote in 3.1-4 and bringing this section to a close.

**Galatians 3.10** "For all who rely on works of the law are under a curse; for it is written, "Cursed be everyone who does not abide by all things written in the Book of the Law, and do them." (Ὅσοι γὰρ ἐξ ἔργων νόμου εἰσίν, ὑπὸ κατάραν εἰσίν· γέγραπται γὰρ ὅτι ἐπικατάρατος πᾶς ὃς οὐκ ἐμμένει πᾶσιν τοῖς γεγραμμένοις ἐν τῷ βιβλίῳ τοῦ νόμου τοῦ ποιῆσαι αὐτά. )

This verse is a continuation of the material that began in the previous section (3.6-9) but also forms a "sub-section." Here Paul introduces again the idea of a curse using similar language from 3.1. He also will, after elaborating on this curse and the contrasting life available by faith, return to "curse" language and show how Christ took on the curse for us, for those who have faith. This verse again uses the grammar from above describing those who are "out of the works of the law" which the ESV has interpreted well as those who rely on works of the law though we should acknowledge that this is not a direct translation. They are what they are, whatever they are "because of the works of the law." Verse 11 gives the modification and focus of "before God" and it applies here too. They are before God whatever they will be because of or out of the works of the law.

Paul uses the term "it is written" to introduce a quote from the Old Testament. He will use the same term again in verse 13 to form an *inclusio* creating a "bracket" around his text. Here he quotes Deut 27.26. This verse introduces the cursing concept that orients this section. The Hebrew quote means more specifically "bind with a curse" so that we might read Paul's wording with the bondage of the curse more clearly. Those who do not obey the law are bound by a curse. This is the same word God uses in the Fall narrative (Gen 3-4) when he states the condition of the serpent and the ground. So, as Deut ends the Torah he identifies that a person who does not do the law is under the same condemnation. This is also the same terminology that God uses toward Abraham in passages that turn out to be about the gospel according to the strategy of the Pentateuch's author. This is the negative contrast to the blessing of Abraham. Who is bound by such a curse? Those who do not continually stick to doing[78] "these things." The verb that characterizes their obedience or lack thereof is a present tense verb and refers to continual action from *meno*. It means in this context "to keep doing."[79] What should they keep doing? Everything written in the book of the law which could also be read as the book about the law or the book containing the law. In the Greek text, the next phrase helps us read this one when it says "of the things to do." This element helps us read the previous phrase potentially as "the book containing the law(s),

---

[78] In Hebrew, Hiphil form of QWM meaning to rise up or carry out. (HALOT)

[79] LN

the things to do." This reading is helpful because it reminds us that the book, the whole Torah (Pentateuch) here, contains the laws but is not itself "the laws." Then, the text also clarifies what is meant by "the laws" when it says "the things to do." Also, some read Paul's admonition here to be against doing the ceremonial laws only, but Paul seems to imply here that all the "things to do" are included.

Another thought is also confirmed by the OT reference itself. This verse in context follows a list of curses related to moral transgressions including adultery, idolatry and beastiality amongst other clear moral violations. The list itself follows closely, though not directly, to the Ten Commandments. Paul says, then, rather clearly, that anyone who tries to do the things written in the law, including the moral code, the Ten Commandments or any other "thing to do" falls under a curse.

In the context of Galatians, this is another moment when Paul uses the language of the metaphysical and speaks to the cursed state of someone who attempts to "be righteous by the works of the law before God" as he clarifies in verse 11. Beyond the ideas included in the OT reference we also still have to see "cursed" within the framework of Galatians and its frequent use of language from the world of magic. The word itself, in Hebrew (*Arur*) and Greek (*kataran*), both can be read and in this context should be read, as "bind under a dark spell." That's what the law does.

**Galatians 3.11** "Now it is evident that no one is justified before God by the law, for "The righteous shall live by faith." (ὅτι δὲ ἐν νόμῳ οὐδεὶς δικαιοῦται παρὰ τῷ θεῷ δῆλον, ὅτι ὁ δίκαιος ἐκ πίστεως ζήσεται·)

As noted above, the first sentence, v 10, forms the beginning of this section and the first line of the chiastic structure which will then get paralleled in v. 13. Verse 11 begins the middle of the chasm where the text follows this structure:

It is evident that no one is justified by the law
The righteous will live because of their faith

The law is not of faith
The one who does them will live because they do them

This middle pattern reflects another parallel structure using an ABAB-type arrangement.

Before Paul introduces his thesis -the righteous will live because of their faith- he clarifies a few details around the concept of justification. First, he clarifies that "the curse" he just mentioned is related to not being justified. Second, he reiterates that justification means to be righteous "with God." Third, he says what may be a surprising statement, that this idea, that no one is justified before God as a result of following the laws of the Torah (any of them), is "evident." The word translated "evident" comes from the Greek word *delon*. It could also be translated as "clear, plain or obvious." The point being this is not mystically understood but rather easily known through simple mental faculties. He may also have in mind the context for the quote he is about to make from Habakukk. The issue of faith for Habakkuk is a vision that God commands him to write down on a table and make really plain, i.e. easy to understand a concept that is similar in meaning to *delon*.

What is so clearly taught? "The righteous will live because of their faith." Here Paul connects a somewhat new idea, "life" or "living" with the ideas of justification and blessings, experiencing the Spirit, etc. that he has been developing so far in this chapter. He also used "life" language in Galatians 2:19a-20, "I am alive with and by God. I was crucified with Christ. I don't actually live myself anymore. Christ lives my life. The life I now live in the body I live by having faith in the Son of God. He is the one who loves me and gave himself for me." As you see this, the central text of Galatians, centers on experiencing the life of Christ taking over for our own lives so that we do not actually live our lives but Christ, instead, lives our lives for us. The issue of life, then, is essential for Paul. Here he connects the idea of life to this cluster of concepts that he is been developing: blessing and the supernatural working of the Spirit. This, for Paul, is what it means "to live." Or, to say it another way, here he is developing the idea he stated in Galatians 2:20, Christ now lives my life by faith.

The quote from Habakkuk gives some interpreters trouble. The problem is that usually the word translated "faith" in Habakkuk 2.4 typically means "faithfulness" or "integrity" so that the meaning somewhat becomes the opposite of what Paul implies here, that man is not justified by faithful obedience but by trusting in Christ, having faith in another person's works. Those from the *New Perspective on Paul* approach point to this as further verification that "the faith of Christ" is "the faithfulness of Christ." As noted above, the book of Galatians conceptually, even if not literally, shows we are saved by *our faith* in the *faithful work* of Christ. So, both ideas are accurate. The only debate seems to be whether or not *this* (in this case) text means "Christ's faithfulness" or "our faith."

In Habakkuk, contrary to many modern scholars, the text can be read as "faith" versus "faithfulness." The semantic range of the Hebrew word translated faith has that as a possibility. It can, like *pistis* in Greek, be understood as either "faith" or "faithfulness." Typically the form for *AMON* (Hebrew for "faith") when it should be read as "faith" is the hiphil verb form. This occurrence of the word being a noun is not in the hiphil form so it's more ambiguous. It is though, placed in a parallel position structurally to Habakkuk 1.5 where the hiphil verb form is used, "A work is being done in your days. You will not have faith in it when it is described to you." This verse is important to the main ideas of Habakkuk. In chapter three he goes on to explain that this "work," (the one they will not believe but that the "righteous" will believe and thereby live) as the same event described in the Pentateuch, mainly in Numbers 23-24 and Deuteronomy 33, where God promises to send a King from the tribe of Judah as the seed that will crush the head of the serpent's "family." (See Sailhamer notes at SEBTS library for more details.) The author of Habakkuk seems to see "faith in the work" as the same faith that the Pentateuch refers to when it says that Abraham was considered to be righteous because he had faith.

With this being the case, it is most likely that Habakkuk, following the Pentateuch, intended us to read "The righteous will live because he has faith." With that in mind, we can see that this meaning also fits Paul's intent. This sentence does, though, seem to speak to the relation of faith to what we might typically call sanctification rather than justification. Those in mind for Habakkuk are already righteous, those who are righteous (by faith) also live because of their faith. In the immediate context of Habakkuk chapter 2, "to live" is cast as "surviving the attack of Babylon." When chapter 3 moves the narrative beyond the immediate historical context into the future "to live" also takes on a new emphasis, so that the finished book of Habakkuk, when read as a whole, explains that those who are justified by faith are righteous and they will "possess life" because of that faith. Paul will explain in more detail what that "life" looks like as he keeps writing but remember the connections to "Christ lives my life now" mentioned above.[80]

One other question related to this oft-quoted text. Does it say, "The righteous will live because they have faith" or "The ones who are righteous because of their faith will live"? The first concept relates to the life of the righteous person after they are righteous or as they are righteous. It reflects the reading we used in the previous paragraph. The second reading reflects an emphasis on justification more than sanctification. Both are equally possible in Greek. In context for Paul, as he works through the Galatians' need "to mature and grow by having faith in the Spirit" might suggest that the meaning is related to sanctification and therefore the first option above. The original verse in Hebrew is written similarly. The fact it's in a "construct" form may suggest that it coordinates with "the righteous" and not "lives" but this is not clear. If this is the case it would be like the second reading above: "The righteous by faith, he lives."

With the context of the following passages and the connection back to Habakkuk and then the Pentateuch we might want to understand "to live" in a more theologically (and compositionally) charged way and translate it as "possess life" or even "possesses real life." Either way,

---

[80] This sentence in Greek could be translated "those who are righteous because of faith, they live."

Paul will soon clarify that type of meaning in the immediate verses. He has already written his letter in such a way that we already know or at least infer that he means "Christ's life" when he says "the righteous by faith live," i.e. Christ lives through them.

**Galatians 3.12** "But the law is not of faith, rather "The one who does them shall live by them."" (ὁ δὲ νόμος οὐκ ἔστιν ἐκ πίστεως, ἀλλ' ὁ ποιήσας αὐτὰ ζήσεται ἐν αὐτοῖς.)

Paul, here in the middle of this paragraph, the third and fourth lines of the two parallel clauses, (Lines 1 and 2 make up 3.11; Lines 3 and 4 make up verse 12) gives a contrasting statement to his previous thought. He has just stated that "the righteous by faith have life." In this sentence, we see a couple of helpful defining grammatical and semantic connections. The first occurs when Paul says that the Law is not "out (ek) of faith." This helps us as readers to understand more fully what the phrase *out of faith* means. Here he uses it, apparently, to denote "not of the paradigm of faith" or maybe not of the spiritual economy of faith. The point is that Paul explains the law as being wholly different from the way of faith. There is a system of being righteous by the law and one that is by faith. The prepositional phrase here might suggest that he intends us to read it, not as just, "people who have faith" when he uses it but as those who are "in the system of faith." Here specifically he describes the two systems as fully incompatible.

Paul also defines clearly the difference between the two systems or economies. He contrasts "faith" as being simply about choosing to have faith in Christ for justification (those who seek justification from Christ. Galatians 2.18) and "law" as those who seek to be justified by "doing these things," i.e. the things written to do, or the entire list of commandments in the law. (Which may or may not include even more laws than what we have included in the Pentateuch.)[81] In more simple terms, "doing" is contrasted to "trusting" which Paul sees as contrasting ideas. (See Romans 4 for another time Paul clearly describes faith as

---

[81] See Sailhamer

the opposite of doing.) For us, the reader this helps us define what Paul is proposing with this system of faith and what he opposes with the system of law. He wants his readers to live by trusting Jesus and the Spirit apart from works, apart from doing.

**Galatians 3.13** "Christ redeemed us from the curse of the law by becoming a curse for us—for it is written, 'Cursed is everyone who is hanged on a tree'." (Χριστὸς ἡμᾶς ἐξηγόρασεν ἐκ τῆς κατάρας τοῦ νόμου γενόμενος ὑπὲρ ἡμῶν κατάρα, ὅτι γέγραπται· ἐπικατάρατος πᾶς ὁ κρεμάμενος ἐπὶ ξύλου, )

The section, at the end of the text, returns to the topic that it started with, the idea of the curse. Paul started this paragraph with a description of those under the curse, those who do not constantly do all of the commands written in the book of the law as he identifies them. Here he begins with a bit of jolt in the text. The absence of any conjunction or relative pronoun to begin the sentence should signal to us its importance generally and its role in closing this section. Every clause since Galatians 3.1 has begun with either a conjunction structure (some Greek conjunctions are always placed after the first word as a grammatical rule) or a pronoun that functions in a similar "connecting" way. Of note is that the last time a similar text-syntax was used was in Galatians 2.20 "I am crucified with Christ." In both cases neither clause begins with a conjunction, both begin with Christ in the Greek text and both follow a rather lengthy set of coordinated clauses. Also, the material of 2.15-19 is parallel to the material in 3.1-4 at least and maybe we should consider the section of 3.1-14 in that concept. Either way, there seems to be an intentional compositional connection between Galatians 2.20 and Galatians 3.13. (Notice also the return to the "life material" in the previous set of clauses.)

Here, the first words of this "closing clause" could be read as the 'aha!' of the previous section and even the clincher of Galatians 3.1-14. With that in mind, we might need to adjust our thesis that the middle material is the theme (though the connection to "life" in the previous material might suggest otherwise.)[82] The content is semantically similar to Galatians 2.20. There, Christ died. Here, Christ "set free at a cost."

The word translated "redeemed" in the ESV means to set free or release with a high cost to the liberator implied.[83] Or to purchase a person's freedom. Paul uses this word four times. Two of them in Galatians meaning "to set free at a cost" (both in Galatians) and one each in Ephesians and Colossians in parallel passages. In the latter case, it has a different meaning, "to use all our time well or carefully."[84] This may imply a structural connection between this section and Galatians 4:4 where Paul says, "Now, when the fullness of time had come, God sent for this son, born of woman, born under the law, to redeem those who were under the law so that might receive adoption as sons. And because you are sons, God has sent the Spirit of his Son into our hearts crying, Abba Father." Notice the similarities between the two texts. (See commentary on Galatians 4:4).[85] The most important aspect of this connection is the further identification of the focus of redemption. We have been made free from the law. In its place, we are "under the blessing of Abraham," "we continually receive the Spirit by faith"",

---

[82] This could adjust the thesis that 2.20 is the "center of the book" if this entire text is considered "parallel" to 2.20 then that could mean that 2.15-21 is parallel to 3.1-14(or later?) This would make the two texts together the structural middle of the book. It would probably leave 2.20 and 3.10-14 as still a peak of the two texts and the book overall. Supporting this new hypothesis is the fact that verse 14 closes out the 3.1-14 section with a return to the material it began with and connects all major ideas together: blessing, life, receiving the spirit. This if it is meant to be connected to 2.20 would suggest that 3.10-14 defines more clearly 2.20. Each halves interpret the other.

[83] LN

[84] He also uses the root *agora* "to purchase" in 1 Corinthians 7 to develop our responsibility to Christ as those who have been purchased. Could this be a intertextual link considering this is next to Galatians? especially if we see the letters as one. (1-2 Cor)

[85] Structurally this could be showing that 3.13 and 4.5ff are "seams." This seems clear even without this as 1) 3.1-14 is clearly ended with an inclusio in 3.14, 2) 3.15 clearly begins a new section with adelphoi, 3) 4.4 comes in a section that ends at verse 11 (4.1-11), 4) 4.12 clearly begins a new section with another "brothers) and new material. This hypothesis suggests that 3.15-4.7 forms a cohesive unit as does 3.1-14. Both end with the idea of Christ "buying our freedom"

and -with the connection to 4.4- "we have received the adoptions of sons whereby God sends the Sprit of his son into hearts crying Abba."[86]

Here, in verse 3.13, we see the nuance that we were given freedom from the "dark spell" that comes on someone who tries to do the law but fails, as all do. And we see how Christ became a curse on our behalf. Paul sees this as being taught in the Pentateuch when it says, "A person who gets hung up on a wooden pole as a criminal is under a curse."[87] In other words, God cursed Christ, who was otherwise sinless, as he hung on the cross. By being cursed, it reveals he took our curse for us. Or as 4.4 says, we were given freedom from being under the law because Christ was under the law and yet fulfilled its requirements. The latter refers to his giving us his own "fulfillment of the law" as he did with Abraham, and the former describes his taking on himself our curse.

**Galatians 3.14** "so that in Christ Jesus the blessing of Abraham might come to the Gentiles, so that we might receive the promised Spirit through faith." ( ἵνα εἰς τὰ ἔθνη ἡ εὐλογία τοῦ Ἀβραὰμ γένηται ἐν Χριστῷ Ἰησοῦ, ἵνα τὴν ἐπαγγελίαν τοῦ πνεύματος λάβωμεν διὰ τῆς πίστεως.)

Paul ends this paragraph (we need to be careful to not read our "grammatical forms" into this concept, maybe just subsection) by connecting Christ's substitutionary work on the cross giving us freedom from the law to his focus for the text of being in the blessing

---

[86] He sent his son and he sent his Spirit. Same root word in the 4.1-4 section.

[87] Sailhamer makes the point that "trees" are significant to the composition of the Pentateuch. They are the source of life in Eden. They are the source of sin in the fall. The man and woman hide amidst the trees from God and make poor coverings for themselves out of leaves of trees. Noah makes a grove of trees before he gets drunk and naked and covered. Trees also play a role in the Tabernacle narrative. If this is accurate, then, when we read about the fact that God binds a curse onto anyone hung on a tree as a criminal. Literally it says, God curses a person hung. In context we know it refers to someone hung on a tree because the previous verse says that when a person is hung on a tree for crimes he must be taken down the same day since he is under a curse. The cursing language and the tree language in context of death also may give structural connection to Gen 1-3.

of Abraham, namely, also receiving the Spirit. As noted above these two clauses serve three functions: 1) to show the ending of the section that began in 3.1, 2) To connect all the big ideas of this section (life, blessing, power of the spirit, spiritual growth and maturation -all of which are experienced by faith) and 3) To add new information to this cluster of concepts.

As it relates to "the blessing of Abraham" the new information Paul gives us connects the blessing to being "en Christo" or in Christ. This phrase could be "inside of Christ" so that it speaks to our unity with him or "by Christ" so that it speaks to Christ being the active agent creating this blessing. The former idea appears to be related to the blessing being for the "seed" and ours by virtue of being one with the seed. The latter idea is implied in the immediate text whereby Christ bought our freedom so that we could have this blessing and so it's "by him."

As it relates to the second clause focused on the experience of the Spirit, the text reminds us that the blessing of Abraham is the same as the "promise of the Spirit." What is the "promise of the Spirit?" It is the same as what Paul described in the first section in three ways, 1) receiving the Spirit (which he repeated here), 2) an entity for being perfected or matured, 3) He gives us "experiences," 4) God supplies the Spirit to us, 5) the Spirit works supernatural miracles in us and through us. Also of course, we note that the terminology of "blessing" connects the concept to "a conferring of good magical power or force." The Pentateuch also connects the idea of blessing back to "life in the garden." So, that's the information that has been revealed. What's new? Paul introduces us to the idea that the Spirit comes to us -as described above- as a promise.

So, Paul introduces two new details about our experience of the blessing and the Spirit. It's in Christ and it's by promise. Paul will go on to develop these ideas more thoroughly in the next section. In that way, they serve as a pivot between one section and another. Paul often, in Galatians, uses this "cross-sectional stitching" to highlight the semantic and conceptual connection between one section and the other.

The last thought on this verse: Paul makes it clear that we are to "receive the work of the Spirit" as described in this section in the many ways detailed above "by faith." So, we are justified by faith and experience the Spirit by the same faith; we trust in Christ to do all the work, have done all the work to make us unfiltered recipients of the blessing, the Spirit.

How can this happen like this? Anyone who seeks to gain acceptance with God by following the commands of the law will find themselves under the influence of the dark magic of a cursing spell. We know this because of what's written in the Torah, "Everyone who fails to continually obey everything that is written in the Laws of the Torah, any of the commands,[88] is under an evil curse." Consider too, just how clearly the law shows that no one is ever righteous enough to be accepted by God through obeying rules, commands or laws. It's clearly stated, "The righteous live by faith."[89] In contrast, the law is not compatible with faith, "The person who does these things will live because of them." So, when we think about the cursed state of those trying to gain acceptance by doing the rules in the Torah we should also

---

[88] The Greek grammar is somethings like "in the book containing the law, namely the things to do."

[89] In Hebrew: "The righteous live because of his faith." In Greek: "The righteous out of faith (because of it) will live." The question in this text is typically related to the word "faith." In Habakkuk 2.22 many suggest that "Amunah" can only be understood as "faithfulness" and, since that fits within the range of meaning of *pistis* it might be what Paul meant. In the new perspective on Paul, this idea dominates. It is then understood to be Christ's faithful act that Paul refers to here. In the structure of Habakukk though another possible understanding is in play. The book of Habakkuk centers on the "work" that God will do in the last days. In a clearly connected parallel passage (1.5) the author of Habakkuk connects the word translated as "faith" or faithfulness here to another form of the same word that clearly means "trust" as in the more common understanding of the word. The point being that Habakkuk should teach others to "have faith in the work" and then in 2.2, he is to explain the vision and make it so easy to understand that someone can read it as they run by it. Then, in Chapter 3 he connects the "work" of 1.5 to a future time that Habakkuk connects to the last days prophecy of Numbers 24 casting the Babylonian events articulated earlier as future events wherein the Messiah moves to the foreground. In other words, Habakkuk calls his readers to trust in the coming seed of the Torah. (see esp. 3.13) (See Sailhamer on Num 23-24)

remember that[90] Christ bought our freedom from this dark curse conjured by the law by becoming cursed himself on our behalf. We see this in the Torah when it says, "The criminal[91] that hangs on a wood pole for his crime is bound by a divine[92] evil curse." When Christ took our curse for us it was so that the supernatural blessing of Abraham might be shared with people regardless of their ethnicity or cultural background or, to say it another way, so that we could begin to experience the promise of the Spirit's presence and empowerment simply because of this faith we've been describing.

---

[90] This additional relative clause is an attempt to show that this sentence connects back to verse 10.

[91] The context of Deut 23 is of a criminal being punished by being hanged so the additional of "criminal." The important aspect missed in a straightforward translation is that this is not a random hanging on a wood pool. This is a capital punishment for crimes via being hung from a wood pole. God curses this one not just because they are hung on a wood pole but because they are hung on a pole as a criminal.

[92] The Hebrew text says "God curses the one who is hung."

# Galatians 3.15-18

**Interpretive Translation:**

My dear family, I am going to pause on the theological language[93] for a moment and use an illustration from your everyday life to help you understand my point. No one cancels[94] or adds stipulations to a human will[95] after the person dies and it has been put into effect.[96] Note though,[97] that these promises[98] were made to Abraham and one[99] of his descendants. But the promise does not say "and to your many descendants" as if it were made to a group of people but it was made to just one person, "and to one of your descendants." This descendant is the Messiah, Jesus. Compare this illustration to God's legal contract with Abraham.[100] The law came 430 years after God's agreement[101]

---

[93] See note on covenant.

[94] The present tense is used, here to convey temporal action.

[95] In context (parallel to inheritance in 4.18), this means will, as in will and testament. He uses the multiple modifiers referring to this being "human" to pull us as his readers away from reading it too theologically. Not, in other words, "a biblical theological covenant" just an illustration.

[96] The word means "to sign into law" or to be in effect, like a law or will. This is used in the context of an inheritance, 4.18 (is parallel to it) and the perfect form of this word basically means that the "will" has become in effect, similar to Romans and Hebrews.

[97] de in Gk but most likely an "epexegetical" usage of the conjunction.

[98] The content of the will, in context, so the plural, but specifically, from verse 14, the Spirit.

[99] singular seed already in the text.

[100] By saying "now I say this" Paul seems to be saying "Before I used a human illustration now let me compare it to the theological truth."

[101] Here the same term as "will and testament" above is used but a connection to an OT covenant might be implied. A OT covenant would have been unidirectional, i.e. because it's from a God it would be not based on stipulations with the other party (BDAG) and it would not include the death of the testator. In the era of the NT it means contract.

was put into effect. It cannot, then, suddenly render it not "in effect"[102] so that it cancels God's promise.[103] The inheritance cannot come as a condition of following the law and as the result of an unconditional promise at the same time. God, though, had already committed the inheritance to Abraham as a promise before the law.[104]

## Summary Commentary:

Paul begins a new section in Galatians 3.15 that runs until Galatians 4:15. He develops here the idea he ended with in the previous section, namely that the blessing of Abraham, the Spirit himself, comes through promise not performance. As a result, to experience this promise we believe it, we don't "do it." You cannot do a promise. Paul uses the example from secular affairs of a last will and testament and explains that the will cannot be amended once the testator has died and the will is in effect. He ends this paragraph by leaving the secular analogy and returning to the theological concept. In the same way, a will cannot be amended after it has been put into effect, the law, which came many years after the promise made to Abraham, cannot change the promise. He ends by making a corollary observation: God gave the inheritance to Abraham through a promise and therefore it cannot be through performing laws because it can't be by both promise and performance at the same time.

In the middle of this paragraph, he also gives information about the heirs of this promise. There were not many heirs; God made the promise of an inheritance (in this "will") to a single heir, the Messiah. By adding this remark here, Paul connects his thinking rather subtly to Galatians 2.20 where the "inheritance" is described in terms of us

---

[102] "in effect" same root, positive and negative reflection.

[103] Promise is synonymous with convenant and "will," i.e. legally binding document.

[104] A lot of interpretive additions here. 1) to showcase the logic of Paul changed the conditional clause into a statement of logical conflict. 2) the perfect tense is used in "he gave" as being "already" and at that time presently in effect. That time was specifically "before the law." I.e. it was in a state of being in effect when the law was given because God had already "signed it into law."

"dying by crucifixion" and Christ "living his life in us in place of our life" as being "In Christ." The promise (blessing, inheritance, Spirit, Christ living in us, etc.) was made to Christ. We only receive it in as much as we are "in him." The "in him" logic is first formulated in Galatians 2.19-20.

**Galatians 3:15** "To give a human example, brothers: even with a man-made covenant, no one annuls it or adds to it once it has been ratified." (Ἀδελφοί, κατὰ ἄνθρωπον λέγω· ὅμως ἀνθρώπου κεκυρωμένην διαθήκην οὐδεὶς ἀθετεῖ ἢ ἐπιδιατάσσεται.)

Paul begins a new section here but continues developing his basic ideas from before: the blessing and promise of the Spirit. This could be seen as a "double-click" into the idea that the Spirit is "by promise," which began in the previous section. The promise and inheritance will dominate this section.

He begins with "according to men I speak." This is a way for Paul, as the author, to guide us as his readers, showing us how to read this next clause. He uses an example from the world of men, a secular not theological example. He will make theological connections to his secular analogy at the end of this paragraph.

The human example he gives relates to a "last will and testament." Some translators use the term covenant here and that is the general term. It can mean many different kinds of legal agreements. It is also the word used to translate "covenant" (BRT) in the Hebrew Bible. Paul guards the reader from seeing it that way in his sentence by the detail "I am speaking from a human perspective or secular mind." He appears to want to make sure we read this in the most non-theological way possible. With that in mind, we should probably read this term as "last will and testament." Consider also the language of inheritance in verse 18 establishing a context of "will and inheritance."

So, with that being the case, we now read the sentence as "a will that has been executed" as in a will that is being applied because of the death of the one who established it. The author of Hebrews uses similar language when he says, "For where a will is involved, the death of the one who made it must be established. For a will takes effect only at death since it is not in force as long as the one who made it is alive." The author of Hebrews goes on to develop the implications of this same concept, namely that Christ's death executed the "will" of the new covenant.

Once a will is in force as a result of the death of the one who established it, then the will cannot be annulled nor can stipulations be added to it. The latter comes from a word used often in official and legal settings meaning "to attach on top of." It could be used, for example, when a soldier's assignment had new details attached to it, or he was given an "additional assignment" to the one he originally received. Here Paul says that this can't be done to an executed will, or more literally, "is not done." In other words, people just don't do this.

Paul goes on, in the next sentence to describe the heirs included in this will and then, as he closes out the chapter, comes back to his appeal to an executed will, this time with a more theological application. "Now, the law, which came 430 years later, cannot invalidate a will that has been executed by God so that it nullifies the promise."

**Galatians 3:16** "Now the promises were made to Abraham and to his offspring. It does not say, "And to offsprings," referring to many, but referring to one, "And to your offspring," who is Christ." (τῷ δὲ Ἀβραὰμ ἐρρέθησαν αἱ ἐπαγγελίαι καὶ τῷ σπέρματι αὐτοῦ. οὐ λέγει· καὶ τοῖς σπέρμασιν, ὡς ἐπὶ πολλῶν ἀλλ' ὡς ἐφ' ἑνός· καὶ τῷ σπέρματί σου, ὅς ἐστιν Χριστός.)

The organizational mechanism in this text seems to be the verb "lego" or "to speak." In the previous verse, Paul *speaks* in a human way. Here, the promises were *spoken* to Abraham. In the second half of this verse, the promise "does not *say*." Then, in verse 17, literally, "Now this I *say*." This gives structure to the text. One argument against seeing the text this way is the parallels between verse 16 and verse 18. Both focus on the "promises" which verse 18 explains is the same as "the inheritance." Because Paul goes on to expand on the nature of the blessing/promise as an inheritance, it is most likely this should be read as a summarizing sentence that transitions to the next topic. As noted above it also links to verse 14 giving a bracketing or "cross stitching" effect at these two seams.

Paul refers here to the promises. What promises? More generally, in the most local text, "the promises" refer to the commitments made within the legal document in the previous verse. The connection, though, back to the previous section also provides more information. The promises are the promise of the Spirit, the life of Christ living in us, the blessing, justification, etc. Paul places "to Abraham" in a fronted position in this sentence. Following the Greek structure, we would write the sentence, "Now to Abraham, they were spoken, the promises and to his seed. He does not say to the seeds, as concerning many but as concerning one; and to your seed, who is Christ." Typically, this would be to emphasize Abraham's role in some way, i.e. the reference to him is moved out of place (one way to emphasize a word or grammatical category) and it is moved forward (even more emphasis). When we look at the internal structure of these two clauses though we something a bit more nuanced. Consider the structure:

A1 - To Abraham
B1 - They were spoken the promises
C 1 - And to his seed
B2 - He does not speak to the seeds, as concerning many but concerning one
C2 - And to your seed
A2 - Who is Christ

The fronting of "to Abraham" serves to emphasize this phrase and to emphasize the A2 phrase below it, "who is Christ." It is a subtle way for the author to draw our attention to the fact Christ is the one the promises were made.

Paul wants to make sure we read the seed as singular. What is interesting about this is that this is not exactly what is in the Hebrew text. The term for seed in Hebrew in the Pentateuch in this quote is singular grammatically but it is also a collective. It can refer to one seed or many. Paul seems to be aware though, that the author of the Pentateuch intentionally and strategically composes his book to show the readers that the seed of note is an individual king of the tribe of Judah who will fulfill the promise to Abraham and Adam and Eve in Genesis 3:15. (For more on this compositional strategy, refer to *The Meaning of the Pentateuch* by John Sailhamer.) It is not the grammar of the "seed" texts in the Pentateuch that shows the seed to be singular. It is the compositional strategy of the author. This understanding of the term seed shows he has done careful exegesis of the Pentateuch (and other Scriptures). This probably is what he means when he describes in Gal 2:2 the presentation he makes regarding the gospel he preaches. It may also connect the statement he makes in Gal 3:1-2, that "Christ crucified" had been shown to the Galatians rather clearly in the "writings" from before, antiquity (i.e. the Hebrew Bible, Old Testament).

This paragraph serves as the head paragraph for the rest of this section (ending in 4:12). As such the emphasis placed on the idea of Christ being the "seed" of Abraham is essential to the logic Paul works through as he progresses onward. Christ is the seed, the "offspring." God spoke the promises of Genesis 15 to Abraham and Christ, his offspring. This may be a moment in the text that surprises the readers, at least us modern readers. We may think, based on what we have read previously, that the promises would have been to us. Paul, though, says something different than what we might expect. The promises, the blessing were made to Christ. With this statement, he begins to show that we are blessed and experience the work of the Spirit by being "in the seed." Remember how Paul started the second major section of this book. (3:1-4:31) "Those who seek to be righteous before God by faith are the *sons* of Abraham." (emphasis mine) Galatians 3:6.

Paul has said, in other words, that we are in the lineage because we have faith. We are sons. He then goes on to show that faith (or not) is the difference, according to the Pentateuch, of whether someone is "blessed" or "cursed." Doing the law (or trying to) leaves one cursed. Having faith attaches us to Abraham, we have faith like Abraham had and thereby we are righteous like him *and we are his sons.* Paul will go on to explain this fully but here he begins explaining that the "blessing" is Christ's and only ours because of our unity with Christ. In 3.14 he stated that Christ became a curse for us so that the blessing of Abraham can come to us *in Christ.* He then adds the clarifying parallel statement, "so that the promise of the Spirit (ie. the blessing of Abraham) we can possibly receive it *through this faith.*" Faith, it appears, in Christ, places us in Christ. As Paul will later say, "If you are "of Christ" then you are Abraham's seed (singular) and heirs as it relates to the promise." (Gal 3:29)

This material is essential to Paul's ultimate thesis: walk in the Spirit, or "step by the Spirit." At the end of chapter 5 he simply gives a bit of a summary of everything else: If we live by the Spirit, we might also step by the Spirit." This is a parallel to "walk in the Spirit and you will not do what the flesh lusts for."

**Galatians 3:17** "This is what I mean: the law, which came 430 years afterward, does not annul a covenant previously ratified by God, so as to make the promise void." (τοῦτο δὲ λέγω· διαθήκην προκεκυρωμένην ὑπὸ τοῦ θεοῦ ὁ μετὰ τετρακόσια καὶ τριάκοντα ἔτη γεγονὼς νόμος οὐκ ἀκυροῖ εἰς τὸ καταργῆσαι τὴν ἐπαγγελίαν.)

After further developing the idea of the seed and therefore the lineage and heirs of Abraham, Paul comes back to the "covenant" or will. Here he moves back into the theological context (as opposed to his secular example above). He replaces the terms from the original sentence in verse 15 with the theological concepts from Scripture. Now, the "will" is the covenant God gave Abraham. It, too, has been executed and was executed before the law came on the scene. So, it cannot be disempowered or be counted as an emendation to the original will. He also adds here that it cannot be nullified or "de-executed." Three words provide cohesion to this text and they all share the same root (kurao).

The word above translated "ratified" in the ESV (v.15) is repeated in vs 17 with the word translated "previously ratified." Then, what we might miss in the ESV, the author states the law does not "annul" the previously ratified covenant. The word annul also comes from the negated root *kurao* but in this case, it means to undo what *kurao* enacts. *You can't un-ratify the covenant God ratified.*

He explains the result and the reason the covenant to Abraham cannot be un-ratified. The result of de-ratifying the covenant would be that the promises therein are voided, or invalidated. The word often refers to being released from a legal contract. A will (or covenant) includes commitments and promises toward the heir. If the law code can undo the "will" that preceded it or even amend it (v 15) then the promises or commitments are also inactive. Paul leaves this sentence as is because it means internally enough to communicate its meaning. If a promise is made and then something else comes along that makes the promise null then the original promise was a lie. Paul considers, it appears, the entire concept self-defeating.

**Galatians 3:18** "For if the inheritance comes by the law, it no longer comes by promise; but God gave it to Abraham by a promise." (εἰ γὰρ ἐκ νόμου ἡ κληρονομία, οὐκέτι ἐξ ἐπαγγελίας· τῷ δὲ Ἀβραὰμ δι' ἐπαγγελίας κεχάρισται ὁ θεός.)

Paul continues the previous clause by adding an explanation. The idea of an inheritance is implied by his use of "last will and testament" language earlier. Here it is explicit. The heir receives the inheritance as a promise. God gave (graced) the inheritance to Abraham through a promise. The term "gave" is a perfect verb denoting a stative aspect to the action of the verb. In other words, Paul emphasizes with his grammatical choice the outcome of God's gift. God *finished* giving the inheritance to Abraham because that's what he promised to do. [105]

---

[105] This use of the perfect shows that it does not refer to past tense per se.

# Galatians 3.19-22

**Interpretative Translation:**

Then, what is the purpose of the law? The law was added[106] to show that we have lived in conflict with God's character, to put the category of transgression into effect. This paradigm was in effect until the seed showed up, the same seed that God promised the inheritance, the blessing. The angels received the commandments[107] from God and then had a mediator write them down for all involved parties. A mediator is

---

[106] Was the law "added?" or "give?" Neg or positive. Only the context can help us decide. Above the language is repeatedly related to "adding" something on which might imply that it was like an addition. In the next sentence it was "added" by the angels. If we consider the thoughts of Sailhamer on this text we might use "add." The law code was added on to the patriarchal religious mode, the faith of Abraham. Nothing can be added to the covenant of Abraham but that dies keep something from being added. IT was not an emendation though. It was a layer with non-conflicting purpose. The sense carries with it "addition" to the original in context versus a positive sense: to give. This could be considered problematic

[107] It could be simply "give" but the word often means to give detailed instructions which fits the spirit of the law in this text as a list of rather tedious dos and and don'ts.

not necessary when there is only one party. God is one.[108] (Or God and the seed are one.) Does the law, then, impede the promises God made to the seed of Abraham? That's not even possible. If the law code was written with the potential to make you alive in God,[109] then real[110] righteousness was by the law.[111] Instead, these writings do the opposite. They draw lines around everything we do turning them into sin and us into sinners. This demarcation causes the promise to be given based on faith in Jesus Christ to those who have faith, not those who do the law.

---

[108] The promises were to the seed from God. The Law is instructions from God to angels to a mediator to man. That is the most clear (but still insinuated) concept in the text. Then he says "God is one" in the exact way he says that the "Seed is one." He doesn't here say why but he in essence says the original (new) covenant didn't need a mediator because only one party is involved. God to God. This hints at a powerful idea: mans involvement in the covenant is joining with a God to God relationship. We will watch for this to be clarified. Also consider Galatians 2:19-20 where Paul defines being "alive in God" to Christ (God) living in me and me being dead because I am in Him and share His (Christ God's) history. ——- I will leave the notes after this to show "working through the text." This phrasing is confusing. Maybe it is intentionally so. Maybe Paul wants to just throw this in there and make us hold it in tension until he answers it. Directly it does not technically say anything except that. A mediator is not one, lit. Or more fluid: a mediator is not "of one" or related to one, or does not mediate when there is only one party. But, God is one. There seems to be no direct meaning given here, in the immediate context. Earlier it did say God made his covenant to not many seeds but to just one seed, Christ. That was the "pre-mediated" covenant. In the covenant to the seed there was no mediator. In the covenant to the Angels there was. (this could be both implied subtly in this text and confirmed by the connection to the earlier statements that are intended to be read with this one: the promises that were made to Abraham were not to many seeds but to one seed, Christ. When the law code came it was given, in contrast, through mediation between multiple parties. BUT/NOW God is one. (No mediation when God is promising to God.)

[109] Compare to Gal 2:19b.

[110] Could be righteous was "really" by the law or as translated.

[111] I am not so sure this text is meant to be read in the subjunctive mood. It does not have subjunctive verbs. "If an able to give life law was given, righteous was from laws." As written it does not seem to me to say "If a law could be given that would give life righteous would have come that way." It seems to be defeating the proposition by suggesting something that he has already disproven: righteousness does not come from the law. If the law with the power to give life was given it would have. It was not.

**Summary Commentary:**

Paul continues his basic line of thought from the previous section. He repeated the last line from 3:14 that ended the larger level pericope from 3.1-14 and was a part of the beginning of this larger section. This helps Paul form a section within a section so to speak. Here he asks the question that he assumes his previous point raises. If the law was an impotent add-on as the previous paragraph suggests then what's its purpose? "Why then the law?" The first point he makes—related to answering this question—shows why it was given, "to cause transgressions." Then he adds a temporal element to the answer, more why it was given when it was given. It is active until the seed comes and receives the promises. When Christ came, to whom the promises were made, then the law was no longer necessary in its original role. The promise receiver (and distributor) was on the scene, the heir had arrived to claim the inheritance. Paul will speak more about the timing element in the next few paragraphs. Here, he then adds a confusing sentence about a mediator. The options are endless. I read it as a hint to the fact that the seed and God being one do not need a mediator. (More below).

This paragraph is broken into two parts each arranged around a question. The next question Paul asks is related to the effectiveness of the law. "Did it work?" Did the Law overcome the promises? Or were they trying? Paul says no and gives two reasons. First, he says that if a law was given (not *could* be given) that could give life (implying the answer is it was not so given), then righteousness was actually from the law. This statement creates an intentional conflict between what has been said previously, neither righteousness nor life come from the law. Here he raises the point those two concepts infer and defeat the counter-thesis. When a "life-giving law" is given (if it could happen), then righteousness, logically, also comes from doing the law. The law accomplishes the opposite effect. It, as was said at the beginning of the paragraph, "captures everything" in the net of sin, or to put it another way, it makes everything sin. Second, Paul also answers the why question related to this statement. What is the purpose of everything being identified as sin? Or as the earlier, parallel statement says it, "causing transgressions." So that people will not try and perform and work their way into being accepted by God. Paul wants them instead to have faith in Jesus. People who see themselves as sinners don't trust themselves for righteousness. That would be illogical. They must trust in another. They must seek Jesus to justify them as Galatians 2:19 says. The law then, by causing or creating transgressions and by capturing everything into sin (by creating the idea of it) pushes people toward faith in Jesus. (Note the difference between the written law and the not written law.)

There are two possible ways to read the sentence that answers the why question.

We could read the next sentence as "it was added because of transgressions" or as "it was added in order to cause transgressions." Sailhamer shows in his commentary on the Pentateuch that the former is implied in the Torah. The more the people of Israel sinned the more laws they were given. The law code came as a result of the Israelites' sin. "The more you sin the more laws you are going to get."

**Galatians 3:19a** "Why then the law? It was added because of transgressions, until the offspring should come to whom the promise had been made," Τί οὖν ὁ νόμος; τῶν παραβάσεων χάριν προσετέθη, ἄχρις οὗ ἔλθῃ τὸ σπέρμα ᾧ ἐπήγγελται, διαταγεὶς δι' ἀγγέλων ἐν χειρὶ μεσίτου.)

Paul answers the question raised by the previous section in three ways: why the law? When was the law in effect? What are the limits of the law?

"It was added because of transgressions" - Here Paul answers why the law was "added." The word added (Greek *prosethe*) is similar to the wording he used above when he speaks of a will not having additions. He wants us to see the law as "an addition" even though no additions can be made. If we could try to bring this out in a translation we might say, "If nothing can be added to the original will, then why was the law added?" or "Nothing can be added to the will, but the law was added. Why?"

The next phrase can be understood in two different possible ways. It can be, as in the ESV above, that the law was added "because of transgressions." Sailhamer takes this view in his commentary on the Pentateuch suggesting that the original covenant with the Israelites in Exodus 19:1-16a was a covenant like the one made with Abraham. But, because the Israelites disobeyed God, he gave them a law code. Every new addition to the law code follows an event of disobedience in the narrative describing Israel's history at this point. So "transgressions" led to or caused the addition of the law.

This phrase can also be understood from a different direction. We may need to read as if the law was given in order to *cause* transgressions. This more clearly fits the parallel statement in Galatians 3:22, "The Scripture captures everything under the heading of 'sin.'" It also connects with Paul's description of the law in Romans 7:7-8 where he says, "What then shall we say? That the law is sin? By no means! Yet if it had not been for the law, I would not have known sin. For I would not have known what it is to covet if the law had not said, "You shall not covet." But sin, seizing an opportunity through the commandment, produced in me all kinds of covetousness. For apart from the law, sin lies dead." Here Paul seems to say that the law produced sin. The Galatians text seems more likely to follow this line of thinking. The Law created transgressions.

This also follows the concept introduced in Galatians 2:17-19 where Paul describes the paradigm of the law. In his description, he says that if this paradigm is no longer active, he is no longer a transgressor because "transgression" means to be in conflict with the law. If the law is inactive then so is the category of transgression. Here, then, he is showing the same idea from the opposite perspective: The Law Paradigm existed to create the category of transgression. Later he will explain in more detail the purpose of this effect, the purpose was (and is) to move people away from trying to do the law (or any system of rules where we know and do good and/or evil -see the tree of knowledge in Eden) and into faith in Christ.

We might bring out the meaning of this text most accurately by saying: "Why does the law code exist? It was an extra layer added to create the idea of transgressions."

"until the offspring should come to whom the promise had been made" - Paul continues the development of the "seed" (translated offspring here) and the promises made to the seed contrasting the one paradigm (law) to the other (promise). This sentence modifies the previous sentence telling us that the law "caused transgressions" until the seed came. This could either mean that the "law existed" until the seed came or that transgressions existed until the seed came or both. Paul suggested in Galatians 2:18-19 that the law is an "economy" or paradigm that has been disempowered. Paul suggests in Galatians 4:1-11 that the timing elements of these events are both historical, there was a moment in history when the seed came, and spiritual, "when you do not know God you are enslaved" to the law. (4.8) So, the coming of the seed, historically and personally, is the end of the reign of the law paradigm and the beginning of the reign of the promise paradigm. The result of this is as he says in Galatians 2:17-19: the category of transgression has been dissolved.

Paul will wrestle with "why" the coming of the seed dissolved the economy of law in chapter 4. Here he suggests something interesting that may intentionally raise dramatic tension in the mind of the reader. He has said in the previous text that the original will or covenant (with Abraham) preceded the law code addendum which is not really an addendum. He has now said here that the "era of promise/seed" follows the "era of law." Paul is playing with time elements to paint a picture of what is happening with each of these two economies. (Galatians 4:1-10 will return to this same material and explain it in it more clearly. Here he is making the point from more of a "Hebrew Bible" perspective.)

He also identifies the seed again. The seed is "the one to whom the promises were made." This serves as a reminder and a point of emphasis. He just said a few verses back that the promises were "to the seed, one seed, Christ." Here, he alludes back to that text. This will also help us understand the rather difficult clauses that follow.

**Galatians 3:20** "It was put in place through angels by an intermediary. Now an intermediary implies more than one, but God is one." (διαταγεὶς δι' ἀγγέλων ἐν χειρὶ μεσίτου. ὁ δὲ μεσίτης ἑνὸς οὐκ ἔστιν, ὁ δὲ θεὸς εἷς ἐστιν.)

Some have suggested this is the most obscure text in Galatians or maybe the New Testament. Let's work carefully through each line to assess how Paul, in these three clauses, adds new thoughts to his major argument: the promises, inheritance, blessing, Spirit, come through faith and not doing the law.

"It was put in place by an intermediary." The first of these fragments modifies the subject "law." Paul has said "it was added to cause transgressions until the seed comes." Now, he describes the law even further with a participial phrase. This participial phrase, by coming after the main clause, "the law caused transgressions until the seed came," may also be intended to explain why this is true. So, it is either simply describing "the law" or it is explaining the main clause. Either way, what does it mean? The lexeme is similar semantically to the main verb, "added." It is the same root that was used in Galatians 3:15 "adds." In this context, it probably means something like "instructed." It is a passive participle or "the instructions were added." The word itself means in some contexts, "to give detailed instructions as to what must be done." It was often used to describe the act of giving orders to a subordinate. This phrase is positioned so that it parallels the phrase "the promise…might be given." The contrast between "rules commanded" and a "promise given" is significant.

How were they given? The ESV simplifies the original statement as you may read it in another translation: "through angels in the hand of an intermediary." The text may be intentionally piling up prepositional phrases to show that the set of commands that were given had a complicated process and is several layers from direct God to human contact. He seems to want to cause the reader to see the law code as being from God at a distance, through multiple steps. We tend to read "mediator" as between two parties. The concept though potentially includes multiple parties. The mediation process or "legal arranging" of the mediator may involve multiple parties. The role of the mediator is the role of arbitrating an agreement between individuals or groups. In this context, Paul has been using legal language and most likely intends for us to keep that in mind here. The new "legal stipulations" of the law code were executed and arranged by an arbitrator.

We might ask: who are the parties involved in the arbitration? the angels appear to be on one side of the table. The Israelites must be on the other side of the table. Ironically, in Paul's description, God is not directly in the picture, though we naturally read, and so likely did the Galatians, that the angels represented God in some way. The conceptual separation, though, between man and God must be intentional in this paradigm.

The natural reading of the next text follows closely on the implications that there was an "arbitration" from a mediator that instituted the law code as a "stand beside" covenant. (Not one that was meant to replace the Abrahamic covenant, but was meant to stand beside it temporarily.) The law was added by a person who mediates between two or more parties, not one party. "But God is one party." This comment seems to come out of nowhere.

The author though does seem to intentionally create a parallel to what he had said in the previous paragraph when he says "the promises were made to Abraham's seed. It does not say "to many seeds" referring to many but referring to one, "to your seed" who is Christ. The parallels are rather clear: 1) seed, promise language are in both places. 2) Both clauses refer to "adding stipulations" to the covenant. 3) Both use language related to counting:

"'Not to the seeds'" as many." COMPARES TO: "A mediation is not for one."

"But to the one seed, who is Christ." COMPARES TO: "But God is one."

This suggests that the author wants his readers to understand this material as a further description of the material above. We might read this then as: Referring for a moment back to the statements that "the promises are not to multiple seeds but just one seed and that seed is Christ." Consider also a mediation occurs between multiple parties not just one. God, however, is just one party. Paul implies that no mediation is necessary in the "promise" economy because only one party is involved. Or, to say it more clearly, God the Father made the promises to God the Son, Christ and they are one. This passage is by no means clear. I would suggest that Paul is hinting at the idea though that the seed is God as is the one who made the promises. He will soon say, spoiler alert, that we are also, by faith, the seed of Abraham. (He has already said we are his sons but he will more clearly designate us as his seed, the one promised the blessing.) This is not a small theological moment. If this is the meaning intended by Paul then he is saying that the Son and the Father are One and we are, by being one with the seed by faith, also now one with the Father and the Son. Also remember he has hinted at this idea already in Galatians 2:19-20 where he says, we are alive with God. He explains this life as being in Christ, so that he was crucified when Christ was crucified and as being "Christ living in me." Later in the text, possibly the climax of this sub-section, he says that we have put on Christ-like clothing and that the Spirit has been sent into our hearts crying Abba to God the Father.

**Galatians 3:21** "Is the law then contrary to the promises of God? Certainly not! For if a law had been given that could give life, then righteousness would indeed be by the law." ( ὁ οὖν νόμος κατὰ τῶν ἐπαγγελιῶν [τοῦ θεοῦ]; μὴ γένοιτο· εἰ γὰρ ἐδόθη νόμος ὁ δυνάμενος ζῳοποιῆσαι, ὄντως ἐκ νόμου ἂν ἦν ἡ δικαιοσύνη.)

The second question follows the logical conclusion of the first and introduces the second half of the paragraph. It also suggests that we should read the first answer with a negative answer, one that might suggest that the law is against the promises of God.

"Is the law then contrary to the promises of God?" - The meaning of this sentence is rather straightforward in English. The one word that could be read somewhat differently is the term translated "contrary" from the Greek preposition kata. As in the case of most prepositions, there are many possible meanings. Consider a few examples of other possible meanings:

"Is the law lower than the promises of God?"
"Is the law inside of the promises of God?"
"Is the law against the promises of God?"
"Does the law contradict the promises of God?"
"Does the law defeat/stop the promises of God?"

This breakdown reveals that the phrase has the potential to have somewhat opposite meanings. Is the law in the promises of God? i.e. the law is a part of the promises, synonymous with them; OR Does the law contradict, stand against, or shut down the promises of God? Or even, "are the laws beneath the promises of God?" The first basically says that the promises include the law. They are 100% compatible. Paul says this is impossible. The second says that the law is against the promises of God. Paul again states this is impossible. The third suggests that the law is beneath, under the authority of the promises. If Paul didn't negate this statement it would be an accurate description. With the negation, we can rule it out.

Based on the context of the previous sentence and paragraph I lean toward reading it as another form of what has already been said many times: Can the law annul, add to, change, etc. the promises of God? So, with that, the preposition should be read as "defeat" or shut down the promises of God. This is similar to what most English translations suggest but slightly different. Instead of bringing up the possibility that the law is against the promises and negating that idea, Paul appears to ask a question that is somewhat more antinomian, a question he has implied already: Can the law render the promises null and void? He answers -as he has already in other ways- never.

"For if a law had been given that could give life, then righteousness would indeed be by the law." - If the understanding of the previous sentences is correct then it will cause us to read this sentence a little differently as well. The translation in the ESV suggests a subjunctive mood: "If it was possible for a law to be given." This potentially reflects the inference of this sentence but it does not fit the structure of the grammar. The actual forms used should be translated as "If a law, one able to give life, was given." This reading fits both the grammar and the context of the text more accurately. This is a way for Paul to simply state, "No law was given that gave life."

He follows this up by stating what was true if the condition was true (though he has clearly stated that the condition is not true). If the condition is true then true righteousness was from the law or righteousness was truly (actually) from the law. (It is unclear what part of the sentence "truly" or "actual" modifies.) Since the conditional sentence works to negate the apodosis, we could read this as "righteousness did not actually come from the law since a life-giving law was not given." This seems to be the sense Paul is suggesting here.

**Galatians 3:22** "But the Scripture imprisoned everything under sin, so that the promise by faith in Jesus Christ might be given to those who believe." (ἀλλὰ συνέκλεισεν ἡ γραφὴ τὰ πάντα ὑπὸ ἁμαρτίαν, ἵνα ἡ ἐπαγγελία ἐκ πίστεως Ἰησοῦ Χριστοῦ δοθῇ τοῖς πιστεύουσιν.)

Paul ends this paragraph by explaining the conclusion to the question of the reason the law was given and by adding an inclusio to the section starting in verse 15 with material returning to the promise being given by faith in Jesus. At the beginning of this paragraph, in verse 19, he says the law was given to "cause transgressions" or to make transgressions a thing, the establishment of transgressions. Here, he says something similar but adds more nuance to his point.

"The Scripture imprisoned everything under sin." - Paul says that the law was given to establish transgressions. Here he switches from the Law to the Scriptures. This either clarifies his original meaning or elevates it to a new concept. Or, to say it another way, either when he says Law he means the version written in the law and/or the Torah itself, or when he says Law above he means that which was "added" or included in the Torah/Pentateuch. He appears to elucidate something about the development of the Pentateuch. The Law was originally given to establish transgressions. They were included in the Pentateuch to point out the sinfulness of all things.

It is important to pause and try to understand "all things." What is Paul referring to when he says "all things" are under sin? What does the context suggest is the meaning of all things? Paul does not appear to answer the question very clearly. Most likely, he directs his comment toward those who "transgress" but he could also imply more than this: everything is cursed. We know that Paul is working directly from the Pentateuch and reading it very carefully as he builds his theology. This may mean he says here -as he says elsewhere, Romans 1- that the entire created order is under sin, or beneath sin.

What does it mean that all things are "imprisoned?" The simple most common meaning of the word is "to enclose." It is often used to describe catching fish in a net and in other contexts to imprison. Louw Nida adds the figurative meaning: to cause to happen with significant restrictions, to restrict. Its root is also used at times to refer to ships encircling the entry to a harbor to prevent other ships from entering or exiting. Here, the idea seems to be confinement and imprisonment so much so that one's actions and freedoms are thwarted. The same concept is also stated in Romans 11:32 "God confined all people in disobedience so that he might have mercy on all people" which means, so that God can work through the paradigm of mercy and grace, he has caused everyone to be confined and limited to disobedience. God, in other words, built the universe with the intent to show grace and mercy. He loves to show mercy. Even, it might be said, that God prefers to answer sin with grace and mercy more than he does to reward righteousness.

The two concepts in the word, as used in this context, appear to be restriction of freedom and designation. A circle has been drawn around all things so that they are labeled "sin" and their freedom is restricted so that they have no other option but to sin. Paul will continue a similar thought in the next verse when he says, "Before faith came we were held captive by the law." Romans 7 teaches that by being aware of sin through the law (even the law written by nature in our conscience - Romans 2:15) we are caused to sin (Romans 7:7-12). We might translate the sentence this way: "The Pentateuch caused everyone to be gripped and stained by the unbreakable grasp of sin's smudgy hand."

"So that the promise by faith in Jesus Christ might be given to those who believe."- Paul repeated what he has said a couple of times. This phrase most closely mirrors verses 14 and 18. Two new concepts are introduced. First, he explains the purpose behind the law "causing everything to be under sin" and "creating the concept of transgressions." The purpose was so that the promise would be by faith. Paul, similar to Romans 11, wants us to see that God's original and better plan was not a system of rewarding righteousness. The plan has always been grace and mercy. That is God's first and best plan. He built the system of the universe, it is not too much to say, so that he could show grace to the undeserving. Here, he points out that he wants this "grace system" to be built on faith (as opposed to works.) This implies that faith and works are contrary, incompatible forces in the system of God (compare Romans 4). God wants to give the blessing, the Spirit, as an unearned gift, or, as he calls it here, an unconditional promise. Man's only possible response to the promise is faith or not faith, believe the promise or do not. (As Dudley Hall says, you can't do a promise. You can only believe a promise.) Similarly, the second element he contributes here to his argument is the concept of "giving" though it is not really an addition. He has said in verse 18 that it was graced to us from the Greek word *charizomai*. Here he returns to the word he used earlier for the idea "to give" *didomi* (Galatians 1:4; 2:20 - both texts at essential peak or seem locations). This may imply a connection between this verse and the "main peak" of 2:20 so that the giving "by grace" of the promise is accomplished as Christ gave himself for us. This is also how he delivers us from the present evil domain. This could even imply a semantic and conceptional connection between the "confinement" and "capturing" of sin and the domain of evil he speaks to in 1:4. Paul may be showing what he originally hinted at: that Christ's substitutionary death and resurrection justifies us for certain, but, as we live in faith in his work, we experience the blessing and promise of the supernaturally energizing of the Holy Spirit and by him we are given freedom not "to sin" but "from sin." He implies that to be "under the law" is to be both "labeled a transgressor" and then, by virtue of being so labeled, "under the power of sin." By moving into faith in Jesus and out of faith in doing law, we move out of the category of "transgressor" and therefore we are no longer in the "confinement of sin." We, then, are free. In other words, to try to do law is to live by the flesh. Both leave one under the law and being under the law leaves us under the power of sin.

# Galatians 3.23-29

**Interpretive Translation:**

Now, before any of us have faith in Christ, the law scrutinizes every move we make looking for a chance to catch us in sin and condemn us as guilty sinners.[112] It designates us as criminals and keeps us walled behind bars like prisoners until we finally respond to the revelation of the gospel with faith.[113] The law has a job to do. It operates as a strict, straight-laced governess driving us toward Christ. This care-giver has one goal: that we would trust Christ to make us righteous in God's eyes and not our moral performance. Once we move from trying to please God with our obedience and begin to trust in Christ alone to make us righteous before God we also stop answering to this governess. The authority of the babysitter comes to an end for you because you all become full-grown, free sons of God when you have faith in Christ. God completely covers every person with Christ once they have been absorbed into Christ so that their identity is "Christ." They are no longer labeled, Jew or Greek, servant or wealthy, male or female because they are all, you are all, one with Christ Jesus. And get this, if you are one with Christ, then *you* are the seed of Abraham. *You* inherit the promise -the blessing, the Spirit.

**Summary Commentary:** The three paragraphs that start at verse 15 and end with this one all deal with the idea of the "one seed of Abraham." They also contrast the promises made to this one seed to the performance/reward system of the law. The previous paragraph asks about the purpose of the law and if it is superior to the "promise"

---

[112] This is an expansion on the idea of the word "ἐφρουρούμεθα" meaning "to watch out in order to apprehend."

[113] "the lingering faith" in the original text. This is an attempt to smooth out the language and interpret the phrase as *our faith* versus what also might be, "the gospel message of faith." If we were to translate this portion of the text with the latter option in mind it may be, "until the gospel message that invites us to have faith in Christ" is revealed."

paradigm. Here, Paul continues the discussion related to the law further describing its purpose and the superseding of the promise paradigm. He says that the law scrutinizes a person's life and captures them as criminals. Here he uses the same terminology as he had previously when he says that the law "labeled" or "hemmed" in everyone to being transgressors. The law in its scrutiny and condemnation serves as a disciplinarian watch-guard over people, like a babysitter or tutor might give to a child. Through the harshness of the discipline, the child is nudged away from the "rule-driven" life and towards trusting in Christ to justify. At the center of this paragraph, Paul repeats an idea that he had stated in Galatians 3:7. Because you have faith for justification and not works, you are sons, in this case, of God. This justification is described as being "of faith," and then Paul connects the idea of "being baptized" or immersed into Christ with being of faith. Those who are "of faith" are "immersed" into Christ. Faith in Christ puts one in unity with Christ. Those who are immersed into Christ are covered with Christ-like clothing covers a person. He becomes their identity as opposed to other potentially defining elements: religion, cultural, economic, sociological, biological, etc. This is because this person is "one with Christ" via "the faith in Christ." Since they are one with Christ, they are the seed of Abraham just as Christ, and also they are heirs of the promise made to the seed.

The author uses a subtle mechanism to connect these three paragraphs together and ultimately shed a lot of light on the meaning. In the first, he says as an aside that the seed was not to many but to one and the seed is Christ." Then in the next paragraph, he uses similar language and with another aside where he says that "A mediator is not one but God is one." This connects the idea of the one seed being God himself. Then, here, he says that those who have faith are not "Jew, Gentile, etc." They are, instead, one with Christ. In using this mechanism he is saying that we who are one with Christ are one with God and that is our reconciliation, i.e. we are in Christ and are therefore in the Trinity positionally and relationally.

**Galatians 3:23** "Now before faith came, we were held captive under the law, imprisoned until the coming faith would be revealed." (Πρὸ τοῦ δὲ ἐλθεῖν τὴν πίστιν ὑπὸ νόμον ἐφρουρούμεθα συγκλειόμενοι εἰς τὴν μέλλουσαν πίστιν ἀποκαλυφθῆναι,)

Paul in this verse and the one below works with a time dynamic describing the paradigm "before faith came" and the one that followed "now that faith has come."

"Now before faith came" - This time designation could refer to either a dispensational idea so that it refers to the coming of Christ or it could refer to a personal idea, a person having faith. Which one fits the text? Galatians 3.8 begins to introduce the time dynamic. The Scriptures are aware of a future when God justifies by faith. They also recorded the gospel in the words: "In you the saints will be blessed," referring to Abraham. Abraham was the first instance referred to in Scripture as being "of faith." This implies that the coming of faith is personal and not dispensational. Abraham, too, was of faith. The text even centers one of its arguments on the fact that the faith/promise paradigm preceded the law by 430 years. (Galatians 3.17)

On the other hand, a time dynamic is introduced in Galatians 3.10 that suggests a more dispensational context: the law paradigm reigned until the seed came, the one to whom the promises were made. Paul echoes this sentiment in the statements he makes in Galatians 4.4: "When the fullness of time had come God sent forth his Son, born of woman, born under the law, to redeem those who were under the law, so that we might receive the adoption as sons." Here in the immediate context, Paul also connects the coming of faith to the coming of Christ. Note though, that only this reference "before faith came" actually includes the terminology of "coming." In the second half of this verse, as we will see, faith did not come. It was revealed. In the next verse, Christ did not "come." The law was a guardian "until Christ." Then, in verse 25, a person is no longer under the guardian once faith comes, where the same lexeme for come is used again. "Until Christ" appears to be then a personal experience of Christ as we compare this section to Galatians 4:1-9 where Paul makes it clear that a person needs to move by faith from law as a tutor and guardian into faith in Christ where they are not under the law.

Most of us can probably see it from both perspectives. Paul may intentionally create this tension for us as readers so that we hold both options in hand, and both options could be valid in the grander context. Though, it most likely only means one of the two concepts here. For me, the phrasing in Galatians 4.8-9 connects most clearly to this text when it says: Formerly when you did not know God, you were enslaved to those that by nature are not gods. But now that you have come to know God, or rather to be known by God…" Paul appears in this verse to connect these elements to a personal faith experience shifting a person from the law to God.

Here, there may be both clarity of how a person was justified before Christ, faith like Abraham in the coming seed, and how a person experiences the "full" promise made to the seed: the blessing which is the fullness of the Spirit. So, while both may be in play, the idea that fits the logic is "when a person has faith." In this case, "before a person has faith they are held captive by the law."

Paul does present faith in a possibly surprising way. Faith *comes* to the believer and is *revealed* to Paul's readers. This could make us look at faith as "the gospel" or even, to fit *The New Perspective on Paul,* "the knowledge of the faithfulness of Christ." It could also be that there is an "awakening of faith" that happens in the believer. This, too, is a place of tension, as are the many *New Perspective* passages. Paul may appear to be aware of this tension and intend it when he says in Galatians 4:9, "You have come to know God, or rather be known by God." If the same dynamic is in play here then Paul wants us as readers to conclude that ultimately the primary and defining experience is not "knowing God" but "being known by God."

"We were held captive by the law" - Before we have faith, we are scrutinized by the law. The word translated *captive (φρουρέω - phroureō)* in the ESV can have a positive meaning: to watch over like a guard to protect. It can also have a negative connotation: to watch out in order to apprehend. On the negative side of the meaning, it can focus on the "watching" hence "scrutinizing" or the apprehension. In the latter case, it can mean to capture or imprison. With this range in mind, we might consider the context to determine what it means here. It occurs in between two uses of the word *sygkleiō* (συγκλείω), a similar word translated as "imprisoned" in verses 22 and 23. We will look in detail at the meaning of *sygkleio* in a moment. For now, we see that it has a similar meaning as what we have seen for the word translated *captive* in the ESV. The law will also be portrayed as an authoritarian governess in the next few verses, notably including verse 25 which is in a parallel position structurally with this sentence in verse 23. This word, though, could also be seen in both a positive light, "caregiver" (also similar to *prhoureo* - to watch over in order to protect), or with a more negative tone: "a disciplinarian governess." Again, we will look more carefully at this concept below. While the semantic context can be read either positively or negatively concerning the law's operations, overall it appears to be negative so that the law "watches over to apprehend" those who are "pre-faith." We ultimately lean this way because of the overall context of negativity towards the law and the priority of the "imprisonment" terminology that we see in the previous verse and as a modifier here.

As implied above, the concept of *phroureo* relates more to the process of apprehending someone than it does to the state of apprehension. It is often used to describe the imprisonment of someone as they wait for their trial. The overall picture seems to be one of a person being scrutinized as a probable criminal. Those who police the behaviors of others are watching this person looking for a chance to apprehend, or even if they are apprehended those who might look to condemn this person are looking for every possible proof of their guilt. So, while imprisonment is a part of this concept, it is the scrutinizing process that leads to the final conviction that it emphasizes. Paul uses an imperfect form of the verb here denoting a continual process versus what we might expect if he wanted us to think of the state of imprisonment. This may be more than we should expect from the grammar but it does fit the context. The law constantly watches those under its authority and takes note of any error so that it can pronounce them guilty and imprison them as a result.

While the preposition transited "by" above could also be *under*, "by" is most likely the idea. The law is the actor in the sentence. If we read it as under it gives the reader a sense of ambiguity as to what is doing the scrutinizing only stating that the action is a result of being under the "domain" of the law. The context suggests that both ideas are true though I understand the idea as instrumental.

"imprisoned until the coming faith would be revealed" - As we referenced previously, the term imprisoned (*sygkleiō* - συγκλείω) occurred previously in verse 22: The Scripture imprisoned everything under sin. Above, as we looked at verse 22, we made the connection between verse 19: The law was added to make us transgressors. The picture of this word in the context above is the guilty verdict caused by the law. We might say "imprisoned as guilty criminals." The point above was that the law causes someone to be "guilty" of sin by creating the rules that define it. A person cannot be considered guilty of illegally speeding until a law is codified that says speeding is not legal. That appears to be the idea Paul writes as he clarifies the purpose of the law. So, here, as a result of the process toward condemnation denoted in the term *phroureo,* we are actually "condemned and imprisoned as guilty." The present tense form of this word suggests that this process happens over and over.

The picture contains an element being in a holding cell waiting for the next step in our punishment as the authorities (prosecutors) bring more and more condemning evidence against us. We might even hold in our minds an "imprisoned in our house" concept so that we are continually proving our guilt over and over even as the trial continues. The main verb has that specifically built into its meaning: we sit imprisoned as the law continually builds its case against us. Paul contrasts this idea, of a temporary and rather hopeless state, to another future state: until the delaying faith is revealed.

The first observation we might make from the phrase describing this state is that it is a repeat of what Paul has just stated: the law scrutinizes us until faith comes. Here we might simply say: condemning us until faith is revealed. Paul, in essence, repeats himself. The second phase helps us understand the first. He adds here the elements of the condemnation that we have seen in the term *sygkleiō (συγκλείω)*, that faith was "coming" -a different word than what he used for "coming" above- and that the faith was "revealed." We have already looked at the idea behind *sygkleio*. Let's look at the other two nuances Paul adds.

The term translated "coming" can mean the faith that is about to occur, the delaying, waiting, or lingering faith, the faith in the future, inevitable faith. All possible nuances of meaning make sense in this context. The idea that appears to fit best may be the idea of a faith that "is about to occur" but with a sense of "lingering." Paul has painted the picture of a person waiting entrapped in a prison with little hope. Now, he describes faith as if it was "pending" at the scene as if it is waiting until the right moment to appear. We might read it as "the pending faith."

A question discussed above becomes relevant here as well. Is the faith referring to an individual's faith or the message that is believed, i.e. "The Faith?" Because of semantic connections to verse 4:9, it appears to be described as a personal journey: you have come to know God and are therefore not under the law. Paul says that this personal, pending faith was "revealed" (ἀποκαλύπτω - *apokalypto*). Faith's *revelation* ends the authority of the law. The term *apokalypto* means to reveal, to make fully known, disclose, uncover, to take out of hiding, bring to light and simply to appear. This interesting depiction personifies faith as an existing but lingering, pending rescuer. Faith exists in the micro-narrative analogy Paul creates *before* the law ends, or while it reigns. Faith does not start to exist in this picture. He "appears" or is "disclosed." We might even say that this text at least implies that faith "is given" to the one under the law.

The word fits into the imagery Paul has used throughout this picture. The Law continually watches for any chance to condemn. It layers charge upon charge condemning us as more and more guilty as we sit captured in prison with no real hope. All of these are present tense verbs. Then faith "pends" or "lingers" - also in the present tense. These present tense forms are used to show the continual experience of being under the law: faith pends, the law scrutinizes, prosecutes, condemns and keeps us imprisoned. Then, faith is disclosed. It shows up on the scene, in the experience, interrupting the procedures. It changes the rules. Paul uses an aorist verb for apokalypto to contrast the present tense situation. Faith appears and changes the situation. In the plot line, the imaginary judge discovers the person's faith and it changes the terms. Imagine a person being charged with a crime and then it is discovered that they were a citizen of a different country or a child of a diplomat. That revelation changes the dynamics as does the revelation of faith.

**Galatians 3:24** "So then, the law was our guardian until Christ came, in order that we might be justified by faith." (ὥστε ὁ νόμος παιδαγωγὸς ἡμῶν γέγονεν εἰς Χριστόν, ἵνα ἐκ πίστεως δικαιωθῶμεν·)

Paul here gives us what he sees as *what follows* ("so then" in the ESV). He has just described the law as an individual who tries to catch those under it in a crime so that it can condemn them and hold them in prison as criminals, i.e. transgressors or trespassers. Now, he moves to the next concept: the real purpose of this scrutiny and condemnation.

"So then, the law was our guardian until Christ came" - Paul began his challenge to the Galatians and the leaders who misled them by accusing them of "toddling in your faith in the gospel" using a term that denotes a child as they teeter-totter while learning to walk. Paul now moves in his language from "imprisonment" concepts to "child-care" concepts though, as we saw above, there is a crossover. The law as one which "watched over waiting for a chance to apprehend and imprison" now acts as the guardian of a child, the picture Paul uses to describe someone before faith comes. The idea behind the position of *guardian* (παιδαγωγός - paidagōgos) comes from a role often seen in Greek culture to provide a watch care over a child. From birth to age six a mother or wet nurse would take responsibility for the care of a child. From around six to twelve the child was then placed under the care of the *paidagogos*. This caregiver gave basic oversight to the child, a "care-giver." There is debate as to whether we should understand Paul's usage here in a negative sense: the slave-master who provided discipline to the child -"disciplinarian" in some translations- or more positive as in the ESV here, guardian. There is also debate whether or not this role in this context should be seen as a teacher or just a person who gives oversight. The context suggests that this person should be seen as a "rule giver and rule enforcer." This has been the implication of the previous discussions of the law. It also is the picture in the next part of the text where the law is the *paidagogos* and the "household manager" who is in authority over the child so that the child's life is the same as a slave. This slavery is also pictured as being under rules and regulations that are then compared (in a later text) to observing the law. (Galatians 4:10)[114] Some lexicons suggest that this role was not a teacher. Spiq and NDNTT suggest that it can be used in that way.

To me, in this context, it is both the strict disciplinarian (as seen in the overall context of the law being rather negative and the slavery experience of those who were under its watch) and educational (as seen in the fact this tutor, even with its discipline has a goal in its program -faith in Christ- and in the fact these tutors lessons are "elementary level education principles" -the law.)

"Until Christ came" - More literally Paul said "until Christ." As we seek to determine the chronological and time-based elements of Paul's thoughts it is important to understand that he may not be referencing Christ's incarnation or death. The phrase could also be "toward" or "into Christ" so that the idea is not a time-based process but a purpose-based process. The law's education program's purpose was to move us

---

[114] From the opposite perspective, can we be sure that an "overseer" should be read in a "disciplinarian" light? And the "basic principles" may be rules as the context somewhat implies but it may also be "elementary school lessons" so that the *paidagogos* is the teacher.

to Christ. The next phrase "in order that we might be justified out of faith" suggests this should be how we read the sentence.

"in order that we might be justified by faith" - Paul repeated the mantra of the text: justification is by faith. Here he suggests that the law's education program has this as its purpose and possibly its duration, *until Christ*. Whether or not the previous phrase is temporal or instrumental, this phrase indicates purpose beginning with "so that" or "in order that." Here he does not use the article with faith. He uses the same form that dominates Galatians 3:5-14. (Note that verse 14 introduces the author's usage of faith for this pericope: "through the faith" or "through *this faith*.") While an object of the preposition can sometimes be understood as a definite noun the usage here at the peak of his argument could imply that he wants to clarify that a person is justified or given righteousness out of *their* faith. The execution of justification does not come out of "the faith" but out of "faith." This suggests a more traditional Pauline view on justification versus *New Perspective* thinking.[115] (See note: Abraham's faith event is 100% a traditional view.)

So, we might understand this sentence as "If the law acted as scrutinizing criminal lawyer holding us under lock and key as he presented a case against us proving that we are guilty, the law, then, serves as a strict, disciplinarian tutor whose intense training program makes us give up on our ability to please God by doing rules of the law and pushes us towards the Messiah so that we are given righteousness because we trust him not by doing good deeds or refraining from sin."

**Galatians 3:25** "But now that faith has come, we are no longer under a guardian" ἐλθούσης δὲ τῆς πίστεως οὐκέτι ὑπὸ παιδαγωγόν ἐσμεν.)

---

[115] Just as aside, was Abraham's faith "faithfulness" or "trust"? He believed God and he counted it as righteousness. What did he do? God promised the blessing would come through his seed and he responded to this promise with faith, he trusted God to fulfill this promise.

Paul echoes in a parallel the idea he started with: the coming (erchomai) of faith. As we have discussed above we take this to mean the time when a person has faith versus the coming of a dispensation of faith. This seems to be more clear in this clause and then in the clauses that connect the concept to a personal spiritual experience in Galatians 4. Beyond that, this verse makes a simple point. Once faith arrives on the scene so that we become "out of faith" or what faith makes us, then the tutor/law no longer has a role to play. He explains more of the reasons this is the case below, specifically in the next verse, and then builds out his argument thereafter.

**Galatians 3:26** "for in Christ Jesus you are all sons of God, through faith." (Πάντες γὰρ υἱοὶ θεοῦ ἐστε διὰ τῆς πίστεως ἐν Χριστῷ Ἰησοῦ· )

As noted in the commentary above, this verse justifies the statement Paul makes in the previous verse "once faith comes" the guardian no longer is active or in authority. Why? Because you are all sons through faith. While he makes this point in a rather matter-of-fact way here, this has been a major theme of the previous section of text starting in Galatians 3:5. This faith is in Christ.

This verse could also say something like: "Because through faith you are sons of God in/with Christ." Greek does not always connect ideas logically using word order like English does. Because of this, this sentence can mean either that our faith is in Christ or that we are in Christ through faith. The former is most likely when we look at the structure of the sentence, but the latter fits the context that follows. As we often suggested, the ambiguity could be intentional because both may be true in Paul's thinking and intended as a part of the reading.

**Galatians 3:27** "For as many of you as were baptized into Christ have put on Christ." (ὅσοι γὰρ εἰς Χριστὸν ἐβαπτίσθητε, Χριστὸν ἐνεδύσασθε.)

Paul continues to layer levels to his argument. In this subsection, he began with a thesis: when faith comes we are not under a disciplinarian, the law. Why? Because by faith we are sons of God. Or by faith, we are sons of God in Christ. This verse will now explain why that is the case. (The second because or *gar* clause in this list.)

For as many of you as were baptized into Christ - Two main questions come from a comparison of the Greek text and most English translations. The first relates to the phrase translated *as many as*. The second relates to the meaning of the word transliterated *baptized*.

The first word can mean "as many among you were baptized" referring to the possibility that some of Paul's audience were baptized and some were not or possibly to a more universal idea, that as many have been baptized *generally* have also put on Christ. Another way it can be read focuses on a more qualitative comparison, "to the same degree you were baptized." Both make sense theological, but in this context, Paul has assumed again and again that his audience is in Christ. So, he seems to make a similar point here and then explain what exactly that point infers. I lean toward the latter understanding: to the degree that you were or just like you were.

The more essential pivot occurs with our understanding of the word transliterated baptized. The word in Greek is basically the same as *baptismo*. As has been discussed thoroughly among theologians for centuries, it has a large range of meanings. Consider a few of the following usages:

- to dip a cloth into dye to dye it, so much so it commonly is used to mean "to dye."
- to immerse into water or another liquid
- to sink, as a ship into the ocean
- to wash with water or liquid
- to participate in a cultic ritual where one is immersed into water
- plunge into as in a sword into flesh

Our question then should be what does it mean in this context? Notice that Paul clusters the term together with "being clothed with Christ" and being in Christ. This suggests that we understand the word as "immersed into" or something similar. We should also consider Paul's theology of baptism to help us decide. How did Paul describe *baptismo* in other texts? In Romans 6, we have a very similar text where Paul says "As many as/to the same degree as we are baptized into Christ, we were also baptized into his death." He repeats a similar concept in Colossians 2:12 "Having been buried with him in baptism." 1 Corinthians 1 emphasizes the cultic ritual, "No one was baptized in my name." In 1 Corinthians 10:1, Paul says that the Israelites were "baptized into Moses" where Moses potentially refers to the Law. In the latter case, the exact meaning is not clear but it is clear what Paul *does not mean*. He clearly does not mean an actual ceremonial water baptism. Paul appears to freely use the term in a conceptual way where it means "to be immersed into something or someone" or "to be placed inside of something or someone."

With all of this in mind, we might consider translating this phrase: As much as you are merged together with Christ.

*Have put on Christ* - What has happened to those who have been merged together with Christ? They have put on Christ, or they have been clothed or covered with Christ. Here Paul could mean that a person has been covered in Christ so that they are hidden in Christ as we see in Colossians 3:4 where Paul says, "Your life is hidden in Christ by God" (My translation). He could also want us to think of the positional or identity aspect of clothing. Clothing has always represented something of one's status. In this culture the dress of a Jew would have been different from that of a Greek, slaves would have dressed in attire that showed their position as would the free, or male and female. Paul, with this in mind, may want us to read about Christ being a new identity, a new clothing so that we are identified as Christ. Whether this illustration is overt or simply a nuance of the language, it most likely plays some role in the construction of meaning in the text. An original reader would most likely start thinking of the unique clothing of the identities that follow this sentence and their clothing.

So, when Paul describes us as either "being covered" in Christ (in a more general way) or wearing Christ-like "position identifying" clothing, the context suggests something positional and culturally related like in the identity designations below it. Also, consider the fact that Paul has already said we are "merged into" or hidden into Christ. So to say simply we are covered has no meaning. To say that Christ has become an identifying dress moves the text forward and fits the context.

To understand the nuance of the original language in the text we would restate it as, "Because when any of you were merged together with Christ, you put on Christ like a new uniform, as if he were your new identity."

**Galatians 3:28** "There is neither Jew nor Greek, there is neither slave nor free, there is no male and female, for you are all one in Christ Jesus." (οὐκ ἔνι Ἰουδαῖος οὐδὲ Ἕλλην, οὐκ ἔνι δοῦλος οὐδὲ ἐλεύθερος, οὐκ ἔνι ἄρσεν καὶ θῆλυ· πάντες γὰρ ὑμεῖς εἷς ἐστε ἐν Χριστῷ Ἰησοῦ.)

This impacts our thinking as readers in two major ways. First, the direct wording itself contrasts being "clothed with Christ." If Christ alone is our new identity then we are no longer supremely identified with other distinctive. We might be tempted to think more deeply into this analogy than we should, wrestling with how the clothing analogy shows the balance between us keeping our identities individually and culturally. But we should be careful here. Paul's main point is not to show the balance between the two extremes but to show the extreme reality of our oneness with Christ.[116] Within this concept is an emphasis that before God, in justification and experiencing the Spirit (within context), there are no more distinctions culturally, religiously, biologically, sociologically, economically, or based on gender.

---

[116] Though we might also consider the other analogy: baptism where a cloth or boat or sword does not cease to exist but changes occur in it in someway. A cloth is still the same cloth, but just a better (maybe ultimately intended purpose of the cloth if it was designed for some use that required the color.)

**Galatians 3:29** "And if you are Christ's, then you are Abraham's offspring, heirs according to promise." ( εἰ δὲ ὑμεῖς Χριστοῦ, ἄρα τοῦ Ἀβραὰμ σπέρμα ἐστέ, κατ' ἐπαγγελίαν κληρονόμοι.)

The final verse of this paragraph brings together much of what Paul has been arguing since Galatians 3:15 specifically and in someways since Galatians 2:15. He begins with the summary of the small elevated verse that began in verse 26: "You are sons of God through faith in Christ Jesus."

"And if you are Christ's" - The way the ESV translates this verse it understands the genitive construction as possessive: "Christ's." The genitive form can also be used to describe a qualitative aspect as it is often used in the verses above: "of faith" and "of the law." It most likely takes on that sense here as well. Those who have been inserted into Christ, clothed with him, and are one with him are also "of him." The wine is "of the vine." The painting is "of the artist." Christ is the characterizing and defining source of all things coming into the life of the believer. By using a rather vague description of our union with Christ, Paul has expanded it to mean the most it possibly can mean. As a comparison he says in 1 Corinthians that we are "out of God in Christ Jesus." (1:30) Our life is now a divine life because a divine being is creating it. God through Christ is creating our life now moment by moment. Christ creates us. To capture the possibilities of Paul's meaning we may need to think of concepts like belonging and Christ as our source. "When you belong to Christ and your life flows from his life, as you do when you are in him, then…"

"Then, you are Abraham's offspring." - This sentence may barely get noticed by readers in our culture. No more meaningful sentence could be written in the context of Scripture and for the minds of Jewish believers who have been studying the Scripture for years. The very beginning of the Bible begins with the basic plot line we see fleshed out throughout the rest: God created all things. His crown jewel was humanity which he created to connect and commune with himself. Humanity chose to go their own way, away from God's grace and presence. God promised that he would send a human who would undo the brokenness that resulted from the first humans' rebellion. This human is simply referred to as the seed. Then, throughout the rest of the Hebrew Bible, our Old Testament, the authors turn again and again to this character, the seed. The story of the Old Testament was the story of a "Seed" that would come, a Messiah who would undo the curse of the fall. Paul traced a part of this plot line through the Pentateuch, especially focusing on Genesis, and says that this promised seed was the seed of Abraham. The seed of Abraham is the Christ and Jesus is the Christ. Then, here, he says something rather earth-shaking, those who are in Christ by faith, we too are the seed of Abraham. Because we are one with Christ, we are the seed of Abraham with Christ.

Exegetically, this phrase serves as a peak moment in the text. One important grammatical consideration comes from what Paul has already said about the term "sperma." He has noted that it should be understood as a singular seed. He has also said that this singular seed is "one" and that one is Christ. Later he connects the language of the "one seed" to the concept that God himself is one as well suggesting that the promise made to Abraham's seed was not between two parties -God and man- but dealing with one party: God himself, Father and Son. The seed, then, is Christ and Christ is not just "Christ" but the second person of the Trinity, God himself. Then here, he says we are the singular seed too because we are one with Christ so we have joined the Trinitarian community. This is the peak of grace.

"heirs, according to the promise." - He continues his logic and gives one more deduction. If you are one with Christ, then you are "of Christ." If you are of Christ, then you are also Abraham's seed like Christ is. And, if you are Abraham's seed (singular), then you are heirs, those who will inherit the promises made to the seed of Abraham, i.e. the blessing, the Spirit. (See commentary above on Paul's layering together the concepts of blessing, Spirit, inheritance and promise.)

To bring out the details and implications of what Paul wrote we could restate it as: If you belong to Christ and your life flows out of him as it does for those who are in Christ, then you too, along with Christ himself, are the seed God promised to Adam and Eve and Abraham. God promised to bless this seed with an inheritance. That inheritance is Christ's, and, because you are one with Christ, the Seed, that inheritance, that promise belongs to you, too.

You are also this one promised seed of Abraham.

# Galatians 4.1-7

**Interpretive Translation**

Concerning these concepts let me share more. While the heir is young he is not treated any different from a household servant even though he is actually the owner of the entire estate. Instead, he lives under the oversight and direction of the estate's supervisors and managers until he reaches the age designated in his father's will when he can take over. We were in the same spot when we were young. We were as like those in servitude. Just like a child under tutors and administrators, we were under the strictest rules commonly[117] reserved for little children.[118]

Then, when the appointed time arrived, God dispatched his Son to fulfill his mission. A human woman gave birth to this Son making him fully human. Just like us, he was born under the obligations of the performance-based religious system described in the Law. Why did God become a human under the authority of the law? So that he could pay off humanity's spiritual debt accrued through its demands. Being free from having to pay off our spiritual debt through servitude to this law, we received a new position in the estate: full legal sons and daughters of God. What does God do for his sons and daughters? He lavishly pours out the Son's Spirit into our spirit as if we were the Son himself. The Son's Spirit cries out deeply and passionately in our hearts, "Daddy!" to God our Father. Can you see it? You are no longer slaves required to pay off an infinite spiritual debt with God based on moral actions and attitudes. You are God's beloved son or daughter. You are God's heir and your inheritance is God himself!

**Summary Commentary:**

---

[117] This may be how "cosmos" should be understood here. Also "the rules given to children in the world" i.e. common basic rules. Paul likely wants us to read this phrase in line with the law.

[118] See Acts 21:24 where the root verb is used "to walk in line keeping the law." The verb means originally "to march in line" like a military. Most suggest it does not have that idea here but that does seem to fit the context.

Paul gives commentary on the thesis of his previous section. What does it mean that we are no longer under these imprisoning caregivers, the law? What does it mean that we are now the seed of Abraham? And the heirs? What's the point? Namely that we have arrived at a new state. The pre-Christ state is a state of law. It is juvenile, restrictive, and driven by childish rules and structures, marching orders. Every step is ordered. The father of the household has declared a date in his will where we transition from a position underneath governors, caregivers, tutors, administrators and managers of the house, oikos, into our rightful position as head of the oikos, the owner, the lord over "all things." In the picture, the believer is not the steward of the house, he owns it. He possesses it and is chief over it. When we experience Christ -the language still appears to be mainly personal in this description not historical- we take on our new position of full sons. We can do this because Christ purchased our freedom. In this portion of the text, Paul connected the material he writes about here back to the material in Galatians 3:13 where he introduced the idea within the Galatians argument that Christ procured (redeemed) our freedom by becoming a curse for us. Here he adds more information about this liberation. Christ was able to purchase us because of two qualities: 1) he was born of a woman, i.e. he possessed human nature, he was the seed of Eve and 2) he was born under the law. These two statements imply that these qualities were required to "purchase our freedom from the law." He had to do so as a man while meeting the standards of the law. Not only did he purchase our freedom, but he put us in the position of sons. This event, the purchase of our freedom and establishing us as full sons, refers to what he spoke of earlier in the paragraph: "the time appointed" by the Father. They share a root connecting the two events and making them one. This also signifies a rather radical event in the life of the servant -us under the law. We are freed and made a son. As sons, we can receive the inheritance. The inheritance is the Spirit, here described as the Son's Spirit sent into our inner being crying and moaning "in our place" to the Father, Abba Father, a reference to our position with the Father and our endearment to him and towards him. He summarizes the text by once again delineating our identity. Instead of saying what we are not (male/female; jew/Greek/slave/free), he says that we are no longer slaves; we are sons and heirs.

**Galatians 4.1** "I mean that the heir, as long as he is a child, is no different from a slave, though he is the owner of everything" (Λέγω δέ, ἐφ' ὅσον χρόνον ὁ κληρονόμος νήπιός ἐστιν, οὐδὲν διαφέρει δούλου κύριος πάντων ὤν)

Paul gives his description with a marker that somewhat shifts his line of thought "I mean" or "Then I say" in the Greek text. Knowing that this text (4.1-13) has parallels to Gal 3:13 (which ends the section of Galatians 3:1-14 - the material occurs in the seam between the two.) and Galatians 3:29. He potentially uses this shifting language to bring his argument to a close. It may crescendo his thoughts in this section. We see that in the ESV translation "I mean that."

"the heir, as long as he is a child, is no different from a slave." - After ending the previous paragraph (3.29) with a summarization of the implications of our oneness with Christ "you are the seed of Abraham, heirs according to the promise," he explains a further take away. (As if to say, "Now I want you to consider."). The heir, generally speaking, is no different (or could be no better) than the servant when he is a child or "young." The slave in this case simply refers to a household servant. Paul paints a picture contrasting the "servant in the house" who has no rights and must do whatever he is told with the heir. A young heir while still a child has no rights over the house.

"though he is the owner of everything" - More literally in the Greek Paul wrote "being lord of all" though the meaning expressed in the ESV captures the sense well. Paul explains the real, potential position of this individual "lord and owner over all the properties and actions of the household" as compared to "no different than a slave."

**Galatians 4.2** "but he is under guardians and managers until the date set by his father." (ἀλλὰ ὑπὸ ἐπιτρόπους ἐστὶν καὶ οἰκονόμους ἄχρι τῆς προθεσμίας τοῦ πατρός. )

In the first stages of life, instead of being lord of the entire household, the child lives the same as a servant under "guardians and managers." Both titles represent the role, in this context, of having authority given by an even higher authority to give direction, administration and oversight to the servants beneath them. The idea of stewardship is implied, management versus ownership. This heir, because he is young, is like a servant under the managers and supervisors of the properties and household.

This relationship to the household changes for the heir at "the date set by his father." The picture appears to be of a father who has died and bequeathed the household (oikos) to his heir. Because of his age, though, he remains under the authority of temporary supervisors before the time set by the father in the will. If this view is correct, then in verse 4, "the fullness of time" refers to the arrival of the "time appointed by the father."

Either way, the word picture communicates a clear message, a personal experience that changes before and after Christ. Before Christ, a person is under the law and as such is under supervisors, stewards, managers. Because he or she is under the authority of these stand-ins he or she is no different than a servant.

**Galatians 4.3** "In the same way we also, when we were children, were enslaved to the elementary principles of the world." (οὕτως καὶ ἡμεῖς, ὅτε ἦμεν νήπιοι, ὑπὸ τὰ στοιχεῖα τοῦ κόσμου ἤμεθα δεδουλωμένοι·)

Now, Paul begins to shift from describing the historical situation as an example to describing the lessons we learn from it. "In the same way we also," he says shifting from the example to our own experience. He then refers to our spiritual childhood. He makes it clear though that he is referring, not to our actual childhood, but to a stage of youth spiritually. We know that based on the fact he makes the contrasting statement in the following verse "But when…God sent his son." So, he connects here the state of his audience to the state of being young (same Greek word) in the preceding example. We were just like these children, in other words. And when we were like these children we were also servants as they were servants. Notice that Paul is using terminology related to the stages of human growth again as he has repeatedly in the earlier parts of Galatians. Also, just as Peter was a toddler in the gospel by returning to the law, so here the law is shown as being in effect only "before Christ."

"We were enslaved to the elementary principles of the world." - Within the framing of the previous example, Paul says that metaphorically when we were children we were also slaves or servants (just like those in the analogy). To this point, Paul has re-applied to his audience all that he had said about the "children" or heirs in the previous verses. Then, he adds something new. In a way that is comparable to servanthood above, under managers and supervisors, we are under "the elementary principles of the world." This phrase can mean a few different things. Consider the possible ideas below:

1) The basic materials that compose the world

2) The spirits that are behind these materials (and thereby control much of the seen world)

3) The basic educational principles or concepts of the world

4) The steps one takes at the direction of another (like a soldier marching at direction of a commanding officer)

So, which meaning did Paul intend his readers to understand? Consider a few contextual elements that may help us decide which meaning fits the best. First, Paul immediately described a scenario of slavery where managers and stewards give direction to the child. This suggests a meaning related to either directed steps or, since an educational focus could potentially be in mind, basic educational concepts. The other two options could also be implied within this context but that seems less likely.

Second, the phrase occurs again in the next paragraph. In this section, it is in context with two different concepts. In verse 8 Paul says (my translation), "But when you did not know God, you were servants with those that were nothing like gods." Another option might be, "When you did not know God, you were servants to nature not being gods." Some translations suggest that this verse repeats the authority entities under whom we are enslaved, and with this meaning, the translation suggests that our enslavement is under "spiritual entities." If this is right then we would see a contextual influence here in favor of understanding this phrase as "spirits." The sentence could be translated more like either of my options above. If so, it creates a context related to the weakness of those in servanthood. In the commentary on these verses below, we will look more closely at these verses. For now, know that the context seems to either be related to spirits or the limitations of nature. This verse is in parallel to the next verse which will add more clarity.

Third, in Galatians 4:9, the wording occurs again (in the Greek text the addition "of the world" does not occur). "After God knows you how can you turn back again to the weak and poor elementary concepts?" With that, we know that this is something that a person can turn from and back to again even after they know God or are known by God. Then, the next verse clarifies what these elementary concepts are: "You observe days and months and seasons and years." This appears to be a reference to the observation of the law.

Paul uses the same root several times throughout Galatians. He describes in an allegory about Hagar and Sarah that Hagar, in the allegory, is in *step* (same Greek root *stoikeo*) with "present Jerusalem" for she (Jerusalem) is in slavery with her children. Hagar is also connected to Sinai or in other words, the law. This would be an inner-textual connection that suggests a connection between "elementary principles" in 4.7 and 9 and Hagar, as an allegorical representation of the law in the next section. Then Paul, as he develops his thesis, suggests that someone who walks in the spirit "steps" (*stoikeo*) in the Spirit. The root means to step or to march following orders. Then Paul says we should respond to the rule that "a new creation" will experience peace and mercury. "Rule" may be intended to be contrasted to *stoikeo* where here the "basic principle" is a new creation and not the law ("circumcision").

Paul uses the exact phrase in Colossians 2:8 "See to it that no one takes you captive by philosophy and empty deceit, according to human tradition, according to the elemental spirits of the world, and not according to Christ" contrasting this concept to circumcision. Then again in Colossians 2.20–21, "If with Christ you died to the elemental spirits of the world, why, as if you were still alive in the world, do you submit to regulations— "Do not handle, Do not taste, Do not touch." Here he appears to clearly refer to the law.

With this in mind, it looks like Paul may be somewhat inventing a usage of the term that relates to its root. He basically means "the ordered or commanded steps or rules" of the world. By using this phrase he may infer a couple of other ideas. One, and I think this is likely, the rules of the law code are more than simply rules written into portions of the Pentateuch. We do see that much of what is written in the law code (both moral rules and the priestly code that guides worship practices in the Tabernacle) comes from the culture around Israel. The laws and religious practices arise from nature it appears. Paul could be implying this principle with the phrase "of the world/universe." He could also imply a relation to the "basic rules necessary for children" when we consider the context of the preceding example. Lastly, he could also imply a supernatural connection to the law code itself. He may intend for us to read this phrase in connection to the magic language in the earlier parts of chapter 3. This text does occur in parallel to those texts. In a magical worldview these "elements of the physical world" would have been seen as having spiritual forces behind them. To control "the elements" one needed to be in connection to these spirits. While we need to be careful not to read all the possible meanings for a word in every context, Paul, by using multiple contexts for the same phrase could be implying a connection between several elements: 1) the rules or law code of the Pentateuch, 2) the moral laws that arise form nature and are common to all men, 3) the childish, elementary nature of these rules (and maybe that they are the first, or basic theological concepts that we should graduate from) and 4) the spirits that witches might connect with to control the elements and forces of nature. In other words, the law is not just the partial selection of rules written in the Torah; it's all attempts at pursuing an acceptable life through good works, morality, or human efforts. Behind all of this Paul may be suggesting a cacophony of spirits. The law way is the demonic way.

As we have said many times, we want to keep some of these elements in mind as we read to see how Paul develops the ideas further but we know that Paul will go on to use the root *stoikeo* as "rules" or "marching orders." here in Galatians and again in Colossians. He at times clearly understands the term to refer to the law code in its entirety. That is most likely the emphasis here with other concepts possibility implied.

**Galatians 4.4** "But when the fullness of time had come, God sent forth his Son, born of woman, born under the law," (ὅτε δὲ ἦλθεν τὸ πλήρωμα τοῦ χρόνου, ἐξαπέστειλεν ὁ θεὸς τὸν υἱὸν αὐτοῦ, γενόμενον ἐκ γυναικός, γενόμενον ὑπὸ νόμον, )

As we stated above, the "time" in the immediate context may refer more to the event in the heart of a believer than the moment in history, or both could be implied. Paul has stated that the heir remains as a servant until the time appointed by the "father." The time in the life of the believer when this occurs when Christ enters the scene. Paul could also use the first concept as a launching point to unveil a way for us to think about his plan and the universal events that are happening in history.

The major independent clause in this section, the one that begins the second half of this paragraph, gives the first of two actions where "God sends" someone. The first clause, here, states that God sends his son. This half of the clause parallels the first half. Notice the language around "time" that begins each sub-section. Most likely this text suggests that the sending is mainly focused on historical events related to his birth, life and redeeming death. He adds two elements to his description of the son.

Paul declares that the son was born "out of a woman." Think about how this relates to the overall scheme of Paul's message. He has multiple times referred to the seed of Abraham. This seed, according to the Pentateuch, as we saw in the commentary of earlier passages, is the same seed that God promised in Genesis 3:15. The one that will "crush the head of the serpent." For any individual to matter messianically, or qualify as the messiah, they had to come from a woman. This seems rather redundant as we read today, but in the early years of the church and throughout much of antiquity divinity often had to be "not physical." It was often argued that Jesus could not have been genuinely human and divine at the same time. Paul makes it clear that Jesus was human. He was born out of woman. He was fully human. As we keep reading we will see that Paul states that this qualification leads to the son's "redeeming" of humanity. While Paul does not fully develop this concept here, he implies what is taught elsewhere, that the Son of God also had to be the Son of man for his redemption to affect humanity. Or, to say it another way, only a human can redeem humanity.

Beyond simply being human, the son was "born under the law." He, too, was born under tutors, supervisors, stewards and managers. He too was "as a servant." There may be something to the fact that the term *doulos* here is often used to describe a servant who is in the position of servant because of debt. While it is not always used this way, and we need to be careful not to assume this is the intended use, Paul's contextual clue related to "redemption" or purchasing freedom might suggest that this concept of servanthood is implied. If this is the case, Jesus was born into the debt of the law too, just like we were, but he was, as we will see below, able to purchase his and our freedom by paying off the debt of the law.

**Galatians 4.5** "to redeem those who were under the law, so that we might receive adoption as sons." (ἵνα τοὺς ὑπὸ νόμον ἐξαγοράσῃ, ἵνα τὴν υἱοθεσίαν ἀπολάβωμεν.)

The word "redeemed" comes from the Greek word *exagoradzo*. It has a few different possible meanings. It can simply mean to buy or pay a price for it. Louw and Nida suggest here the meaning "to cause the release or freedom of someone by means which proves costly." It also notes that a literal translation might be "to release by means of paying a price." While we should use caution when looking at the parts of a word to understand its definition, it may provide insight here. The root word "agoradzo" is also the root word for "agora" which would have been the public square in Paul's time. It would have included the marketplace. In this public square, one would make many different transactions including the buying and selling of humans as property. Spicq simplifies the action denoted as "a transfer of property and noting that the price has been paid." Paul uses this terminology, it would appear, to specify the work of the one born under the law and born out of a woman. He was like us. He amplifies the word picture by showing that the father accomplished the appointment of the appointed time by sending his son to "free us from our debt." Louw and Nida suggest that the term focuses more on the freeing and less on the purchasing, though a cost is always implied. If this is the case, we might understand the reference being to the Son, who was also originally born into the same servitude we were, having "freed us" from our servitude.

What is the purpose of the Son's work? Why did he free us? He freed us so that we might receive something from him: sonship. This term may refer to adoption and it may refer to "full sonship." Both concepts could also be in play. If Paul is using his analogy tightly -from above- then we are actual sons and the freedom "the Son" procured also made us transition from being "under stewards" to being full sons, i.e. lord over all things. If Paul uses the picture more loosely, Christ purchases our freedom from slavery by paying our debt (the picture has evolved and now we are indebted slaves) and we, as freed slaves, are now considered full and real sons with the legal rights implied.

**Galatians 4.6** "And because you are sons, God has sent the Spirit of his Son into our hearts, crying, "Abba! Father!"" (Ὅτι δέ ἐστε υἱοί, ἐξαπέστειλεν ὁ θεὸς τὸ πνεῦμα τοῦ υἱοῦ αὐτοῦ εἰς τὰς καρδίας ἡμῶν κρᾶζον· αββα ὁ πατήρ.)

Paul then moves into the second "God sent" clause set and begins to explain the logical association to the previous action: God sent his son to make us sons. If God has made us his sons, God sent the Spirit of his Son into our hearts. A couple of reflections on this sentence. 1) God sent the Spirt of *his son.* Theologically we often emphasize that the Holy Spirit is the Spirit of God. Several NT texts make this clear. 1 Corinthians 2:10-11 comes to mind. Here Paul emphasizes that the Holy Spirit is also the Spirit of Christ. John 14:17 makes the same point. (The Spirit of truth, whom the world cannot experience because it neither sees him nor knows him. You know him because he has been living with you already. He's me! And he will be in you." (My translation) Paul repeatedly refers to the Holy Spirit as the Spirit of Jesus. The Spirit of God is the Spirit of the Son, of Christ Jesus. He is Christ dwelling with us.

God sends the Spirit of Christ *into our hearts.* Paul, at the end of chapter 3, shows that we are "in Christ," merged together with him, one with him. Now he revisits the logic to show that Christ, though the Holy Spirit, is in us. He has been sent into our hearts. A couple of thoughts about "the heart," the location of the Spirit in the human being: 1) we understand the non-material self differently (at least on some levels) than Paul or his audience. That doesn't make us more accurate or correct, but it does mean we should not read our understanding into his words. 2) at the simplest level the heart, the *kardia*, refers to the total non-material part of a human being, his spirit or his inner man. 3) Louw and Nida give this definition: the causative source of a person's psychological life in its various aspects, but with special emphasis upon thoughts — 'heart, inner self, mind.' BDAG says, "seat of physical, spiritual and mental life."

The heart is a place of all the inner actions of one's immaterial self. It desires. It feels. It thinks. It chooses. It has aptitude and attitude, a way of thinking about things. It has beliefs. The Spirit is "in" our immaterial self. He is in our mind; God's mind, Christ's mind, in our mind. So much so that Paul says elsewhere (1 Cor 2: 12ff) that we have the mind of Christ. The Spirit has been sent into our inner-self, the part of us that feels and thinks. And, he too thinks and feels in us so that at least some of the thinking and feeling in our hearts is from the Spirit and not directly from us.

"crying Abba Father" - the Spirit's place, in this text, his role in the divine conversation is *our role.* He joins our inner-self and thinks and feels what we should feel, according to truth, according to the gospel, towards God and by extension towards all reality. Paul chose the word "*kradzo*" to cry out to reflect the Spirit's "thinking and feeling" inside and beside our feelings and emotions. The word choice appears to reflect more than just "words" or speaking. The Spirit does not just say Abba. He cries out Abba Father denoting deep feeling in his call towards God. He *cries* to God. We could say "he yearningly and passionately calls to Abba" and he is doing this "alongside and within our own emotions and thoughts." The verb form suggests an ongoing action too being a present tense participle. The Spirit continually cries to the God within us. He does not stop.

The term "Abba" paired here with Father has a somewhat debatable meaning. All agree that it is an Aramaic word meaning father. The debate revolves around the issue of affection. Is it a uniquely affectionate term or simply another word for father? BDAG suggests that it is a term of endearment. Other lexicons suggest that there is simply no evidence in the papyri. I lean toward the former, that it is a term of endearment for two reasons. First, by being paired with the rather emotionally charged word "to cry out" the concept seems to imply a rather emotionally charged semantic nuance. Second, the word appears to be simple in its pronunciation similar to Dadda in English and matching the corresponding *imma* for mama in Aramaic. Sometimes we may allow academic rigidity too much authority in determining obvious potential meanings. BDAG is typically considered the better lexical resource when definitions are debated. With all of this in mind, we will go with the idea of "Abba" as referring to the more affectionate reference to one's "Daddy." The tendency to lean one way or the other, towards the *affectionate* understanding or away from it probably says more about theological leanings than it does our exegesis, but both meanings are possible as BDAG suggests. Beyond all of this, we have to explain the reason that Paul does something he never does before or after, uses the Aramaic version of father, not Hebrew or Greek. It is least likely that he was simply being repetitive.

A paraphrase that brings out the meanings we have seen may sound like: Now that you are God's sons, He has sent the Spirit of the Son to join you in your mind and emotions. Now, inside of you, he continually calls out to God on your behalf, Daddy, Father.

Consider this statement as an outcome of several thoughts Paul has said about our life in the Spirit. First, at the beginning of chapter three, Paul challenges the Galatians. Are you now made mature by the flesh? He contrasts maturity in the flesh with a life of ongoing faith that he describes as "the Spirit working supernaturally miracles in you." He then begins to develop the idea that the "Spirit's work" comes out of faith by showing that Abraham was blessed by faith: the blessing was the promised inheritance, the promised inheritance was the Spirit - and in context, not just the Spirit, but "the Spirit's working supernatural miracles in you." Then, he begins to contrast being in faith (and therefore living in the blessing/Spirit) with being under the law or "of the law." Those under the law are trapped, imprisoned, servants following "orders." Here, as we reach near the end of his development he says that this "work of the Spirit" looks like this: the Spirit of the Son crying in our hearts "Abba." The Spirit, in other words, is making our theological position real and true in us. Our response to what he is saying and doing inside of us is faith.

As we read this text, we want to pay special attention to what Paul is telling us is true and what he is telling us to do. For the former, he says that it is true that we are one with Christ, merged together with Christ, and have inherited the blessing/Spirit with Christ. Because of this, we are sons. Christ freed us from the law wherein we were enslaved. We are no longer under the law and its requirements, rules or stipulations. The law -written in the Torah or nature- no longer applies to us. The government and economy of the law have been deposed and replaced by the government and the economy of grace and the Spirit. Now we are "out of faith." Is that our response? Is that what we are to do? Have faith? First and foremost yes. We are to be "out of faith" or what faith (as opposed to doing rules and laws) makes of us. Paul originally, in this section, says that we should "respond with faith" or "listen with faith" or "listen and believe." Then, he suggests that "to listen with faith" means to "be made mature by the Spirit" which is very different than being made mature "by the flesh," "the words of the law." Now, what does our faith "cause?" Our faith, according to verse 5, causes the Father to supply us with the Spirit and supernatural energy or action inside. What does this text then help us understand in coordination with these ideas? First, the giving, sending, or supplying of the Spirit comes to us because we have faith. So, what do we actually have faith in? It appears, that we have faith in what was written before "Christ crucified" or, the work of Christ to free us, to deliver us, to die for us to "save us." That is what we respond to with faith, "the message that Christ was crucified on our behalf." When we do that originally we "begin in the Spirit" and as we continue to do that we "mature in the Spirit." And how? He keeps crying out, over and over, Abba Father. He relates to God on our behalf. He proclaims in us and for us our identity in Christ. The more we hear him and believe him the more we live in this identity and all that it means. I think if we were to say to Paul, "We've read Galatians 3 and 4. What do you want us to do?" He would say "have faith in what Christ did on the cross for you, what he turned you into there and then keep listening to the Holy Spirit as he speaks, thinks and feels inside of you. He will tell and remind you who Christ made you into. Have faith in what he says. Mature by having faith in what the Spirit says to you. You begin by believing the gospel. Now, listen to the Spirit and respond with faith as he proclaims in our hearts the benefits of the gospel. In the same way that Christ lived and died on your behalf, the Spirit is thinking and feeling on your behalf before the Father, towards the Father."

**Galatians 4.7** "So you are no longer a slave, but a son, and if a son, then an heir through God." (ὥστε οὐκέτι εἶ δοῦλος ἀλλὰ υἱός· εἰ δὲ υἱός, καὶ κληρονόμος διὰ θεοῦ.)

In the last verse of this paragraph, he summarizes his conclusion. Since you are redeemed you are adopted as sons. Since you are sons the Spirit is in you crying father. Therefore: you are no longer servants. Notice he returns to the topic of "servants" where he began. You, in a past state, were no different than servants. Or as he put it here, you were servants (under the law). Then, by coupling together four "be verb" clauses, he closes out this sub-section with a few summary statements. First, as we have seen: You are no longer slaves. Second, you are sons. Third, because you are sons you are heirs of God through Christ.

Some Greek manuscripts say "you are heirs through God" and others, most of them, say "you are heirs *of God* through *Christ.*" Depending on one's perspective on textual criticism you may go either way. I lean towards a more "geographic" perspective where we should consider the version that has the broadest utilization geographically. This would be the latter option. Most translations follow the more commonly accepted approach of critics which is to choose the version that is oldest with considerations toward the shorter version, the harder reading and the reading that best explains the other.

We are heirs of God and because of God's plan no matter which reading we choose. Both theological points are made in the text. Christ put us into this standing through "redemption." If the older reading is correct the somewhat tenuous reading places an emphasis on God's sovereign working out of the plan. If the broader reading is correct the emphasis is on a structural summarizing of two points: together with Christ, we are God's heirs (and the inheritance is the Spirit) and Christ made us so. This latter reading does state more emphatically that our inheritance is from God or maybe even God himself. This would be a layer added by Paul. He has said we are one with Christ and therefore the seed of Abraham and heirs with Christ. This may be considered the harder reading from some theologically. That we are actually God's heirs or heirs of God. But, this idea has already been taught. Our inheritance is God the Spirit. I believe Paul is stating something he believes to be rather profound, and it is, that because we are sons of God, not just sons of Abraham, we "inherit God."

# Galatians 4.8-11

**Interpretive Translation:**

So, you are not servants anymore. You are sons. It follows too that if you are a son, you are also God's heir through Jesus Christ. But when you did not really understand God, you served under those who do not possess God's nature.[119] Now though, once you began an intimate relationship with God and even more, once God shared himself intimately with you, how can you go back to living your life[120] based on[121] these impotent, inadequate rules meant for children? Do you want to go back again and keep serving under *their* authority? You refuse to stop practicing the law keeping religious customs like feasts and festivals as if they benefitted you. You make me afraid that all my efforts [122]are now worthless in your mind.[123]

---

[119] This is a difficult phrase to me. It could mean that "you served along side of/with those by nature not being gods." It appears that Paul is referring to the authorities from verse 4.1 and he says, in contrast to the Son and the Spirit, these administrators did not possess God's nature. And, to Paul, that is important. If we compare that to Galatians 2:19, the fountainhead of this argument, then the whole point is to be "alive with God's life."

[120] See LN on Acts.

[121] This partially comes from the meaning of the verb as we see it from LN and the preposition "epi" upon.

[122] Perfect Lit "Lest indeed in vain I have labored all my labors for you."

[123] In your mind not in the text. Trying to capture something of the reflexive or passive nature of "phoboumai"

**Summary Commentary:**

This paragraph should be read closely with the preceding one and it should be considered the final word of the major section that started in 3.1. Paul, after stating in 4.1 that a person as a child lives like a servant under administrators and under "elementary-like, universal rules and regulations." Here, he returns to the same concept and defines the era of spiritual adolescence and servitude as the part of life when a person does not know God and is not intimate relationally with God. The answer, it seems, to spiritual maturity and growth, is to move away from a life based on doing the commandments and rules written into the law code or in the fabric of the universe and to begin, instead, living in the intimacy that is ours through justification by faith. Paul rebukes the Galatians (and with this rebuke defines again their error or "now being made mature by the flesh") for "living life according to" the rules. The problem with these rules, these regulations and commands, is that they are not God nor are they really intrinsically like God. Here, Paul uses a play on words. He describes the "stoicha" the "universal elements and the spirits that guide them" and connects the idea of the rules-based religion to a popular view of the world: one in which the most basic elements of the universe are controlled by spiritual beings. The rules are like these "universal elemental ingredients" and behind them are demonic spiritual forces. They, though, are not really like God. They do not possess his nature or his qualities. He goes on to define what he means with this note by saying that they are "weak and poor," or to put it more as he intended: powerless and spiritually bankrupt. In 3:4 God richly supplies the Spirit through faith. Here the rules system supplies all that it has: nothing. This replacement for this system of religion and commandments is the one "of faith" whereby in faith we are giving the blessing, the Spirit of the Son talking in our hearts and declaring "Abba" to the Father. Or to say it like Paul says it here: The other option, beyond living according to powerless rules, is to live in the intimacy God provides us in the Spirit. The ultimate pivot explained here is that the Galatians *want,* will and desire to live as servants of the old system. As Paul stated about justification "those who seek -want- to be justified by Christ" he now says by implication about our maturity. It is simply a matter of what do you want. Do you want the Spirit? Do you want intimacy? It's yours! Paul defines what this choice looks like in the case of the Galatians. They are continually observing religious feasts. They refuse to stop. Paul has already connected their law-based living to circumcision, the types of food they might eat, the moral code. Now he also connected the idea to the celebration of feasts. In so doing, he leaves no doubt that nothing about the law code, not even the Ten Commandments themselves, is meant to be followed as a way to please God. In his final statement of this section (and probably a way to introduce the next section simultaneously) Paul admits a worry. The Galatians cause him to worry unless all his labor and toil -note that he still speaks of effort for Christ even during a focus on grace- is in vain. This connects back to the experience of the Galatians when Paul says they may have experienced so much in vain and potentially back to his presentation before the Galatians council when he presented his argument so that he made sure he did not "run or labor in vain."

**Galatians 4.8** "Formerly, when you did not know God, you were enslaved to those that by nature are not gods." (Ἀλλὰ τότε μὲν οὐκ εἰδότες θεὸν ἐδουλεύσατε τοῖς φύσει μὴ οὖσιν θεοῖς·)

"Formerly, when you did not know God" - Paul transitions into a new subsection by grouping several conjunctions. The ESV has "Formerly" but in Greek, it would be something more like "But then indeed not." So a transition has occurred from the previous paragraph, but this material should be read in conjunction with what has preceded it. This entire section (Galatians 4:8-11) appears to be in parallel to 4.1-4. Both contrast what Paul writes between where the Son redeems the Galatians and sends his spirit into the hearts of the believer, the sum of what it means to be "an heir of God." Here Paul says that this means to "know" God using the term *oida*. (In the next verse he uses a different term, *ginosko*.) The most important insight Paul adds with this phrase results from this connection. Before the gospel, before a person is an heir or a son, before the one is redeemed and the Spirit cries out in their heart, they do not know God. To not have this positional change is the same as not having a relational "knowing" change. If we were to try to bring out the meaning of "know" as much as we can we might, in this context suggest it means "be aware of" or maybe even "meet." Something like the following translation might be helpful: You are heirs but remember when you had not really met God..."

"You were enslaved to those that by nature are not gods." - Before a person meets God or gains a relational connection to Him -in this case characterized by sonship and the presence of the Spirit of God himself- they remain as servants. Remember this idea dominated the previous paragraph. There Paul describes the pre-Christ servitude as being to administrators and stewards and, being under their authority, also under strict regulations meant for little children. (He will mention that latter part specifically again in the next verse.) He characterizes these authorities that supervise the pre-Christ believer here a little differently. (Note that he refers to the regulations of the law in the Torah and any other kind of "rule system" one might lean on to gain approval with God.) These authorities "by nature are not gods." What is his point? Let's cover what seems to be clear and then what may be less clear in this phrase. It is at least more clear that Paul states that the Galatians serve "those being not gods." So, the entities expressing authority over the pre-Christ individual are not gods. The form of "gods" occurs in the dative form. It can be translated as "gods" as if it is to be understood more accusatively or it can be translated in a more literal dative "to gods" or "in gods" or "by gods." You served those who are not with gods, by gods, etc" What is less obvious is what Paul means by "in nature." The word means "the characteristics possessed by the nature of one's *being*" versus those gained. For those who are born it would describe the qualities one possesses at birth, not those gained by education, discipline, etc. Our concept of "nature versus nurture" applies here with this term referring to the qualities of "nature" not nurture. The point is that these entities and authorities do not possess the qualities and characteristics of real gods.

We need to settle into the worldview of the Galatians here and think about the context Paul has established. As we said in the previous commentary on the previous text, Paul here describes these authorities

-these that have already been clearly connected to "the rules of the law" when he called them tutors, then administrators- as "not genuinely being like real gods." In a moment, he will say that they are impotent and impoverished. He could be saying a few different things and even intended a multi-layered understanding. He could simply be continuing in his personification of the law as administrators and noting that these stewards are not really god. The laws are not God Himself. In the Jewish mind, the law was very closely aligned with the person and mind of God. Paul may be intending to object to this thesis. He could also be simply trying to contrast the two states: in one case a person is under administrators -rules and rule givers- that are not actually "God" but the other person has the son of God himself inside of them. Another possibility we looked at above relates to the possible view of the universe that Paul engages in and has engaged throughout the book.

Paul has used the language of witchcraft and engagement with spirits repeatedly in the book. (See commentary on Galatians 3:1-5) He repeatedly sets the blessing and cursing of the gospel and the corresponding experience of the Spirit in contrast with the spiritualism reflected in the Galatians' cultural worldview. He could intend us to think about the law and the rules of the law as being similar to the basic elements of the universe. The Greek mind that Paul engages believed that the basic elements of the universe (*stoicha*) were controlled by different spirits like earth, water, fire and wind. To me, it is clear that he wants us to read the "stoicha" mainly as orders or rules but, he could also intend a play on words that challenge the worldview of the Galatians. As he personifies the rule system as "authorities" he may intend us to think of the laws in a similar way that someone might think of these basic elements and the spiritual beings that "direct them" as if he says "in the same way that you believe authorities rule through these basic elemental forces you are under the authorities of these overseers and administrators that rule through these "basic elementary rules." Ultimately his system puts you under the power of demonic spirits that gain leverage through the law code. Paul likely wants us to connect "the law code" to the dominance of spiritual forces the Galatians understood as being behind the "stoicha" of the universe. In contrast to the "spirits" who do not possess God's real nature, we have the Spirit of

God himself and we engage him relationally. (As we will see below the opportunity we have within the gospel is to engage the Spirit relationally or it may be better said, to engage God relationally through the Spirit.)

With all of this in mind to bring out the many nuances and probable inferences and connections, we might restate this verse: You are heirs but remember when you had not yet really met God you served under demonic spiritual forces that gained their leverage over you through the rules of the law. These spiritual forces have nothing in common with God. They are nothing like him. Nor, do they possess his power, yet these ruled over you before the Spirit of God himself joined himself to you in our inner being.

**Galatians 4.9** "But now that you have come to know God, or rather to be known by God, how can you turn back again to the weak and worthless elementary principles of the world, whose slaves you want to be once more?" (νῦν δὲ γνόντες θεόν, μᾶλλον δὲ γνωσθέντες ὑπὸ θεοῦ, πῶς ἐπιστρέφετε πάλιν ἐπὶ τὰ ἀσθενῆ καὶ πτωχὰ στοιχεῖα οἷς πάλιν ἄνωθεν δουλεύειν θέλετε;)

"But now that you come to know God or rather be known by God" - Paul continues his contrast by describing the state of the Galatians after Christ freed the believer and the Spirit joined himself to the heart of the believer. In this state, the Galatians "know God." Paul uses a different word for *know* here than he used in the previous verse. Most likely he wants us to think about the intimacy nuance implied in the contrast. Also, if we look at the full semantic range of *ginosko* used here then we see that "relational intimacy" is a potential part of the meaning. Considering the context of the intimacy implied in the "Father/Son" or even "Abba/Son" relationship we should probably understand something related to that as the intended understanding of *ginosko* here. The word itself can mean relational intimacy at multiple levels: friendship, parent/child, and marital (including sexual intercourse) amongst other aspects. The intent of Paul here seems likely to show that in the contrasted stated of the believer he or she "is intimate with God."

Next, he says in the ESV "or rather be known by God." The term "rather" implies "instead of" so that Paul represents knowing God intimately as being insignificant. The term can also be "even more" so that in the second phase "being known by God" is not instead of knowing God but an even better addition to it. You know God and are known by God. The simple translation "know" could be misleading. If we translate it as "experience intimacy" the verse takes on a different concept. You share intimacy towards God but even better, he shares intimacy with you. When we compare this text to the previous wording where "the Spirit cries Daddy" in our hearts this seems to be the "that but also this" to that phrase. The Spirit cries Daddy in us. But God cries "Son" back. The most important point Paul makes is the reciprocal nature of the relationship between God and the believer and what he implies may even be more important than that. It implies that our engagement with God relationally, intimate connections back and forth with God through the Spirit, is the essence of the life Paul calls the Galatians into. In other words, as he builds layer upon layer describing the life he calls the believer into he begins by making sure we know it is the life of spiritual maturity and it's of the Spirit, a supernatural working of the Spirit in us, and it occurs in the context of faith and it's the opposite of "being made mature by the flesh." He then goes through a lengthy explanation of the original promise made to Abraham being by faith and not by doing rules. This promise is the blessing and the inheritance that is also the Spirit Himself. Then, in this chapter, he makes it very clear the Spirit joins himself to us and operates in us as the Son in us or a son in us. This is the experience of those who live in faith the the gospel, the life of Christ living in us. Now, he further defines this life of faith as not just the Spirit being in us but of a reciprocal sharing of intimacy between God and the believer.

"How can you turn back again to the weak and worthless elementary principles of the world?" - If you are now living in such intimacy with God how are you turning back to the "stoicha?" Louw Nida suggests that the term translated "turn to" can be in some cases understood as "to live according to." This seems to be the emphasis here while the obvious "back" or "again" aspect also should be understood. The question in this term relates to whether or not the context suggests behavioral or belief-based actions. The person who does this work may return to a former way of thinking or a former way of living, acting. So, we could either read this as the Galatians going back to trusting in these rules or trying to live by them. While both ideas are probably included in this usage the translation "go back to living by" captures the essence. Paul in question form challenges the Galatians because they have returned to a life based on "rules" instead of a life based on faith in the gospel and the promise of intimacy it provides. Also, Paul shifts to a present tense verb as opposed to an aorist form. This could simply be to diagnose their present condition temporally. It could also infer that they keep going back to the law over and over.

The Galatians have returned to living by the *stoicha*, the orders or regulations and rules he mentioned in verse 3 above. Paul characterizes these *stoicha* here as being powerless and impoverished or literally "weak and poor." This may be in contrast to God's provision of the Spirit in 3.3 which is supernatural and rich. (Placing this sentence at the end of the section that started in 3.1 aligns the two texts, implying they should be read together in context.) These rules not only lack "the nature, quality, and characteristics of God's being" as Paul said in 4.8, but they are, to continue his disparaging, without power and bankrupt of value or useless. (See a similar statement from Paul in Colossians 2:23.) While, as we presented above, these rules could be seen to be connected to demonic spirits, Paul could be simply saying "they are not actually connected to any real supernatural power." He makes it clear, either way, immediately following this text that "living by these regulations" in the case of the Galatians looks like "observing" the law.

"Whose slaves you want to be once more" - Paul connects the ideas of verse nine to the ideas of verse 8. (Also remember the parallels between 4.1-3 and 4.8-10.) When you did not know God you served the "not gods." Here, you know God so why do you choose to serve the impotent and useless *stoicha*? A couple of important aspects of this service are included here. One, it is by will or choice. The Galatians "want" to live in this position of servitude. Ultimately, Paul suggests, that whether one lives according to rules or intimacy and faith is a matter of choice and desire. Which one do you want? He said practically the same thing about justification when he said some "want to be justified by Jesus" in Galatians 2.18. The opportunity for a better way is freely available and given. One must simply make a choice. As the Galatians show though, this choice has to be reaffirmed over and over to truly "live in it." Second, the service is present tense and should be read as "constantly serving." You always want to keep continually serving the powerless and useless regulations.

**Galatians 4.10** "You observe days and months and seasons and years!" (ἡμέρας παρατηρεῖσθε καὶ μῆνας καὶ καιροὺς καὶ ἐνιαυτούς)

In case his readers are not clear on the type of behaviors he rebukes he gives an example. The Galatians still observe religious festivals. This verb occurs in the middle voice so we might need to read it reciprocally in some way. "We observe for ourselves." If we only had this verse to understand what Paul taught against as it regards the law code we might conclude that his concern focused on the ceremonial law. This though is one of many references to the law. He has rebuked a life built on trying to do any part: clean and unclean animals, circumcision, ceremonial and most notably, the moral code. Additionally, his use of the *stoicha* of the cosmos terminology implies that he sees this as not just a Torah problem but a universal religious issue. He contrasts not just the Torah to believing the gospel but the paradigm of all religions that require the performance of "commands" to gain God's favor.

**Galatians 4.11** "I am afraid I may have labored over you in vain." (φοβοῦμαι ὑμᾶς μή πως εἰκῇ κεκοπίακα εἰς ὑμᾶς.)

Paul wraps up this major section (starting in 3.1) with a subtle return to the language of "vanity." "You petrify me," Paul says to the Galatians. He is petrified that his toil and labor might have been "meaningless." This serves as an end to this major section and also to set up a bit of narrative which may form a structural bracket to the biographical material in chapters 1-2:14. Notice the semantic similarities between this sentence and the phrase in 2.2 where Paul explained why he presented to the Jerusalem leadership: "to make sure I did not labor meaninglessly." Between this sentence, the titular reference to brothers in the following verse (12), and the shift back into biographical material about his time with the Galatians, we should read this as a major seam in the book. It might even warrant placing the idea of "meaningless effort" as a major theme of the book. Either way, it appears that 2.15-4.11/12 has been structured so that it is the semantic peak of the book overall. As stated above this most likely also means that 2:19-21 lies at the center of the material.[124]

---

[124] Or it could be the launching point, i.e. it climatic ends 2:15-20 and then 3.1ff is set as the "now lets talk about what means" aspect. Clearly Paul includes many subtle references back to the 2.20 poem in 3.1-4.11. Note the poetic nature of 3.27-29. Also note that verse 29 ends with the statement that we are heirs of the promise and then the next text has the same statement as its peak. Note also the lexical link back to 2.12 "fearing the circumcision party Peter drew back." So in the space of a couple of verses he links uniquely back to 1) language about laboring in vain 2) "fear" language, 3) Then "brothers." Note also that after the shift he says the Galatians received him as "an angel, as Christ himself." which may be a connection back to 1.4-5. (also "brothers" could serve as both an ending to the section and the "re-beginning.") This could potentially infer that 3.15 to 4.10 is the actual semantic peak of the book. It could also infer a A1, B2 parallel between 1.-4.10 and 4.11 - End of Galatians. It appears that either the idea of the idea of the end of 4 being the peak with the OT analogy or Galatians 2.20 being the peak with 5.1ff being an added on element structurally.

# Galatians 4.12-20

**Interpretive Translation:**

Oh, dearest family, originally I became more like you and now you should become like me. I will never stop begging you to abandon your attempts to obey the law!

Indeed,[125] you know well that when I originally visited you and shared this gospel with you my physical health was very poor. It caused you a lot of difficulty but you displayed authentic[126] love and kindness toward me. You saw the value in taking care of me and refused to send me away even though I was no doubt a burden. Instead, you took me in and treated me like I was an angel sent from God or even as if I was Christ Jesus himself. What happened to this deep, overwhelming favor you had for me? I can tell you clearly about what it was like before. If it was possible to cut out your own eyes and give them to me, you would have done so. How is it that I became your enemy just because I kept sharing truth with you?

They obsess over the wrong things when it comes to you. They want to keep you under their restrictions so that you are you become obsessed with them just like they are.[127] But, it's always beautiful to obsess over beautiful things, good and right things, the gospel. This applies when I am with you and when I am not with you. You are like infants in my womb, and my labor pains will not stop as I wait on Christ to be formed in you. I want to be with you as soon as possible and then change my attitude towards you because right now it's not good. Right now you are causing me a lot of anxiety and worry.

---

[125] From de, not but here, or "now" or "and" but more of a way emphasis the sentence.

[126] You did not reject or despise the your test regarding my physical health.

[127] "Them" may refer to the "resections" implied by the verb "to forbid" or to lock up. This word connects back to the rules of the law and their "locking up" effect.

**Summary Commentary:**

Structurally this paragraph plays an important role in Paul's strategy. As of Galatians 2:15, Paul has moved into an expository tone teaching and exhorting the Galatians to strengthen their faith in the gospel as opposed to observing the law. Here he returns to the biographic narrative discussing his time with the Galatians. There are also many verbal links back to Galatians 1. Most likely this forms an inclusio to the front of the book. The basic thesis of this paragraph is that the Galatians should see in their relationship with Paul reason to turn from the heretic's false gospel and back to believing the gospel Paul preached. Additionally, he uses this story to paint a picture of the kind of life the gospel creates. In so doing, he shifts the focus of his teaching towards the active, selfless love and person will be filled with as they grow close to God. He gives several motivating reminders. 1) He lived the freedom of the gospel "I became like you." 2) He gospeled the Galatians through much suffering and they served him too. (He not only reminds them of his suffering but that they are already deeply invested in it.)

**Galatians 4.12** "Brothers, I entreat you, become as I am, for I also have become as you are. You did me no wrong." -ESV (Γίνεσθε ὡς ἐγώ, ὅτι κἀγὼ ὡς ὑμεῖς, ἀδελφοί, δέομαι ὑμῶν. οὐδέν με ἠδικήσατε· )

This sentence serves as both a transition from the previous paragraph and an introduction to the next. It also makes a major shift in the structure of the text. The titular "brothers" provides an end to the section that began in Galatians 3:15 where Paul also uses the same word "Brothers." The literary type shifts to biographical from hortatory signifying a shift even further back to before Galatians 2:15 where Paul made a shift in the other direction, from biographical *to* hortatory. He also uses several verbal and literary links back to chapters 1 and 2:1-15 showing intentional inclusio. Less so, he includes a couple of links back to 3.1 showing a parallel structure there as well. The point of these links is to show that this paragraph is emphatically to be read as a shift.

Note here too that the next section is an allegorical reflection on Sarah and Hagar. This could be either a unique text or a return to "exegesis of the Hebrew Bible." We will watch closely for comparisons to chapters 3:5-29ish.

Paul begins his shift by stating that he wants the Galatians to be "as I am." In some ways, he has spent the entire book describing what that means: his faith in the gospel and freedom from the law. He also clarifies that here and adds "because I am also like you." In other words, Paul shifted his approach to be that of a Gentile, just like the Galatians and this is the preferred approach in the gospel. This is one view of many as to the meaning of this text. If we do our best to let the literature be our guide then Paul's earlier meaning fits well. We might also consider the parallelisms to Chapter 1 and reflect on how that might also give more clarity to meaning. To say that point another way, Paul says here (possibly) be like I described myself in the first section of this letter because I am also just like you. That, if it is the intended reading, begs the question: in what way does Paul describe himself in the first section of this letter and how does that relate to the Galatians? In this first section the most fitting comparison would be 2.11-14 when Peter, being tempted by the Jerusalem cohort, separated from the Galatians and Paul "became like them." Also of importance, as we wrestle with Paul's meaning, is the immediate context. Paul says "I became like you" and then begins to describe what may be the same event. He joined them and lived with them as they were. This makes his overall argument tighter. If this is the case he is saying, because I came to you, lived among you and lived like you, be like me now. This is also supported by the immediate movement in the text toward Paul's description of the Galatians not mistreating him at all when he "became like them." Also, compare this phrase to the inclusio of this section, 4.16, Paul says "I become like an enemy to you when I tell you the truth?" (I became like one of you; like your family.)

"I entreat you" - This present tense verb suggests a very intense and emotional entreaty. Paul passionately pursued the Galatians' spiritual fidelity. "I am begging you" may be a clearer translation.

"You did me no wrong" - This sentence suggests the previous one refers to Paul's original missionary visit so that the context of the first verse implies Paul "became like them" in a missional or even incarnational sense. When he joined them and "became just like them" they did not wrong or harm him. The word translated "do wrong" in the ESV can mean simply to do a wrong or injustice. It often has the nuance of harm or even violence. The idea of mistreatment may fit best here. "You did not mistreat me in any way." This root is the negated form of the word translated "justify" in previous texts. It most likely occurs to connect the text back structurally with the first section of the book. If more is meant maybe Paul is saying "you acted towards me as if you were justified." The connection would be subtle and based on the literary connections, even implied and subverted, but Paul could be emphasizing justification as an impulse for their actions and service toward him. He does soon (5.1-5) shift from an emphasis on justification by faith to living out one's justification in service to others. Maybe this hints in that direction as do many other elements described below.

The microstructure of this text has two features: 1) the parallels between the "ginomai" verbs in 4.12 and 4.16 that form a bracket for the text and 2) the series of second aorist verbs that describe the action. "You did this. You did this. You did this." The first occurs here "You did not mistreat me."


**Galatians 4.13** "You know it was because of a bodily ailment that I preached the gospel to you at first," (οἴδατε δὲ ὅτι δι' ἀσθένειαν τῆς σαρκὸς εὐηγγελισάμην ὑμῖν τὸ πρότερον )

The second verb (this time perfect) continues the action. First "You did not mistreat me." Now, "You knew that." What did they know? They knew that Paul "gospeled" or "shared the good news" with them in weakness of the flesh on his "first visit." What does he mean? Most likely, based on the context below, related to the implied issue of eye trouble, he refers to an actual physical ailment. A lot has been written about the possibility of what ailment Paul possibly faced. We will be careful to simply see what the words of the text actually say about the situation. The text itself could either mean that Paul has a sickness or ailment of some sort or that his ministry with them was characterized by inadequacy caused by his flesh. In the latter case, it may be something similar to what he describes in 1 Corinthians 1-2 when he says he came to the Corinthians preaching poorly or it could be some sort of moral failure. Most likely, according to context, the issue had something to do with his eyes.

The ESV suggests that this inadequacy or ailment was the cause for his being in Galatia. "It was because"… I preached. This is a possible translation of the preposition *dia*. It could also describe the condition of this ministry. "I gospeled *while* having a weakness." Notice the term "gospeled" is used a few times in this commentary. That is a more exact translation of the actual Greek word typically translated as "proclaim the gospel." The actual word is a verbal form of the word "gospel." "I announced something good" could also be an acceptable translation. The focus of the verb is on the content of the message more than the way it's communicated. The closest simple English equivalent may be "I cheered you." Here, Paul's main point is an interesting contrast: During difficulties, I cheered you.

**Galatians 4.14** "and though my condition was a trial to you, you did not scorn or despise me, but received me as an angel of God, as Christ Jesus." (καὶ τὸν πειρασμὸν ὑμῶν ἐν τῇ σαρκί μου οὐκ ἐξουθενήσατε οὐδὲ ἐξεπτύσατε, ἀλλὰ ὡς ἄγγελον θεοῦ ἐδέξασθέ με, ὡς Χριστὸν Ἰησοῦν.)

"And though my condition was a trial to you" - The ESV works to smooth out a rather difficult phrase in Greek. The text reads "and the trial of you in my flesh you did not despise nor reject." The takeaway of a more literal reading is that the thing the Galatians did not reject was not Paul but the "trial." Paul states rather plainly that the weakness of his flesh described in the preceding verse was a trial for the Galatians. What does he mean by "a trial?" Spicq uses the gloss "sounding" with this term. The idea behind the word is probably simply that this was a difficult situation. And the Galatians embraced the opportunity to serve Paul. There may be a nuance to the word here (there often is) of proving the authenticity of their affection for Paul.

"You did not scorn or despise me" - As noted above it was not Paul the Galatians did not scorn or despise (though this fits better in English) but the trial, the difficulty. These two verbs continue the structure described above. You did not mistreat me. You did not despise me. You did not reject me. Scorn (*exoutheneo*) means to despise. It is the word Jesus uses when he describes the Pharisees looking down on others as being "not good enough" for their company. The Galatians were not "repulsed" by Paul. This implies that they could have been. Despise (*ekputo*) means to reject and even literally "to spit out" or throw away. Disdain is another way to translate it. The idea of "spitting out" may be to reject like one might do with bad food or drink. It may also be the result of a symbolic gesture one would do to show disdain. "You are repulsive."

"But received me as an angel of God, as Christ Jesus." - Paul gives both the negative and positive descriptions of the Galatians' treatment of him during his ailment. They did not disdain or reject Paul. Instead, from the positive perspective, the Galatians "received" Paul as an angel of God, or even as "Christ Jesus." Some commentators accurately highlight the possibility of translating "angels" as "messenger" or in this case "messenger from God." While this is possible the structural parallel back to chapter 1- "Though I or an angel from heaven preaches another gospel" and the connection to "Christ Jesus" here suggest a spiritual entity, specifically an angel. The connection back to Chapter 1 suggests that Paul's bigger point here is that the Galatians received not just him but his gospel as if it was "from an angel of God, as from Christ Jesus." This also is an example of intentional hyperbole as to the level of "reception" the Galatians showed Paul, to the same level as if he was Jesus. A subtle challenge comes from this thought. Any reader of this text now begins to understand the kind of treatment we should give other people, especially believers, and especially those who are suffering, especially when that suffering causes most others to "reject like they were repulsive."

We might restate this verse as "You did not despise or get repulsed by the opportunity to serve me even though I was ridden with a gross and potentially contaminating disease, even as difficult as the experience might have been for you."

**Galatians 4.15** "What then has become of your blessedness? For I testify to you that, if possible, you would have gouged out your eyes and given them to me?" (ποῦ οὖν ὁ μακαρισμὸς ὑμῶν; μαρτυρῶ γὰρ ὑμῖν ὅτι εἰ δυνατὸν τοὺς ὀφθαλμοὺς ὑμῶν ἐξορύξαντες ἐδώκατέ μοι. )

"What then has become of your blessedness?" - The phrase more literally might say "Where then is your blessedness?" We can see that the ESV attempts to bring out the inference. *You previously treated me with "blessing" but not now. What happened?* The word blessing means most specifically "a state of happiness" and can also mean "a recipient of special favor." Paul seems to say something here like "Formerly, you served me with so much happiness. What happened?" Or "What happened to the happy favor you had towards me?" It suggests that "happiness" characterized the lives of the Galatians before -a happiness that gave impulse to free, joyous service and favor towards others, even the most despicable- but did not do so any longer. Legalism steals the possibility for happiness and then "serving out of joy." Most plainly, Paul says "Where did your happiness go?" -which might come across as a strange challenge. "You are no longer happy like you used to be." Paul does imply that this happiness was an impulse for "gospel" service towards others, especially him, but no longer. (Paul has used the same word to describe the freedom of grace and justification in Romans 4:5-10.)

"For I testify to you that, if possible, you would have gouged out your eyes and given to me?" - Just how extreme was the Galatians' passion toward Paul? Just how much happiness did they have in serving him? His malady must have been related to "seeing" or at least that seems to be the best guess. The possible literary connection in this case might be between what Paul says in Galatians 3.1 and this text. Remember the phrase "bewitch" means "to give the evil eye" which was a way to say hex via the gaze or typically a gaze and a mutter. Of course in this same immediate text Paul not only says "hex through the eye" he also says that Christ was crucified in their eyes (before their gaze). These two lexemes move forward and emphasize Paul's very "witchcraft" oriented language. He started with it (cursed, anathema in 1) and then he will continue to use these semantic ideas to describe the spiritual realities of the gospel. If there is a connection, then Paul might be suggesting the transformation of the gospel in their lives in juxtaposition to the condition they are experiencing now: under the evil eye hex.

If not, he most likely refers here to specifically his eye malady and their willingness to serve him happily. Of course, both options could be intended without any hermeneutical issues. Generally speaking, Paul does seem to have elsewhere 1) a physical ailment - 2 Cor "thorn in the flesh" and 2) an issue seeing well - "see what large letters I am using" (Gal 6.11). It is no accident that Paul makes this note in the same letter.

**Galatians 4.16** "Have I then become your enemy by telling you the truth?" (ὥστε ἐχθρὸς ὑμῶν γέγονα ἀληθεύων ὑμῖν)

Paul finishes this paragraph (or subsection) with a return to the "ginomai" verb he began with. Verse 12 says "Become like me." Here he says 'Have I become your enemy?" In the latter case he uses the perfect tense to show the stative aspect of "becoming" the enemy. In other words, through regularly telling them the truth (present tense: continual action) he does not exist in the state of the enemy. (Perfect tense is process + result/state.) So much of this text then hangs on what Paul was. First, they were to be like Paul which he defines as the same as when "I was as you." Now, though, he -even after so deep a connection between Paul and the Galatians and such a powerful movement of the gospel in their hearts producing happiness- is their enemy.

**Galatians 4.17** "They make much of you, but for no good purpose. They want to shut you out, that you may make much of them." (ζηλοῦσιν ὑμᾶς οὐ καλῶς, ἀλλὰ ἐκκλεῖσαι ὑμᾶς θέλουσιν, ἵνα αὐτοὺς ζηλοῦτε·)

The next two verses are hung onto three uses of the verb "make much of" from *zelo*. (It also includes a bracketing of "to be present" connecting verses 18 to verse 20.) The word has a broad range of meanings including: "to be concerned over; to make much of; to obsess over; have a deep devotion to." It appears that the idea mainly relates to "obsessing over." Their obsession is with the Galatians and it is "not good." The obsessing is not a good obsessing and it is an obsessing over "not good." What do they obsess over? Beyond the Galatians generally they "want/seek to restrict you." The term translated as "shut you out" can refer to being excluded. It can also refer to not being allowed to do something or participate in something "to restrict." It shares a root (*cleo*) with the term translated "imprisoned" in Galatians 3:22 and again in verse 23. The connection between the law as an imprisoning tutor and the false teachers is clear. In 4.21, in a sentence connected by the verb "thelo" (to want, also used in the present verse), Paul says some "want to be under the law." This phrase here then refers most likely to the fact that these false teachers obsess over making sure the Galatians are appropriately "restricted" under the "not goods" of the law. We might say it as the "rules" or "Don't do this and don't do that."

With this in mind when Paul ends this clause by saying "so that you obsess over them" he could refer to a desire by these false teachers to become gurus. Any legalistic system has to have its exegetes of jots and tittles and even more so, all the restrictions that lie between what is written. This could be the point. He could also imply that they want the Galatians to become obsessed over "rules" just like they are. While either could be possible, and most translators go with the former option, the connection to the "laws" makes more sense to me. If this is right we might translate this sentence as "They obsessively make sure you don't do anything bad; they want to tie you up with tedious restrictions so that you also obsess about them." Or "They obsess over the wrong things when it comes to you. They want to keep you under their restrictions so that you become obsessed with them just like they are."

**Galatians 4.18** "It is always good to be made much of for a good purpose, and not only when I am present with you." (καλὸν δὲ ζηλοῦσθαι ἐν καλῷ πάντοτε καὶ μὴ μόνον ἐν τῷ παρεῖναί με πρὸς ὑμᾶς.)

In verse 18, Paul contrasts the "obsessing" of the false teachers with an alternate obsession. "Now good to obsess in good always is" is a very wooden way to translate the first half of the text. The takeaway of this wooden translation should be the emphasis on a new obsession: "good" instead of "not good." Also, note that the term "to obsess" means to continually obsess so that Paul is saying that "Constantly obsessing in 'good' is always good." This also appears to somewhat give us an idea of what Paul means when he says that the Galatians obsess over "not good." He could mean to obsess over "doing good" as he has just described, i.e. the behaviors of happy service as described above. Or, if the broader context is in mind, the gospel, the "good news" itself may be in mind. It may be impossible to know for sure; the bigger point is to stop obsessing over the restrictions; the "not goods." But, if we asked Paul, "what do you mean by good?" He might say back to us: "What do you think I mean?" And to me, it is clear that the only thing "good" Paul has written about is the "good news." The literary structure and the connection between this text and Chapter One suggest the same.

"And not only when I am present with you." - As often is the case with the churches Paul has planted they seem to operate differently in his absence than they had in his presence. Paul wants the churches to operate according to sound doctrine, according to the gospel, but he needs them to be able to do so without him. In some ways this becomes the ultimate goal of missions; independence from the missionary "even while I am not there." Remember that Paul began this paragraph with a reminder of what it looked like while he was there "I became like you" and because of that, they should "become like me." Now, he suggests his ultimate goal: for them to be "good news" obsessed even when he is not there.


**Galatians 4.19** "My little children, for whom I am again in the anguish of childbirth until Christ is formed in you!" (τέκνα μου, οὓς πάλιν ὠδίνω μέχρις οὗ μορφωθῇ Χριστὸς ἐν ὑμῖν·)

This sentence may suggest a movement into the next paragraph. As Paul often does in Galatians though, he may use this verse (and even the next two) as a transitional crossover - "cross stitching" between section and the next. Either way, Paul calls those formerly referred to as "brothers" as "my children." Notice the terms of affection. This terminology also prepares the reader for the next paragraph where Paul compares the law and the gospel to Sarah and Hagar and their "giving birth." Paul is "anguishing with birth-pains" while Christ is being formed in the Galatians. A few notes: First the term "anguishing" is a present tense verb. Paul does not stop "anguishing." He compares the constant suffering in birth pains to what he experiences while he waits for Christ to be formed in the Galatians. He uses the imagery of a child growing in the womb to Paul's vision of Galatian spiritual maturity. Louw Nida suggests here that the *morphow* (form) means "to cause something to have a certain form or nature" and he reminds the reader that it derives from the word *morphe* which actually means "nature or character." This verb has a similar semantic range as the word "by nature are not gods" in verse 8 so that Paul may intentionally connect the two ideas here. You are servants to those who are not gods "by nature" but I want Christ's nature to form in you. (Also note the similar language from Paul between 4.11 "labor in vain" and here "toiling in childbirth.") Beyond that, this sentence paints a picture of the ultimate aim of the gospel: Christ's nature and character being formed "among" those who believe the gospel. If the comparison between verse 8 and this verse is intended then it shows an essential difference between Paul's gospel and potentially another version. In the other version "doing good and not doing bad" in its many forms does not lead to having the nature of god. The law cannot confer what it does not possess. But, the gospel, "faith in Christ" actually does something better than what the law appears to intend to do: produce righteousness. But, the righteousness the gospel produces is more than that. The righteousness of the gospel is Christ himself being formed within us. This was Paul's aim. It required labor and pain. It also required patience.

**Galatians 4.20** "I wish I could be present with you now and change my tone, for I am perplexed about you." (ἤθελον δὲ παρεῖναι πρὸς ὑμᾶς ἄρτι καὶ ἀλλάξαι τὴν φωνήν μου, ὅτι ἀποροῦμαι ἐν ὑμῖν.)

Paul, in verse 18, says he wants the Galatians to "obsess over good" even when he is not present. These law-focused teachers want the Galatians to obsess over restrictions in his absence. Now he says he *wants* (same Greek verb *thelo*) to be present with the Galatians. He wants to change his voice or as the ESV says, "tone." The Galatians were "bewitched" before, they were the "foolish Galatians." in 1.5 they make Paul "astonished." Now, they cause Paul to stay continually "perplexed" (Present tense verb). These similar descriptors serve to create cohesion and structure. The word "perplexed" means just that with an emphasis on the worry and anxiety that such a perplexing might cause.

# Galatians 4.21-31

**Interpretive Translation:**

Tell me. Those of you who want to do the rules written in the law code, do you actually understand the law code? The Scriptures tell us that Abraham had two sons: one son from the slave girl and one from the free woman.[128] But, the son that came from the slave girl was created and formed according to natural physical processes while the son of the free woman was created and formed as the result of a promise. These events are an analogy of the different ways a person might seek God's approval. The two women represent the two different paradigms[129] we have been discussing, law and faith. The first, the woman who gives birth to children who are in slavery, Hagar, connects to Mount Sinai. (Mount Sinai, Hagar, is in the deserts[130] of Arabia where I journeyed when I began to prepare for my mission and where Israel wandered faithlessly before they came into the promise land.) It corresponds with the present, physical Jerusalem and the authorities that operate from there.[131] You read about them earlier. This Jerusalem is in slavery with her children, her spawn.

On the other hand, spiritual Jerusalem is free. She is our mother. The Scriptures also tell us this:

Listen to me, childless mother.

---

[128] This word can be "independent" or unbound, free. This means it could be a reference to an "unmarried woman" but in context, it most likely is not that sense.

[129] This is a "in context" translation. It could be "covenants" or treaties or legal documents or legal systems. He writes this example at the end of chapter 3.1ff section. It is clearly a referent back to the end of 3 the "law" paradigm versus the "faith" paradigm. Of note is that the difference is between faith and law not grace and law. Same as Romans 4.

[130] Arabia was a zone of deserts. Sinai specifically was in the Sinai peninsula and is the "wilderness" or desert wasteland where the Israelites wandered.

[131] Paul potentially rebukes the legalism that has taken hold in Jerusalem under James.

You who cannot have children, sing with joy.
You who have never felt the pain and toil of labor burst out in uncontrollable shouts of pleasure.
Because so many more are the children of the woman who was abandoned to her lifeless womb[132] than the woman who was paired up with the man.[133]

You, dearest family, were created as the result of a promise, similar to Isaac. Just as in the case of Isaac and Ishmael, the one who is created and formed through natural physical process still refuses to stop harassing[134] the one who is created and formed[135] supernaturally through the Spirit.

What does the text say about Sarah's response to Ishmael's mockery of Isaac? She told Abraham, "Send the slave girl and her son away from the camp. The son of this slave girl will not get access to the same possessions as the heir of those possessions himself, the free woman's son. So, dear family, we are not in the lineage of the slave girl. We are in the lineage of the free woman. Christ set us free to actually be free, to live like free people. So, be free! Stay free. Never stop being free![136]

---

[132] Because the children of the /no life/no fruit/no humans/not having life/land having no vegetation/no produce/ in ruins are many. She has more than that the woman who has a man. The picture is of an abandoned dead land that produces no life, fruit, or negation.

[133] In Greek "woman who has a man/husband." In Hebrew "Married" or "Under authority of a man." It most likely refers to Hagar who was connected to Abraham as a second wife or concubine. Sarah, in a way, was abandoned by Abraham for a time. Her womb was dead. In Isaiah, the Lord "abandoned" Zion but then returned to her and restored her and in doing so she had more children than the land could hold. This is used as a picture of salvation, comfort in the scheme of Isaiah. It is also a "restoration back to Eden." See Isaiah 54:1-6 and 62:2-5

[134] In Genesis the word ironically is from the same root as "Isaac" to laugh. Ishmael was picking on Isaac. Mocking him. "Toying with him." OR possible, "molesting him."

[135] The word means "to bear" but the concept can picture the entire process from conception to giving birth and then to rearing the child. More fully we might better say "created."

[136] The actually text simply says "Keep standing free" but the terminology is stronger than that literal translation might imply.

Be free from the reign of evil that has dominated the universe for millennia through the law.[137] Stop burdening yourselves[138] again and again[139] with this heavy yoke of slavery.[140] Don't put it on again. Go run wild and free.

**Summary Commentary:**

This text, along with the previous paragraph and the one that follows appears to be an "echo" parallel to the first section of the epistle. It also, in that way, appears to be a bit of a "restating" and deeper description of elements. He uses the story of Sarah and Hagar and their corresponding sons, Isaac and Ishmael, to teach his readers about the state and life of those who are "of faith" or "of the law." Those who are under law have the same life force as Ishmael. That life force is the flesh: natural human abilities. This life results in "a yoke of slavery" being on those who try to live under the law, a yoke that we tend to return to over and over. Paul also suggests that this life of slavery comes out of Jerusalem (during his time) and the teachers there. Those who "are of faith" are like Isaac. They are children of promise and the Spirit. Freedom, just as Sarah was free, characterizes their life. Paul also quotes from Isaiah 54.1 to describe the flourishing of the believer's life. Like Sarah, even though her womb was dead -as is our "flesh" dead in its ability to produce life- we will break out in singing and rejoicing and flourish (which he describes via the analogy of having many children." This text connects deeply to a restoration of Eden and an end to the curse of Genesis 3. In this text, we are "being fruitful and

---

[137] This a direct copy from my translation of Galatians 1.2 which I believe Paul intentionally connects to this passage. He uses the same root "histimi" to stand and in the context of "freedom." The root is different but it has very similar phonetics so much so Paul might have even thought it to be the same word. This is the parallel to that phrase. "to deliver us from the present evil age," -Galatians 1.4 ESV

[138] Also, this is a reflexive middle take on "enexo"

[139] Attempting to bring out the present negative as "stop keeping."

[140] Structurally this text is parallel to 4.21 "Tell me. Those who want to be under the law, Have you heard the law?" Notice the connection that happens in the seam of the next verse "I say to you."

multiplying" and childbirth looks like "singing and joy" instead of "pain and labor." (Note that there are many other places in this section of Isaiah that suggest a spiritual restoration of Eden. Specifically Isaiah 51:3) The text ends with instruction on how to deal with "righteousness through the law or flesh." Cast it out. It cannot be mixed at all with a life of faith. Christ set us free so that we could stay free or live in freedom. We should learn to stand in that freedom or stay in it. We do this by refusing over and over to put back on the yoke of slavery, the law. This, by the way, is an expansion of a small statement Paul gives at the beginning of the book: Christ sets us free from this "standing evil domain" which here he connects to the law economy.

**Galatians 4.21** "Tell me, you who desire to be under the law, do you not listen to the law?" (Λέγετέ μοι, οἱ ὑπὸ νόμον θέλοντες εἶναι, τὸν νόμον οὐκ ἀκούετε;)

Paul shifts into a new paragraph but uses a repeat of the lexeme "thelo" from the previous paragraph, beginning here as he ended there which he often does. He addresses the Galatians directly and asks them to explain to him or simply tell him if they "listen" to the law. He either suggests here that they do not listen to the law well or that they do not understand it when they do listen. The latter seems to be more likely. One question in this text relates to Paul's reference to the law. Does he mean the law written within the Pentateuch or the Pentateuch itself? It might be suggested that, since he immediately refers to a text in Genesis he must refer to the Pentateuch. A couple of observations suggest otherwise. 1) He seems to use this story as being about "the law" and not "from the law." So, this reference teaches about life under the law but it's not the law itself. 2) In a parallel text, he quotes from Isaiah. Here he seems to be continuing his description of life under the law versus life in faith. He even in this text makes clear he sees a "spiritual" application and he is reading the entire thing as an analogy or allegory of law versus faith. In the next paragraph, beginning in 5.2 he returns to a familiar refrain specifically referring to circumcision as a microcosm of the kind of issue he is challenging, any attempt by the false teachers to require obedience to a law to gain acceptance with

God. This contextual clue, along with the other elements above, suggests he is speaking in this verse about the law within the Pentateuch and not the Pentateuch itself. (Though a play on familiar terminology could be happening too. "You want to be under the law but do you even listen to the "Law?")

The first clause could be simply "tell me" or it could be "explain to me." With the likely contrast of "you do not understand" the law following immediately, "explain" may make more sense within this context. Even if we use a broader term like "tell" the idea of "explain to me" is implied and that understanding is within the possible range of meanings for the term *lego* used here.

Who does Paul expect to make an explanation? "Those who want to be under the law." This terminology repeats regularly throughout Galatians. Here Paul returns to a familiar concept, introduced in 2.18, that one's "wanting" or desiring ultimately indicates one's dependence. Previously Paul says that some "want" to be made righteous by Christ making "faith in Christ" and wanting to be justified by Christ synonymous. Here he does the same with "wanting to under the law."

Lastly, as hinted at previously, what does he mean by "listen" to the law? It could mean simply *to hear* but it most likely means more than that, *to understand*. "Explain something to me," Paul says, "Do you not understand what the law does? What it requires? How it works?"

**Galatians 4.22** "For it is written that Abraham had two sons, one by a slave woman and one by a free woman." (Λέγέγραπται γὰρ ὅτι Ἀβραὰμ δύο υἱοὺς ἔσχεν, ἕνα ἐκ τῆς παιδίσκης καὶ ἕνα ἐκ τῆς ἐλευθέρας.)

This verse begins stanza A of the paragraph about an event in Scripture. He will give another reference from Scripture in verse 27 which begins the second half of this paragraph. This does not appear to be a direct quote. He simply says that Abraham had two sons, one by a slave girl whom we know as Hagar and Ishmael and one by a free woman which we know as Sarah and Isaac. This story appears to be connected to the material in Galatians 3 at some level when Paul explains based on other texts from Abraham's life the nature of the law and promise from a different perspective. That would mean that structurally this text may both end 3.1-ff and 1.1-ff while also potentially being a restart of the first section for the beginning of a new one. We will watch closely. [141]

**Galatians 4.23** "But the son of the slave was born according to the flesh, while the son of the free woman was born through promise." (ἀλλ' ὁ μὲν ἐκ τῆς παιδίσκης κατὰ σάρκα γεγέννηται, ὁ δὲ ἐκ τῆς ἐλευθέρας δι' ἐπαγγελίας. )

Paul continues describing the differences between these two children. The first, the son of the slave girl, was born according to the flesh. What we know from both the meaning of these words and the example they arise out of tells us a few things. This child -and the life that it defines- is just that, it is birth, creation, life, conception, forming, etc. The idea of birth establishes the concepts attached to the picture. Paul used the same picture above when he said he toiled with labor pains waiting for Christ to be formed in the lives of the Galatians making it clear that a life that looks like Christ is the promised outcome of this process, or within context, a life lived by Christ. This is an important point. The goal is not just to look like Christ. Christ must live the life. The picture of birth suggests this end. The picture of forming in the womb and being born suggests it's a process. The entire process is wrapped around the basic concept of life: life begins or is created and the life forms a being into an image. The being is the "outcome" of this creation and forming of life. So, the question implied in the analogy, which is how one must engage analogies (by trying to discover what picture it paints, asking it questions) is "where does this life come

---

[141] Maybe this is the introduction of "freedom from present evil reign" which here, in 5.1, he shows to be freedom from the law but also shows it to be freedom from the lusts of the flesh as he further develops into chapter 5. It may be: 1.1-5.6 is section 1 and 4.12-6.18 is section 2 with 4.12-5.6 serving as both the end of section 1 and the beginning of section 2, truly a "seam.' It may also somewhat be either 1) in a parallel position to 2:19-20 because they both quote from the intro at the beginning or 2) the actual peak of the book. If the latter is the case we might say the book is about "stop putting on the yoke; stand in your freedom" which would make sense.

from?" And the answer is given as "according to the flesh." This life (as pictured in the mechanistic approach to conceiving Ishmael) was created and formed by the flesh.

Remember what Paul has already suggested about the flesh: it is an energy that can be looked on to produce "spiritual maturity." So, it is more than the body and its desires and drives. It is the "self." In Galatians 1.16 it is the "the whole self" of a person that might be consulted with, heard from, engaged with including their words, thoughts, and knowledge. It is in contrast to "revelation" and the Spirit. It is "not god." It is the part of self that "does religious works as written in the law" in 2.17. So, a moral, thinking entity, but the same entity, in this text that can have faith or "want or seek" instead of "perform works." In Galatians 3.3 this entity can be looked upon as a source of "perfecting" or maturity and is contrasted to the Spirit. Again, here, in many ways, he is the person without God, or, all that the person is without God. In the immediately preceding text, Paul described his ailment as being "in the flesh" which may be a way to infer, even slightly, that this entity is the broken and cursed part of the self. In summary, the flesh, the *sarx*, is the thinking, believing, wanting, feeling and potentially moral self that is characterized by the brokenness of disease. It is not, in the thinking of Paul, just the body and what we might consider its natural desires: eat, drink, breathe, reproduce, experience pleasure, protection from pain and danger, etc. He thinks of the entire self, the entire human and all that the human does. In some ways, Paul's view of a human is similar to our modern view: a person who is defined by his physical self but a physical self that thinks, feels, believes, etc. He would add two elements to this though. One: the human being is broken and so all of its desiring, thinking, feeling, etc is also tainted and ultimately unable to produce "godlike-ness." Two: It is "not god" but can become dominated by God through intimacy and faith. Ultimately when we read *sarx* in Paul we should think: human or self. It is all that the human is physically and "spiritually" but without God.

So, the son of the slave girl represents a creation and forming of life that arises out of self or our "humanity," to put it simply. If we want to say it in more detail we might say "religious and moral life" that comes from our own thinking, wanting, believing, willing, etc. The analogy connects, of course, to the story of Ishmael who was conceived -not in "immoral actions"- but in an abandonment of dependence on God to fulfill his promise miraculously. Ishmael was "created and formed" by natural processes and from human ingenuity, thinking, scheming, etc. "The best of humans humaning."

**Galatians 4.24** "Now this may be interpreted allegorically: these women are two covenants. One is from Mount Sinai, bearing children for slavery; she is Hagar." (ἅτινά ἐστιν ἀλληγορούμενα· αὗται γάρ εἰσιν δύο διαθῆκαι, μία μὲν ἀπὸ ὄρους Σινᾶ εἰς δουλείαν γεννῶσα, ἥτις ἐστὶν Ἁγάρ.)

In case we missed it as readers, Paul clarifies that these two women and their sons represent the same two "covenants" or treaties or possible wills that Paul has been referring to: Law and Faith. He makes the connection from the Law (Sinai) to slavery (Hagar was a slave girl.) to specifically Hagar. "Hagar is the Law: She is Sinai. She bears children that are born as servants."

**Galatians 4.25** "Now Hagar is Mount Sinai in Arabia; she corresponds to the present Jerusalem, for she is in slavery with her children." (τὸ δὲ Ἁγὰρ Σινᾶ ὄρος ἐστὶν ἐν τῇ Ἀραβίᾳ· συστοιχεῖ δὲ τῇ νῦν Ἰερουσαλήμ, δουλεύει γὰρ μετὰ τῶν τέκνων αὐτῆς. )

Paul continues to give commentary on the analogy. He comments that Mount Sinai is in Arabia which could be for one of two reasons. 1) He may be connecting "life under the Law" to Israel's wandering in the desert, in Arabia. 2) He could also be connecting this text back to his own journey to Arabia. The former idea makes sense theologically but less so literarily. If this is Paul's impulse then the reasoning is clear. He wants the Galatians to see life under the law in as negative terms as possible. If the latter option fits better then Paul may want us to see this paradigm (law) in contrast to his own approach as described in Chapter

1. He did not go to "present Jerusalem" when he wanted to connect with God. He went to Arabia and operated out of revelation. If this is the intent Paul subtly connects here, via literary structure and parallelism, his experiences in Chapter 1 with what it means to "walk in the Spirit" or the faith paradigm. The law paradigm has strong connections to "present Jerusalem." The faith paradigm abandons Jerusalem and lives by faith, inheritance, the promise, and revelation.

Either way, Paul connects the Law to "present Jerusalem" and in in so doing continues his "anti-Jerusalem" message. As discussed above, this could be either 1) against legalistic teachers like the Pharisees, in or out of the quickly expanding church -under which Paul trained in the ways of Torah or 2) the Christian leaders of Jerusalem -mainly James but also Peter- who have fallen into legalism. As we have said multiple times though, the real answer might be both. He appears to make a connection between the false teaching he has addressed in 2:15-pres and the cohort from James in 2:10-14.

Paul's last comment relates to the condition of present Jerusalem: Jerusalem is still enslaved. A few thoughts on this comment: This may imply that Paul sees the "prophetic kingdom" in spiritual terms. He contrasts "present Jerusalem" or physical Jerusalem; i.e. "The Jerusalem that is here" with "spiritual Jerusalem." So the kingdom appears to be "spiritual Jerusalem." Note that the Jerusalem of Paul's time was not rescued from their submission to Rome. Paul appears to make this point and use it to condemn the teachings and authority of present Jerusalem as if to say "The Law way corresponds to the physical Jerusalem right here in my time. Both leave a person unaffected by the new king Jesus. Both are still slaves. Jesus wants to free us. This is a spiritual reality for those who live not by the physical but by the spiritual, the kingdom, faith, the promise."

**Galatians 4.26** "But the Jerusalem above is free, and she is our mother." (ἡ δὲ ἄνω Ἰερουσαλὴμ ἐλευθέρα ἐστίν, ἥτις ἐστὶν μήτηρ ἡμῶν·)

Paul continues with his contrast between present Jerusalem (which he connected to Hagar, Sinai, the Law and slavery) and "spiritual Jerusalem" or "Jerusalem above." "Above" in the biblical mind doesn't typically refer to something in the cosmos but an entity that is "in the sky" where the sky is anything that is above the land or anything that's in the atmosphere. The point is more that the entity is "spiritual" than its position in the cosmos. (This is the idea any time something is referred to as "above" of "heavenly.")

Paul says that this spiritual Jerusalem -the one corresponding to Sarah, Isaac, Promise, Spirit, etc- is free and that she is our mother. So, we too are free because we are born out of one who is free. The major idea is that we are free because we are spiritually out of the lineage of Sarah and Isaac and spiritual Jerusalem.

**Galatians 4.27** "For it is written,
> "Rejoice, O barren one who does not bear;
>> break forth and cry aloud, you who are not in labor!
> For the children of the desolate one will be more
>> than those of the one who has a husband.""

(γέγραπται γάρ·
  εὐφράνθητι, στεῖρα ἡ οὐ τίκτουσα,
    ῥῆξον καὶ βόησον, ἡ οὐκ ὠδίνουσα·
  ὅτι πολλὰ τὰ τέκνα τῆς ἐρήμου
    μᾶλλον ἢ τῆς ἐχούσης τὸν ἄνδρα.)

For the second time in this pericope, Paul quotes a text from the Tanak. This begins the second half of the subsection. Here Paul quoting from Isaiah 54.1 describes "Spiritual Jerusalem." Isaiah develops the same idea around "Zion" in Isaiah 48-54 (and even until Isaiah 66). In Isaiah, the author develops the idea of the "seed" starting in Isaiah 1. He shows that this seed, the same seed from Genesis 3:15, is the servant or arm of Yahweh, who takes on our sin and takes it away like a sacrificial lamb. (Isaiah 53) This servant, through resurrection, creates what Isaiah calls "comfort" in some places (Isaiah 40) and salvation often also. He characterizes this comfort with many different images: marriage between Yahweh and Israel, a renewal of Zion (Jerusalem) back to Eden, and a flourishing of Zion (which he compares to Sarah) as having "many children." This is the context of Isaiah 54.1.

Note that Paul uses the same root as he introduces this story (*odino*) when he says that he was experiencing "labor pain" while he waits in Christ to be formed in the lives of the readers. This sets the contextual horizon for this story and the corresponding material. The quote itself suggests a very positive experience for a person who "does not bear" and who does not experience labor pains. Instead of crying out in pain this woman cries out with singing and in pleasure. The imagery appears to connect to a return to before the curse, before "labor pains" are associate with child bearing. Paul is not talking about the events that led Sarah to give birth to Isaac. He is really talking about the events in our life that lead to Christ living our lives through us. (This also speaks to the progressive nature of sanctification.)

"The children of the desolate" - the translation "desolate," while possible, does not show the clear meaning of the text. The desolation connects more to her womb than to her generally. The term in Hebrew (and in Greek at times) refers to a land that no longer bears fruit or is lifeless. It also implies that the land has been abandoned. In the strategy of Isaiah, Zion, through judgment has become "desolate," has become barren Sarah. "Sarah" or restored Zion flourishes with many children. The point may be literally that the kingdom of God has a lot of people in it, maybe even that there are more "spiritual children of Abraham" than there are actual Jews. It may also refer to spiritual "flourishing" and fruitfulness.

"The children…will be more than those of the one who has a husband." - The term husband may refer to "a man" instead of a husband. Reading this as "husband" can make us misread the reference in this clause. This is Sarah but it connects to Sarah's life when her womb was barren and Abraham attached himself to Hagar instead of her. At this point, Hagar "had a man" and Sarah did not.

Overall this text has strong implications related to the miraculous nature of Isaac's birth and, by correlation, us. Our birth, our lives and our spiritual fruitfulness are a "miracle" and not natural.

**Galatians 4.28** "Now you, brothers, like Isaac, are children of promise." (ὑμεῖς δέ, ἀδελφοί, κατὰ Ἰσαὰκ ἐπαγγελίας τέκνα ἐστέ.)

We are Isaac and our birth and life is "miracle" because it arises not out of scheming and natural processes but as a result of promise, God's faithfulness, to do what he promised to do. (This verse begins the second half of part two of this paragraph.) This also connects this imagery to the promise described in Galatians 3 which is the Spirit.

**Galatians 4.29** "But just as at that time he who was born according to the flesh persecuted him who was born according to the Spirit, so also it is now." ("ἀλλ' ὥσπερ τότε ὁ κατὰ σάρκα γεννηθεὶς ἐδίωκεν τὸν κατὰ πνεῦμα, οὕτως καὶ νῦν." -Galatians 4.29 GNT-T)

Paul makes a subtle shift here. He now starts to ask us to take action based on the reality of our condition. Here, in the beginning of this shift, he reminds the readers that Ishmael "persecuted" Isaac and so those who are being created by "human processes" persecute those who are born out of the Spirit. For the first time in this reference, Paul overtly connects this material to being born or created out of the Spirit. So, born of promise and into freedom is also "according to the Spirit." The Spirit produces in this lane. The flesh, the law "Hagar," produces in the other. The term translated "persecute" in this text comes from a word that means "to laugh" in the Hebrew version of the text. Interestingly, the word shares a root with "Isaac." They are basically the same word. Ishmael "Isaacs" Isaac. The term can also mean "to fondle sexually." Ishmael either mocked Isaac or molested him. The Greek term behind "persecute" is a general idea of "pursue" or persecute. It contains the possibility of both terms but does not make a choice. It is an imperfect verb suggesting a repeated and continual action.

The question is who is Paul referring to? Is he referring to a theoretical concept? Maybe one's own internal voice and tendency toward the Law paradigm? Or is he referring to the false teachers who promote living by the law? Keep those questions in mind as we read the next text.

**Galatians 4.30** "But what does the Scripture say? "Cast out the slave woman and her son, for the son of the slave woman shall not inherit with the son of the free woman."" (ἀλλὰ τί λέγει ἡ γραφή; ἔκβαλε τὴν παιδίσκην καὶ τὸν υἱὸν αὐτῆς· οὐ γὰρ μὴ κληρονομήσει ὁ υἱὸς τῆς παιδίσκης μετὰ τοῦ υἱοῦ τῆς ἐλευθέρας)

We left the question raised in the previous verse unanswered. Who is Paul referring to? We will keep it unanswered for now, but instead we will focus on a new question. What does he say we should do with "Ishmael"? We should cast him out because he is stealing the inheritance that belongs to the heir just like Sarah requested Abraham to do. We should probably not get too technical with the inheritance issue. If there's any meaning to it it's that the inheritance is being taken away from the heir as long as Ishmael is tolerated, but the connection to the Spirit as the true blessing and inheritance we read of earlier in chapter 4 suggests a possible referent.

The Ishmael paradigm has to be completely removed. It cannot be tolerated at all. We can't just be nice to the Law paradigm. We must be relentless with it. To answer the question from the previous verse, this applies to all faces of the Law system, its impulses in us and those who teach or promote it. As we see in the next text, we cannot mix the two systems. They cannot exist together. That is ultimately Paul's message here.

**Galatians 4.31** "So, brothers, we are not children of the slave but of the free woman." (διό, ἀδελφοί, οὐκ ἐσμὲν παιδίσκης τέκνα ἀλλὰ τῆς ἐλευθέρας.)

Paul, in summary and clarifying fashion, connects all believers to the paradigm or system reflecting by Sarah and Isaac. He says this before he makes his final point in the next verse. (The first verse of chapter 5 is the final verse of this paragraph.)

**Galatians 5.1** "For freedom Christ has set us free; stand firm therefore, and do not submit again to a yoke of slavery." (Τῇ ἐλευθερίᾳ ἡμᾶς Χριστὸς ἠλευθέρωσεν· στήκετε οὖν καὶ μὴ πάλιν ζυγῷ δουλείας ἐνέχεσθε.)

As we suggested previously, 5.1 ends the paragraph. Structurally this verse parallels with 4.21, but beyond the structure there is not much connection lexically.

"For freedom Christ has set us free." - Those of us who are not children of Hagar, the slave woman, but who are children of the free woman Sarah, have been made free by Christ. The phrase "for freedom" modifies "made free" or "set free." It's a dative noun phrase. It can mean to freedom, in/into freedom, with freedom, by freedom, or for freedom -though the latter is not common for the dative. The point seems to be an emphasis on Christ granting of freedom. It reflects a Hebraic tendency to repeat a word to emphasize it. We might say it as "Christ set us free to make us really free, actually free." This concept is supported by the next phase. "Stand firm, therefore."

"Stand firm, therefore" - Paul says factually that Christ freed us to actually live in freedom so "Stand in it." Stand in the freedom or "establish yourself" in freedom. The point is to stand there or stay there without allowing yourself to be moved. Remember the semantic word group that Paul has used frequently in this letter related to "walking" or standing. In 2.13 the false teachers "toddle" in the gospel. That is, they stumble around and fall. Paul then uses the term "stoiecho" to describe the law, the ordered (structured) and *ordered* (directed, regulated, commanded) steps (stepping) required by the law. He also uses the idea of falling in Galatians 5.4 when he says the false teachers and their adherents have fallen down and away from grace. In the following verses, he will describe our call to walk (*peripateo*) and step (*stoiecho*) in the Spirit. All of this imagery relates to this semantic concept in verse 5.1. Instead of stepping in the law or toddling away from the gospel or falling away from grace, Paul says we should all "stand" or stay in it, in our freedom, in the "faith/promise" paradigm. This is an important connection to "grace" in Paul's argument. (via lexical connection to 2.20-21, *tithemi*) You were freed to be really free, Paul says, so stand firm, establish yourself, or simply stay free. Do not move.

"And do not submit again to a yoke of slavery." - The other option, the one the Galatians are guilty of falling back into is subject themselves or "become under the control of" to the yoke of slavery. The structural parallelism suggests what is probably obvious ether way, the yoke is the law. The verb is in the present tense so we could say "Stop going under the control of this yoke." It is something that the Galatians do over and over. If we missed the connection from the "yoke" to the Law, Paul makes it ever more clear when he describes it as a "slavery" yoke. The term "yoke" comes from "zugo"; it is very similar phonetically to the term "zume" for "leaven" that Paul will use below. The point is that the yoke and the leaven are probably the same idea in Paul's mind. It is the law.

Lastly, it appears that Paul makes a connection in this text back to his introductory sentence. He says in his introduction "Christ gave himself for our sins to deliver us from the present evil age." We could translate this text in a way that shows the connections to our present verse. "Christ gave himself... to give us freedom (different word but same meaning as "make free" in 5.1 and a very similar word phonetically) out of the standing (same word that's used in 5.1 "Stand) evil age (paradigm/economy)." These links suggest that Paul is now delivering on the promise implied in his introduction. He has already developed the idea that Christ gave himself for us (see Galatians 2:20-21). Here he connects the "giving" all the way through to "freedom" from the "standing" era. This means that here (explicit) and there (implicit) the deliverance and freedom is from "The Law" paradigm. Notably, he calls the law paradigm "The standing evil era" in Galatians 1.3.

# Galatians 5.2-6

**Interpretive Translation:**

Pay attention to me. I am Paul. You know me. This is my voice, my message to you. When you start circumcising yourselves and others[142] in order to obey the law, The Messiah no longer provides any positive impact on your spiritual fruitfulness. This is the statement that I repeat to every person I encounter. Any person practicing or teaching circumcision obligates himself to do every rule written in the law at all times. This shifts a person back into the system of "spiritual debt" because any system based on obeying rules puts a person in a position where they can never do enough to meet God's standard. This disconnects you from Christ's life -any of you who try to earn God's approval by obeying the rules of the law. You have removed yourself from God's unearned favor. Instead, we wait confidently for what we expect: the righteousness the Spirit does through us when we have faith because neither circumcision or uncircumcision accomplishes anything with Christ Jesus. Strength and power are not increased in any way in when you obey a rule of law. What does increase your strength when you are in Christ? Faith as it awakens love.

**Summary Commentary:**

Paul continues here the same message he has been speaking on since 2:15 (or 3.1). This text may introduce the next section of Paul's letter; the ethical section. (Though the biographical material a the end of chapter 4 describing his visit to the Galatians likely also provides the introduction to this material.) If this is the case, we might find it strange that he immediately revisits the same material of the previous section: trying to do the law does not help a person get righteous, but there are subtle differences in what Paul presents here. (Beyond that he wants to

---

[142] This is an attempt to bring out present tense. It is either stated "when you're in the state of circumcision" or it is more about the ongoing activity of the group. "Y'all are being circumcised." "When you reinstute the practice of circumcision"

continually return to the foundation of the faith system as opposed to the law system being the way God works.) Here his focus is not on "justification" per se but how the faith system "works." He begins by reminding his readers or possibly refocusing his readers on an important issue. The law system and the faith system are mutually exclusive; they are not compatible or mixable. One might expect Paul to shift back to "law" based thinking now that he has moved into the ethical portion of the text. Instead, Paul doubles down on faith. It may be important to remember that Paul has made this his emphasis for several verses now. This entire section is not about justification per se, though he has made sure his readers clearly understand how justification works and how it relates to experiencing the Spirit. This section focuses on "maturing" (contrast that to toddling in the gospel 2.12) through the Spirit (by faith) in the same way a person is justified by faith (and because a person has been justified by faith). Now, having laid the conceptual foundation for how and why the Spirit works in a person by faith, he moves on to the Spirit producing life in the believer. He uses terminology related to a tree producing fruit (5.4) and faith activating and awakening love (towards others) (5.6). He also suggests that law following systems do not have the "capability to activate" or give power to someone or something. With this terminology he makes a shift from language related to forensic justification to language related to how faith "activates" or works.

**Galatians 5.2** "Look: I, Paul, say to you that if you accept circumcision, Christ will be of no advantage to you." (Ἴδε ἐγὼ Παῦλος λέγω ὑμῖν ὅτι ἐὰν περιτέμνησθε, Χριστὸς ὑμᾶς οὐδὲν ὠφελήσει.)

Paul shifts here into a clearly delineated new section. As we read and see different transitions of the text we will work toward a text theory to establish how this text is put together and understand the author's strategy. Here, he returns to a specific example of "following the law." This is the first text since the description of his visit to the Jerusalem council where Paul's emphasis on circumcision specifically is an example issue for slipping back into the law paradigm. This also potentially indicates a strong parallel connection between 2.1-11 and this section. The "circumcision" language occurs six times in chapter 2 and six times here in this section. Beyond that it does not occur until the summary of the book. This clustering forms strong cohesion between the two texts. This may also be why Paul says at the beginning of the next section "You ran well" which is what he said about his own intent when he visited the Jerusalem council: to demonstrate that he had been (or performed well.) Also note Paul's reference to "freedom" in 2.4.

The reason Paul does this is most likely to reorient the reader to the situation textually that motivates his message. He says in essence "this is that and that is this." So what he is addressing here is the same issue that should have already been solved in Jerusalem. This message was "endorsed." From the perspective of 2.1-11 we might ask "What was Paul's message?" He makes clear that this was the answer. In other words, 2.15-the present text or further, was the gospel he presented in Jerusalem. This may be a way for Paul to show that his message included an ethical aspect "activated faith" as well as a conceptual "actual faith." Paul also uses the terminology "activated" or working to describe the grace he was given in 2.8. Later in this text Paul will say that faith connects us to grace and to the "production of Christ" (using the same "ergon" -working- root) and "activates" (energon) through love.

With that in mind as context, Paul, at the beginning of this new section, contrasts the Galatians with Titus (and his own theological implications) and shows the seriousness of them not believing the gospel or "staying in the faith paradigm and not returning to the law paradigm." If one returns to the law paradigm by, for example, participating in circumcision rituals then Christ does not "benefit" them. Paul uses the present tense form of "circumcision" here which may be surprising. We might expect aorist or perfect or pluperfect. He also uses the plural verb. He may use this form to suggest something different than "get circumcised." The Galatians are "getting circumcised" or "practicing circumcision." So Paul's warning comes to those who "practice the ritual of circumcision." We might translate this phrase: "If you keep practicing circumcision." In context, Paul clearly refers to this practice as a part of a religious rite. He will say a few verses later "whoever tries to become righteous with God by the law" showing his readers that the issue is not the actual circumcision event but one's attempt to be considered righteous in God's judgment because they are circumcised (or by doing any of the rules and commands written in the Torah.)

"Christ will be of no advantage to you" - When a person seeks God's approval by doing the law Christ provides no advantage. The phrase "provides no advantage" translates the term ōpheleō (ὠφελέω). Jesus used the term when he said, "What does it *profit* a man to gain the whole world and lose his own soul?" Matthew quotes Pilot describing his frustrating lack of progress in solving the Jesus problem, "When Pilate saw he that we was gaining nothing, but rather that a riot was beginning." Here, with this contrast, we see the term means something like "to move or progress toward a desired end." In contrast, the woman with the issue of blood has spent a lot of money on solutions to her health but did not *improve,* the negation of the same term. (Mark 5.25) Paul uses the term in a similar way. Circumcision never "benefits," advantages or helps. Good deeds done without love "do not benefit" the doer. An especially helpful use of the term with Paul occurs in 1 Corinthians 14.6, "Now, brothers, if I come to you speaking in tongues, how will I benefit you unless I bring you some revelation or knowledge or prophecy or teaching?" Paul contrasts something "in-actionable" with something "actionable" or doable. The idea here relates to providing a tangible and measurable benefit as opposed to simply a nice idea or even an emotional benefit. Bodily exercise gives a measure of *ōpheleō*. Inspired Scriptures give an advantage, progress or benefit (ōpheleō) in regards to "teaching, reproof, for correction and for training in righteousness." James uses the term to describe the importance of joining works to faith. Faith without works does not "provide real benefit." The word picture he uses relates the idea of one who simply wishes a hungry person well when they request food as opposed to actually feeding them. The former does not provide a real tangible benefit. The latter does. BDAG and Louw and Nida both suggest the term simply means "to provide assistance." There also seems to typically be an emphasis on the assistance typically being tangible in some way.

So, the term means something like "to provide a measurable increase in usable, tangible benefits or good to someone." In almost every context the emphasis on the outcome of the assistance being real or tangible in someway. To show the idea intended in this term we might restate this verse as "When you reinstate the practice of circumcision believing that it will make you more acceptable to God, Christ will not assist you in a meaningful and measurable way that shows up in real life." (See also commentary below where the parallelism between this term and "indebted" is explained.)

**Galatians 5.3** "I testify again to every man who accepts circumcision that he is obligated to keep the whole law." (μαρτύρομαι δὲ πάλιν παντὶ ἀνθρώπῳ περιτεμνομένῳ ὅτι ὀφειλέτης ἐστὶν ὅλον τὸν νόμον ποιῆσαι.)

Paul repeats a first person verb related to speaking, here "I testify" or give testimony. This is part B of the first subsection of this paragraph. First Paul says "I speak" and here "I testify." Every person that practices circumcision (notice the parallel to verse 2, A in this subsection) is a *opheiletes* (from the verb *opheilo*). The phonetical symmetry between *owe* here and "*benefit*" above is intentional. The person who practices circumcision experiences no real life benefits from Christ. Instead they are indebted (*opheiletes*) to do the whole law. The choice to be justified before God by any one part of the law means a person has to do the whole law. This shows that Paul's example of circumcision is just that, an example. Any law based pursuit of acceptance with God leaves one short.

Paul has been clear throughout his argument that all parts of the law are still "the law" and must be abandoned if a person desires to be justified by Christ. The issue here, Paul suggests, is not that abandoning "faith" impacts one's justification. That is not the issue. The issue is that abandoning one's faith (and moving back into law) shuts off Christ's assistance from us, making us ineffective. We do not experience the tangible impact of his work in us and through us. (One could say this text -and the following verses- are Paul's James 2: "faith without works is dead" passage.) Instead of having a tangible benefit from Christ's assistance the law keeper has debt. For Paul, law is the entire law and all of its parts, or to say it another way, it is the system of law that must be abandoned. By using financial terminology he connects the law to "economic" thinking. The law is a type of economic arrangement between God and man. This arrangement leaves a person in debt. Faith is a completely different economic arrangement. The follower of Christ starts with faith but also lives in faith in Christ.

Plato uses the same play on words when he quotes Socrates that some say a just person "owes a debt (*opheiletes*) of harm to enemies but benefit (*opheles*) to friends." (Republic 335e) This could imply that this saying was a common statement in these communities during these days. Paul could be taking this common statement and reallocating it to the gospel. A person under the law still has a debt (and he is God's enemy.) A person in Christ is Christ's friend and experiences his bill of "benefit."

The main point of this sentence is that if a person attempts to be seen by God as righteous by doing any part of the law -including circumcision- then he will remain a debtor to do the whole law. Paul will use a different analogy to teach the same concept in 5.8 when he says "A little leaven leavens the whole lump." Any requirement to obey any part of the law spoils the purity of the faith system.

"I am stating it again. Every person who practices the rite of circumcision believing it gains God's approval goes back into debt. If you try to do the law to gain God's approval you have do it all perfectly all the time or you remain short of the required payment."

**Galatians 5.4** "You are severed from Christ, you who would be justified by the law; you have fallen away from grace." (κατηργήθητε ἀπὸ Χριστοῦ, οἵτινες ἐν νόμῳ δικαιοῦσθε, τῆς χάριτος ἐξεπέσατε.)

This text forms the center of the paragraph and operates as the peak semantic concept. When a person seeks to be justified by the law they are disconnected from Christ and remove themselves from grace. The phrasing "you who would be justified by the law" or more literally "whoever justifies himself by the law" clarifies the real issue at hand. The issue is not the act of circumcision specifically but the pursuit of justification by doing the law. The verb is either meant to be read as middle "justify themselves" or passive "are justified." The context of "doing the law" suggests a middle idea here. It may be helpful to remember here that Paul connects "being justified by the law" to any type of human moral performance in the preceding verses. Also it is important to know that this is a present tense verb suggesting an on-going state of "self-justification."

Paul then characterizes those who justify themselves through doing the law in two ways. 1) They are severed from Christ and 2) They have fallen away from grace. These are strong and potentially difficult phrases describing a person who looks to obeying the law as a way to be seen as righteous before God.

"You are severed from Christ." - The term "severed" comes from the Greek word *katargeo* (καταργέω). According to BDAG, it means to cause a person -in this case- to 1) become unproductive, 2) lose their power or effectiveness, 3) come to an end or 4) to cause the release of someone from an obligation. The verb here is passive so those who do the law are the recipients of this action. With these possible meanings in mind, we might say that the law doer is caused to lose their effectiveness from Christ. That would be a rigid connection between the meanings in the Lexicon and the wording here in Galatians. Paul uses the term to describe what happens to a wife when her husband dies. (Romans 7) She is disconnected from the law of marriage or, i.e. no longer under his authority (good or bad). While we typically see this example in a negative light if the relationship with the husband was good -think protection and provision in this context- then a wife would not want to be removed from his authority. In Romans 7 Paul says that a person, through Christ's death, becomes free from the authority of her husband (analogy for the law) because the law says death removes the obligation. Here Paul says that a person is disconnected from Christ (in a similar way) when they go back to the law. Other uses include reference to agriculture. It is the opposite of what the tree does to the ground. (What happens when it is cut down.)

The simple picture almost always represents a removal of a thing (or person) from a source of power (good or bad) or life. The power could be for sustenance, provision, fruitfulness, authority etc. The word at times focuses on the event causing the state and sometimes on the state itself (and the ramifications).[143] We might state it as "When you justify yourself by the law you remove yourself from the fruit-producing life Christ offers you."

"You have fallen away from grace" - In parallel to the statement Paul makes about the law followers above, "You remove yourself from the life of Christ," Paul states, "You have fallen away from grace." The phrase "to fall away" translates the verb *ekpipto* (ἐκπίπτω). E*kpipto* literally means to fall away as translated. It can also mean "to drift off course" as in a ship that drifts off course on a journey. The term "fall" can imply passive action in English that is less emphasized in Greek. It is often a volitional action in Greek so that it can be translated in some contexts "to throw oneself." It can also mean "to die" or be removed from life. This kind of idea seems to fit the context of its parallel statement: to be removed from the life of Christ. The picture is of a person falling or jumping out of the sphere of grace. In the simplest of terms the idea is disconnection from grace at the choice of the law follower.

To understand Paul's meaning it is more important to see what grace is in this sentence than to understand what it means to fall away or, to put it another way, it was what one falls from that is essential. Above the person is disconnected from fruit producing life in Christ. Here they are

---

[143] There may be a play on words here too. A person who practices circumcision is obligated to do the whole law. A person who justifies himself by law is released from the obligations toward Christ. This is a possible gloss of the word. In context it probably means more "to be disconnected from the life producing force in Christ" but this play on words may still be implied. In the mind of Paul and his readers these concepts were more closely tied together (power/authority/energy/life/obligation).

disconnected from grace. Grace means generously providing good to someone as a free gift; to treat with favor as a favorite, i.e free favor. It can be the pleasure given and attractive quality given off by art or the beauty of another person or it can be a literal physical benefit or gift. In this context, it most likely refers to Christ freely giving us his own beauty and life and "benefits."

The point Paul makes relates to the Galatians need to continue in faith even as those who are already justified. When a person stops living by faith and returns to live according to the law -seeks to justify themselves by obeying the rules in the law- they are uprooting themselves from Christ's life and grace. As they drift into law they drift away from grace. The main idea is that a person cannot live in grace or by grace while also living by the law. Grace is an all or nothing proposition.

One possible translation of this verse might be, "Those who justify themselves by following the law leave grace behind" or "abandon grace."

Before moving onto the next verse notice that Paul places grace and Christ in the same position in the text. Christ's life and work in us is so closely linked to grace that the two, Christ and grace, can be seen as the same type of thing so that we might read the latter phrase as "the grace of Christ."

Also see the connection back to 1.4 where the Galatians "deserted" the one who called them to grace. Finally, don't miss that the context is not salvation, but growth. This text is focused on faith activating into action not faith receiving salvation. This same tree/life/fruit-beating imagery will be used in a couple of paragraphs to describe the fruit of the Spirit worked in and through the life of the believer as they "walk in the Spirit."

**Galatians 5.5** "For through the Spirit, by faith, we ourselves eagerly wait for the hope of righteousness." (ἡμεῖς γὰρ πνεύματι ἐκ πίστεως ἐλπίδα δικαιοσύνης ἀπεκδεχόμεθα.)

In verse 5 Paul writes the first of two "for" (*gar*) statements. Together these two statements conclude this paragraph. They are parallel to verses 2-3 where circumcision as a term is used in a similar way. In this verse, Paul elaborates on how a person experiences "the actual benefit" of Christ's presence in their life. In contrast to those who seek to make themselves righteous by doing the law, Paul describes his way is not about doing; it's about waiting. In the context of "grace" language Paul may intentionally paint a picture of a person waiting for a gift or waiting for a "benefit" or power and life. The contrast to "doing" the law is clear. Just like in chapter 3 when Paul contrasts having faith with "doing," here Paul contrasts doing with "waiting." So, for the Galatians, as they look to see their faith "provide a real benefit" to themselves and others (ie. make a difference) what action should they take? They should wait.

Notice a couple of things about this waiting. First, it is a way to describe faith or "what faith does." Faith waits. We see this because it conceptually fills the same position as faith in the previous and following texts. Second, the term has an emphatic meaning: to wait intensely and expectantly; to wait with anticipation. The term in this context suggests a confidence during the waiting as opposed to "wait and see" it is more "we will certainly see soon so we wait." The term also occurs in the present tense form meaning that Paul's says "they continually wait" for righteousness. The point does not appear to be that they have to keep waiting but that this is the constant practice of faith. What does faith look like? It waits on the actions of another. It waits on the grace, the gift, the power, the strength, etc. And, as Paul writes in the next sentence, it waits on the activation of love generally and specifically for others.

What is he waiting for? He waits for a hope of righteousness. (Paul uses the same language in Romans 8:23, 25 - waiting on what is hoped for) Righteousness is in contrast to those who make themselves appear righteous by doing the law. Instead of "righteousness" in law, Paul is righteous "by waiting." He waits for expected righteousness. The term "hope" means just that: it means a positive experience that has not yet occurred but is desired and, in some contexts, expected. So Paul says that we should wait with anticipation for the righteousness we desire and expect. Because the object (accusative) is the "hope" and not specifically the "righteousness" Paul could either intend for us to understand that we are waiting for "the internal compulsion and desire" for righteousness to grow in us or that we are waiting for the righteousness that we desire and expect.[144] In context and grammatically this idea makes sense, that instead of justifying ourselves, we wait for "the inner compulsion towards righteousness" to grow in our hearts. This idea comes from the root concept behind the term "hope." It has a range of meanings from "to desire/wish" on one end to "expect with certainty" on the other. One might argue that Paul used this term to suggest we wait for a movement across that exact semantic range. We wait for the desire of righteousness and then, as the desire grows, it changes into an expectation of confidence. The term is in parallel to "through love" in the following verse where Paul describes how faith begins to activate into productive and beneficial service. It starts, in that verse, with love. So, here, Paul may infer, by the parallelism, that we experience first the heart change of a "desire" for righteousness before we experience actual "righteousness." The coupling of hope with "wait with expectation" may suggest that we should read this as "wait expectantly for the expected -promised- righteousness." Either way, Paul suggests that we wait on the Spirit to execute the entire process from desire to expectation to activation.

The two phrases "by the Spirit" and "out of faith" most likely modify "the hope of righteousness" so that this hope and the righteousness that follows comes from the Spirit and as a result of faith. This helps his readers understand two aspects of this righteousness as compared to that of the law doers. 1) It is "out of faith" which he has described as being a result of waiting eagerly 2) The Spirit does this righteousness.

---

[144] It may be that the parallelism of this text with chapters 1-2 makes this the "sanctification" portion of the same text as Galatians 2:15-ff.

Structurally this sentence seems to be the most out of place, but it is also the most clear point of the text. Doing the law is bad in every way. It disconnects us from Christ's "tangible positive impact," his life and his grace Instead, we should wait on what we expect from him: the desire for righteousness and righteousness itself.

**Galatians 5.6** "For in Christ Jesus neither circumcision nor uncircumcision counts for anything, but only faith working through love." (ἐν γὰρ Χριστῷ Ἰησοῦ οὔτε περιτομή τι ἰσχύει οὔτε ἀκροβυστία ἀλλὰ πίστις δι' ἀγάπης ἐνεργουμένη.)

Paul concludes this section with the second "for" statement and returns to his original challenge: practicing circumcision disconnects a person from Christ's tangible benefits. In the previous verse he discusses the work of the Spirit "in the Spirit." Here, he uses a similar construction "in Christ." This helps us as readers to connect being in Christ with the work and action done by the Spirit of Christ. The Spirit works in us freely because we are in Christ. When a person is in Christ the Spirit works in them freely. To be in Christ is a true fact about a believer but one that must be responded to with regular faith to experience the benefits of the position. Above it says, "by the Spirit because of faith." The parallel nature of the two verses suggests we understand the idea as "In Christ and by the Spirit and because of faith."

He returns to the concepts of verse two when he says that circumcision nor uncircumcision "counts for anything." Do not miss that he now connects circumcision to uncircumcision. This helps the readers know that it is not the act of circumcision specifically that is the problem but the "confidence for justification" one has in the act. Confidence in any part of the law or any moral act or set of acts is the problem *even when that act* is "uncircumcision." No paradigm but Christ. The term "counts" means "to be strong or powerful enough to do a thing." The issue then is one of "experiencing strength." Rules and regulations making or following (including moral rules and religious rituals) do not give the person the capability or strength to do anything where anything implies "righteousness." The term can also mean "make healthy" which has clear connections to "return one's vigor, strength, or capabilities." Also see the parallel to "benefits" in verse 2. The two terms are similar and are in a parallel position. So the capabilities are to "make a tangible impact." The imagery Paul uses here displays what "moral effort" cannot do: give a person the capability or strength for anything good. But, faith -which he has defined above as "waiting for desire of righteousness" does "give one strength." He has already described this process in the previous verse: Waiting on the Spirit to give one the desire for righteousness until that person has the expectation and experience of that righteousness by the Spirit. Now he further elaborates on this process. Faith gives one the capability "to do righteousness" by "working through love." Let's look at that phrase more closely.

"Faith working through love" - As we stated above the verb "gives strength to do" is implied in this text. Also we have already seen how faith "works" in the previous verse. It waits on the inner compulsion of righteous to be brought into the inner man by the Spirit. It waits on this strength. What does Paul add here to this process? What insight? He says that faith gives strength as it urges (from *energon* "to work, activate, urge.) through love. Faith -as it waits in hope and on hope- eventually allows for love to be turned on. Paul redescribes the impulse he called hope (*elpis*) above as love here. Faith moves from waiting to acting as love turns on. Love, in other words, is the impulse (strength, vigor) for righteousness when that righteousness arises from faith, by the Spirit, and "in Christ." *Energon* is also the same word Paul uses in Galatians 3.3 where he says God "supplies the Spirit and *works supernaturally"* in you. Here the Spirit through faith (waiting) gives the strength to act as it urges through love. *Energon* is semantically similar to "to give strength to do" above. It is also "to give the capability to do" or energy to do and often even the next step of that idea. In other words, not only is the concept of "giving the capability to potentially do," it is the actual impulse into action. It's kinetic. We might say "produces."

To bring this out in the text we might say: "for those in Christ practicing circumcision does not give you the strength to do anything meaningful, neither does confidence in uncircumcision. Faith does give you that capability, and that capability grows into action as it is strengthened by love." In other words, whereas law doing cannot even give a person the capability to do good, faith not only gives the capability, it produces an actual outcome and it does so though creating love. Love in this context is affection for a person so that you desire their good so much that you take action to provide it. Agape always assumes a level of emotional affection and pleasure in and towards someone. Here it also moves into service. (Galatians 5.13 "through love serve one another" and "Love your neighbor as yourself.") Faith, by waiting on the Spirit to give the compulsion and strength to do good, gives rise to "producing love" or it produces by causing a person to love.

# Galatians 5.7-12

## Interpretive Translation

You were growing in the gospel like a runner slowly building speed. Who tripped you up? Who made you stop believing in the truth? These beliefs did not come from me,[145] the one who initially invited you into the hope of the gospel. Just as a little bit of leaven leavens the whole lump of dough, a little bit of law-based religion makes your whole relationship with God based on your performance and obedience.[146] Ultimately, I believe[147] that you will not conclude that any other message is the truth other than the message I taught you at the beginning because you are one with Christ and the Spirit is inside of you teaching you the truth.[148] Those who keep confusing you, they don't help you carry your burdens.[149] But, they will carry the penalty of their actions as they try to carry the weight of the law. Ultimately, it will crush them. [OR: Those who keep confusing you will ultimately be crushed themselves by the weight of the law they try to make you carry.] Whoever these people are. Dear family, if I myself am still teaching everyone that they had to be circumcised, why is the circumcision party attacking me? The cross means you could never earn God's acceptance through doing the rules of the law or any kind of performance or obedience. If I did teach that circumcision was required, then the cross would lose the power to halt law-based thinking in its tracks. People could go on thinking they can be good enough to earn God's approval by following the rules. I want those who

---

[145] This text has the same ambiguity as Galatians 1.4. Is it God or Paul who is the caller? In 1.4 both make sense but we decided the text leaned slightly toward God.

[146] This is not a direct translation; Paul's words are ambiguous and open to interpretation.

[147] This could also be "I trust in the Lord regarding you."

[148] Another very interpretive paraphrase but it shows what might otherwise be missed. That Paul connects previous ideas about being in Christ into this phrase here too.

[149] Making the connection to 6.1

cause you to walk away of the freedom of the gospel to not stop at getting circumcised. I wish someone would cut off their testicles too.

**Summary Commentary:**

This text is structured so that it complements the previous section, 5.1-6. That section began with "Stand in your freedom." This section ends with "Those who make you stop standing in..." (ESV "unsettle"). Following Paul's tendency to use "stepping" and walking language throughout the book Paul begins by acknowledging the previous state of the Galatians before they encountered the false teachers. They were running well. The term for run also means in some contexts "to make process." Most likely that meaning is intended here. The Galatians were growing but then someone stopped them; someone halted their progress. (ESV "hindered") The growth and progress they experienced were measured by "truth," a reference most likely to the gospel. They continued, in other words, believing the gospel and understood this truth more and more. Paul, in verse 7, asks "who put a stop to your progress?" using the Greek root "kopto." When he ends this paragraph he will declare a wish that these perpetrators will be "castrated" using the same root revealing the tone of his message and the passion behind his admonition.

Using language from the beginning of the letter he asks how the Galatians could abandon him, the one who originally invited them to believe the gospel.[150] Somewhat out of nowhere he adds a comment about the beliefs they were shifting into: a little leaven leavens he whole lump of dough. Knowing that his reference in this text echoes the strong admonition he made in Galatians 1.6-10, that a person who preaches another gospel should be condemned or "anathema," we can understand why he added this note. Even a little legalistic error ruins the gospel. He follows up this strong rebuke with an affirmation: he still believes in the Galatians. What does he believe? Paul is confident that they will not consider or regard as truth "another" gospel. Again

---

[150] See commentary on Galatians 1.6

Paul uses the same wording here as he did in Galatians 1.6-10. ("another" here and "another gospel" in Galatians 1.) What gave Paul this confidence? The Galatians unity with Christ. As we remember how Paul described what it means to be "in Christ" we will start to understand Paul's confidence. When God makes a person one with Christ, God himself, through the Spirit, begins to live parental intimacy deeply within that person. He also begins to pour out his power and supernatural work. His love becomes our love and he changes our desires into righteous desires. We no longer need teachers. The "Anointing" teaches us. Those who do hinder the Galatians' progress, the ones who who keep confusing them (ESV "trouble), will bear the penalty. Paul most likely makes a connection to the language he used in Galatians 5.1-2, the yoke of the law. Those who bear the yoke of the law will also bear *its* penalty. Paul then contrasts them with himself and his message. They bear the penalty. He bears a "proclamation." Paul explains that his message is not circumcision or these "false teachers" would not attack him. He may, here, be clarifying that he does not teach the same message as the legalists he rebukes. When a person teaches that obedience to the law is a requirement for justification they impact the implications of the cross. The cross operates so that it "shuts down" or stops any law based thinking. It says a person can never be good enough. The teaching of circumcision (and all other law based approaches to justification) disconnects (same word used here for "removed" that Paul used in 5.4 for "severed" in the ESV) people from the power of the cross to shut down law based thinking. How serious is Paul about this addition? He would like for those who are being circumcised to also be castrated. The term in verse 12 "unsettled" can also mean "stir up to rebellion." It shares a root with "stand" in 5.1. Paul, by ending this section (5.1-12) with the same root with which he began, basically says "stand in freedom" (to begin the text) and then ends with a strong rebuke of those who cause the Galatians to stop "standing" in that freedom.

**Galatians 5.7** "You were running well. Who hindered you from obeying the truth?" (Ἐτρέχετε καλῶς· τίς ὑμᾶς ἐνέκοψεν [τῇ] ἀληθείᾳ μὴ πείθεσθαι;)

Paul continues a familiar pattern of the book of Galatians using language related to walking and running to express the nature of he spiritual life. He most likely intends for his readers to make that connection and to also see the concept of this word as "make progress" -one of the possible meanings of the Greek term *trexo*. He has stated in the previous sections the need to "stand" in freedom. Here he acknowledges that the Galatians were previously "growing" in this position. Now, someone has stopped that progress. Paul suggests he does not know who these people are asking the question, "Who is hindering your progress?" Paul had used almost the exact same language to describe the purpose of his visit to the Jerusalem council in Gal 2.1-14. He presented his teaching to those who "think" and discern (same root he will use in 5.9) that he did not "run" or "progress" or in this case probably "give effort" in vain. What is this significance of this connection? Here Paul challenges those who "halt" their progress, their efforts to grow in the truth, this "good" effort. (i.e. not in vain, but valuable.) By making this connection Paul may be intentionally casting this information in the light of his previous presentation. He ran well, gave effort that was not in vain. They had done the same. Someone stopped them. The connection between the two texts suggest that this was the cohort from James. Paul casts the rebuke he makes here as the same or similar event as Galatians 2.1-14. The event of Galatians 2.1-14 is the occasion of this material.

The term *egkopto*, translated here as hinder, took on this concept as a part of its meaning when it began to be used as part of a military strategy where one side would create ditches in the ground ("strike into") making traps for their opponents, pausing their progress or preventing their retreat. The picture here serves to describe the action of the cohort from James. Their false teaching led to holes in the ground, as it were, on the path of the Galatians as they ran closer and closer to the truth. That's the picture Paul paints.

What did they prevent the Galatians from doing? The ESV says "obeying the truth" and that is a possible translation of the term *peitho* in this text. The term can also mean "trust or rely upon" and most likely means that in this context where Paul has repeatedly used terminology and concepts that refer specifically to "faith." If there is a nuance in the meaning of this term as compared to "pistuo" (the term he typically uses for faith), it has to do with "being convinced or persuaded" so that Paul may infer the work of outside forces to influence the beliefs of the Galatians. This outside influence leads them to rely on false ideas and not the truth.

One characteristic we see multiple times in this paragraph is connections to Galatians 1.1-2.14 and especially 1.5-10. Considering this connection, Paul probably has in mind "the truth of the gospel" from 2.5, "We did not yield in submission even for a moment so that the truth of the gospel might be preserved for you." We will see in a parallel text in 5.10 that Paul makes an allusion to 1.6 when he refers to "another gospel" using the same terminology.

Paul shifts in this text away from the advantages and disadvantages of circumcision (or law-based religion) and towards a strong rebuke of those who teach that idea. The Galatians were "growing' in the truth until the James cohort (most likely) showed up and confused them. The issue was "believing the truth," i.e. the truth of the gospel.

**Galatians 5.8** "This persuasion is not from him who calls you." (ἡ πεισμονὴ οὐκ ἐκ τοῦ καλοῦντος ὑμᾶς.)

The term translated "persuasion" in the ESV shares a root with "obeying" in the previous verse. As we saw there, the best way to understand the term there was "rely" or have confidence, maybe "believe." Paul says here that this "belief system" that the Galatians had been persuaded to accept did not come from him. He refers to himself as "the one who called you" the same way he referred to himself in Galatians 1.6. The point seems to be that the Galatians are abandoning the faith and gospel they learned from Paul.

**Galatians 5.9** "A little leaven leavens the whole lump." (μικρὰ ζύμη ὅλον τὸ φύραμα ζυμοῖ. )

This text raises an immediate question to the reader. How does it fit? It feels like it appears a little out of no where. Two textual connections may help us uncover why Paul included it. First the term "leaven" is the Greek for *zume*. The word *zugo* occurs in 5.1. In the ESV it is translated as "yoke" which is its typical meaning. Paul could be simply tying the two texts together to make sure we as readers know we are still talking about "standing in freedom" from the yoke (*zugo*) This would make sense when we see the other parallelisms between 5.1-2 and this paragraph. This would define the "yoke" as the legalistic message of those who "hinder" the Galatians, i.e. the law. This also helps us understand a certain dynamic of "law based thinking." Any little element a person might add to grace, any requirement, any restriction changes the nature of the entire thing. A second connection can be seen structurally where Paul has made and will make several connections between this paragraph and Galatians 1.6-11. Paul appears to have in mind those he referred to in this earlier paragraph. They are those who preach another gospel and those who should be anathema. Paul is making very strong statements against these false teachers, both here and in that first reference. This sentence could be a defense of such harsh criticism.


**Galatians 5.10** "I have confidence in the Lord that you will take no other view, and the one who is troubling you will bear the penalty, whoever he is." (ἐγὼ πέποιθα εἰς ὑμᾶς ἐν κυρίῳ ὅτι οὐδὲν ἄλλο φρονήσετε· ὁ δὲ ταράσσων ὑμᾶς βαστάσει τὸ κρίμα, ὅστις ἐὰν ᾖ.)

Paul uses the root *peitho* in this sentence for the third time bringing cohesion to the four verses of the text. Here he has the "belief" and it is "in you in the Lord." For the first time in this letter he shifts his tone regarding the Galatians. He is confident that they will come to a different conclusion than what it appears they have been leaning toward. His persuasion and trust was toward the Galatians and in Christ. This means that the beneficiary of his faith was the Galatians but the object of his faith was the Lord. The word emphasizes the Galatians as the recipients of the outcome of Paul's faith but may confuse the English reader. Paul had faith in the Lord regarding the Galatians.

"that you will take no other view" - Paul's faith was in the Lord and towards the Galatians; what did he expect the Lord to do? He expected the Lord to protect their thinking, to work among them so that they ultimately "take no other view." A more literal translation of the wording might be, "that nothing other you would think." The word *phroneo* which the ESV translates "take a view" means to think, to think about a matter, to think in a certain way (for example "like Christ" in Philippians 2), or to come to a conclusion through the thinking. Paul identifiers that the Galatians are wrestling with the truth. Eventually they will settle on a conclusion. They will "come to think" in a certain way.

Paul says the they will come to "no other" conclusion. This phrasing is repeated from Galatians 1.6-10 where Paul says "I am astonished that you have believed another gospel so soon." So, when he says that they will ultimately not come to think another is true he means "another gospel." In a way, he is recapitulating as he moves into the last major section of the epistle. He further affirms that his focus here is the same as when he began the letter: those who teach a false gospel, those who are to be anathema. "I myself trust in the Lord even for you that ultimately you will not come to believe another, false version of the gospel."

"and the one who is troubling you will bear the penalty, whoever he is." - This verse may be parallel to Galatians 5. "Who is he who hindering your progress?" Both use synonyms related to a person negatively affecting the spiritual growth of the Galatians. Both also describe a question regarding the identity of this perpetrator. In the previous clause Paul uses another second person plural verb the same as "You were running well." Regardless, Paul adds further light to these opponents. He had stated that they were stopping the progress of the Galatians. Here he states that they continually "trouble" them. The term means "to shake up or stir up." It may here imply either emotional manipulation (see commentary on Galatians 1.6ff) or creating a state of confusion. In context with the "thinking" language that may fit best. "Those who are trying to confuse you."

This person (or group of people both singular and plural uses occur) will bear the penalty (from *krima* -judgment). The inference is that he will either bear the penalty of the message he teaches or the anathema from Galatians 1.10. No one can actually do the law so to place oneself under the law leaves only one possible outcome, judgment. That could be Paul's point here. He could also have in mind his earlier point in Galatians 1.10 where he says that the person who preaches another gospel must be anathema.

This verb "to bear" occurs again in a parallel text structurally, Galatians 6.1-2 where Paul says "bear one another's burdens." When we arrive at that parallel we will see Paul intends to compare those who see righteousness by doing the law with those who walk in the spirit. Those who teach law bear the judgment (of the law) those who walk in the Spirit bear one another's burdens.

Paul ends this sentence by acknowledging again his inquisition regarding the identity of these false teachers. This either suggests that Paul genuinely does not know the identity of the false teachers, or it is a rhetorical device where Paul plays dumb. If the latter is the case then Paul wants to draw us into these questions with him and make us wrestle with their identities. The many textual links take us back to Galatians 2.1-14 to give us our answer. If this is the case the reader can understand why Paul may want to be coy in his approach. "If someone happens to teach this they are anathema and I want them to be castrated… but I don't know who they are." This could also possibly be a reference to "doesn't matter who they are." This would echo the statement in Galatians 1 "whether anyone even an angel of heaven preaches another gospel."

**Galatians 5.11** "But if I, brothers, still preach circumcision, why am I still being persecuted? In that case the offense of the cross has been removed." (Ἐγὼ δέ, ἀδελφοί, εἰ περιτομὴν ἔτι κηρύσσω, τί ἔτι διώκομαι; ἄρα κατήργηται τὸ σκάνδαλον τοῦ σταυροῦ. )

The first question we need to answer about this sentence is how does it fit? What is Paul's argument and how does this relate? Paul will make a clear transition in verse 13 (Galatians 5.13) where he begins to form the ethical process for the gospel he preaches. In Galatians 5.7-10, he forms a somewhat clear unit. He also seems to add an inclusio wrapping up verse seven in verse 12 by using the same root "*kopto*." (See commentary on verse 7 and 12.) This verse in some ways seems to be out of place. One possibility is that Paul is ending this subsection 5.1-12. One justification of this thesis is the fact that Paul returns to commentary on circumcision as he had discussed in Galatians 2:1-5 and uses the same terminology of "severing" both here and in verse 4. If this is the case, then at least structurally Paul is "summarizing" his conclusions all in one major unit. These parallels help us understand Paul's point in both parts.

Paul states a simple question: Why is he persecuted (he implies by the legalists in Galatia) if he preaches circumcision? He obviously implies too that by preaching circumcision he means to teach people the need to obey the commandment to be circumcised in the law as a part of one's attempt to gain God's approval and acceptance by the works of the law. One subtle characteristic of this sentence that may have meaning is the use of the term "kerisso" for preach immediately after using "krima" for judgment in the previous verse. The words have a close proximity and phonetic viscosity. If this is the case Paul may want us to read his work as one who "does not preach circumcision" in contrast to those who do and will bear their judgment. This may be a simple way for us to make sure we correctly identify those who "trouble" the Galatians in the previous verse.

"I wish whose who unsettle you would emasculate themselves." - Paul ends this section with a strong statement describing just how much disdain he has for these false teachers. As noted above he has made apparent effort to connect these statements back to his original target from chapter 1. In some ways, this could be the crescendo of that argument. They are to be anathema, yes, but they are also to "emasculate themselves." Structurally, this sentence has been simply attached to the previous paragraph as an exclamation. This makes sense as it ends the previous section. The ESV translated the participle "ophelon" as I wish; it may be more literally said "would that." Either way it implies that this is Paul's desire and it is stated in a unique way to show emphasis on the emotions behind the desire. This type of phrasing is used to show that Paul is exaggerating but that the emotional frustration behind his words is accurate.

What exactly does Paul wish these false teachers would do? The translation "emasculate" glosses the word *apokopto*. We have discussed the idea above that this term shares a root, *kopto*, with the word translated "hindered" above. Similar to the previous verse this connection helps us understand who Paul refers to. They *engkopto* the Galatians; Paul wants these *engkoptoers* to be *apokoptoed*. The term means "to cut off, to cut from or to cut in two." It may simply refer to Paul's desire for them to be separated from the Galatians. In support of this understanding we see the connection back to Paul's statements at the end of chapter 4 regarding the children of "flesh." They are to be driven out of the camp. According to BDAG the term can also refer to castration. Its more immediate context connects the meaning to circumcision so that Paul may be saying "You focus on cutting off the foreskin of the penis so much that I want you to go ahead and have your testicles removed." While both meanings are possible, the meaning Paul intended could be either. The closer proximity of the circumcision context may suggest that is the best choice. The emotionally charged nature of the phrasing may also suggest this possibility.

Lastly, who are these that "unsettle" you. Before we look at the word meaning review the other ways Paul describe them. They hindered the Galatians (or halted their progress.) They are troubling, stirring up and confusing the Galatians. They are connected to the ones in Galatians 1 who teach another gospel and probably to those in Galatians 2 who tried to spy out Paul's freedom. They may even be the circumcision party from James and in some ways Peter himself. This term includes the root "*histimi*" to stand connecting it back to 5.1 "Stand (root: *histimi*) in the freedom." With this in mind in someways the semantic idea behind the term (context) suggest something like "to cause to stand against the freedom." The term here, *anastatow*, means to upset the stability of a group and in many cases is used to described (similar to the other terms in this paragraph) to cause a revolt. Paul seems to be suggesting that the movement of the Galatians is more volatile than simply "slipping" away from the freedom (and Paul's gospel). They are in rebellion against him and by extension Jesus himself.

# Galatians 5.13-15

**Interpretive Translation:**

You were invited into freedom, my dearest family, the kind of freedom that does not operate out of the natural, biologically driven self. This freedom activates love and this love drives you to endlessly serve each other like slaves because you love each other. The entire law is really about one idea: love those in your Christian community like you love yourself. Contrast this to your current state and you begin to see that as you bite and chew on each other you are devouring each other. Stop it! Don't treat each other that way.

**Summary Commentary**:

As Paul makes his transition into a new section, what we might call the "Walk in the Spirit" section he sets it up by closing the previous section using a reference back to "stay free" in 5.1 and then projecting forward to the content of his next message. Ultimately that message is that our new law, the law of Christ, is to love each other and that is done in the power of the Spirit. One of the most important contributions of this text comes from its connection back to Galatians 5:5-7 which begins to describe the mechanism for "action" in the Spirit-led life. Faith works through love. That text further describes the process as "we wait with anticipation for the desire of righteousness that comes though the Holy Spirit out of faith."

**Galatians 5.13** "For you were called to freedom, brothers. Only do not use your freedom as an opportunity for the flesh, but through love serve one another." (Ὑμεῖς γὰρ ἐπ' ἐλευθερίᾳ ἐκλήθητε, ἀδελφοί· μόνον μὴ τὴν ἐλευθερίαν εἰς ἀφορμὴν τῇ σαρκί, ἀλλὰ διὰ τῆς ἀγάπης δουλεύετε ἀλλήλοις.)

As we continue to work towards a text theory this text seems to be a part of a larger seam that ends the previous section and begins the next. In its ending capacity it reaches back to 5.1 that states the goal "Stay free." Here, Paul describes the freedom itself. Looking back at 5.1 we are reminding this is the purpose of Christ's redemption. He made us free to experience freedom. Freedom was not just the process; it defines our expected, present experience. Why did Christ redeem us? So that we could and would experience freedom. Freedom from what? The next several texts makes clear we are free from the law generally and circumcision specifically. This text will show that we are free to love as the Spirit is free to work in us. Real freedom is both freedom from the law and freedom "of authority" or "of being a son," lord over the oikos, to rule. (And this includes ruling over the regulations of the law so that they obey us instead of us obeying them.)

Most English translations add a verb to the second sentence so that it becomes "Use your freedom." This is a way to smooth out the English translation. More likely, though, Paul is describing "this freedom" in more detail. Literally it would be something like, "You were called into freedom, only the kind of freedom that is not an opening or starting point for the flesh."[151] Flesh, as it has meant previously, means the whole of the natural and physical man, all the faculties, talents and abilities that are given at bitth and developed through training and experience.[152] The term translated *opening* comes from the world of the military where it means "a base of operations" or a starting point. Paul paints a picture of what we might call a "backdoor" for the flesh. Freedom, the freedom that we are called to and should stand in might be seen as a "backdoor" for the "natural way" of living a godly life. Paul's accusers may have used this argument against his teaching. Paul clarifies that this kind of freedom is not a backdoor, a starting point, an

---

[151] Another aspect to this text that makes it parallel with 3.1 and thereby possibly function in a similar way as the beginning of the section major section affirming or at least suggesting what other elements also suggest. This could also mean we as readers should read "only I want" here as it is in 3.1 so that it is "Only I do not want the freedom as an opening for the flesh."

[152] This may be a helpful way to think about "the flesh and the world" - the flesh is the faculties given through birth. The world is other people's faculties given at birth. These latter faculties affect the facilities of the individual.

anchor-hold for the natural faculties and abilities to take over the process. In a few verses he will describe just how contrary the natural system is to the Spirit system. In this paragraph he hints at a reality: to be free from a thing means to be enslaved to another. The believer is free from the law and religion based on the natural system -doing, working, effort, performance. He is enslaved to love in as much as he is now captivated by the presence of the Spirit of the Son who is love.

The last clause continues to describe "this kind of freedom." Instead of being "the freedom as a backdoor for natural systems" those who live in this freedom "serve each other" or are enslaved to each other through love. (Notice the contrast between freedom and slavery.) Remember he has described this system of freedom and Spirit as "as faith activates it activates through love" and described that process as one that the Spirit works in us and that we should wait on. Now he stair-steps from that idea to describe further that in this freedom, (that is, in this experience of the Spirit,) a person grows in their love for others. The freedom that attaches us to the Spirit and the Spirit to us builds a fire of love in our being for others. Now: Faith/Grace - Freedom - Spirit - Love - Service/Slavery of Others. Before: Works - Slavery - Law - Flesh - Serving Self by Serving God. When you look at the way the previous paragraph ends the meaning becomes more clear. In essence Paul says, don't let your freedom turn into another opportunity for fleshly, human legalistic religion.

The term "love" may be an imperative verb (command) or an indicative verb (stating a fact). So it is either "You must love each other" or "You love each other continually." Most likely we should read it with the English translations as a command. A possible translation of this verse might be: "You were invited into freedom dear family, the kind of freedom that does not operate out of the natural, biologically driven self. This freedom activates love and this love drives you to endlessly serve each other like slaves." So, summarily, we can either be free from supernatural love and serve the law as slaves or we can be free from the law and serve others out of a supernatural love worked in us by the Spirit.

**Galatians 5.14** "For the whole law is fulfilled in one word: "You shall love your neighbor as yourself."" (ὁ γὰρ πᾶς νόμος ἐν ἑνὶ λόγῳ πεπλήρωται, ἐν τῷ· ἀγαπήσεις τὸν πλησίον σου ὡς σεαυτόν.)

Paul makes a turn here. He has repeatedly described the law in negative turns. Here, he starts to show the relationship of the law to the believer who does not seek to do it or be justified by doing it. This person ironically fulfills the heart of the law better than the person who tries to do the law. Pause and get that: the person who tries to do the law fails to do it. The person who does not try to do the law fulfills it. What a powerful argument against trying to do the law! Also, see that Paul is not and has not once suggested that one's behavior does not matter. He has stated -and here clearly- that godly behavior does not result from trying be godly. It results from the freedom concept he described at the end of Galatians 3 and the beginning of Galatians 4. Christ made us free. In our freedom as sons the Spirit of the Son flows into us, makes us relationally intimate with God, works supernaturally through us (Gal 3.3) maturing us spiritually, gives us the desire of righteous and here, again as in 5.6, stirs up love in us, or, it may be better said, loves through us. Just as 4.7 describes, he acts out the thoughts, actions, desires, compassion, etc of the Son in our hearts. There, to the Father. Here, towards others. Paul will echo this sentiment in the bracketing text, Galatians 6.2, "Bear each other's burdens and so fulfill the law of Christ."

Much has been written and taught regarding the command "You will love your neighbor as yourself." Little can be added here. The one insight that may be helpful comes from the modifier "as yourself" though I am by no means the first to say it. It is our natural love for self that sets the standard of how we should love others. Even in our most unhealthy states, we love ourselves. We, as it says in the previous verse, spontaneously serve ourselves. Paul (or Moses or God) uses the known to explain the less known. To love oneself is to pursue one's own happiness or more actively to do things that I believe will make me happy in the short or long term. Paul says to do things that will make other people happy in the same way that we try to make ourselves happy.

A question that arises in this verse comes from the term "neighbor." Is Paul specifically saying love those in our community? And if so, our Christian community? Or does he suggest here the command to love everyone? Contextually, the emphasis seems to be on the Christian community. First, the very next verse speaks to the Galatians' apparent issue related to harming each other which we will look at below. Additionally, as we saw above, when Paul develops the idea further he speaks to the community: "When one of you...," "Bear each other's burdens," etc. While Jesus expanded the command of this verse to include God's work in us to "love our enemies," Paul here emphasizes a more specific outcome of what he will call in the next verse "walking in the Spirit." Here he says the Spirit bears the fruit of love in us, yes, and specifically we should expect that love to be directed towards those in our local Christian community.

**Galatians 5.15** "But if you bite and devour one another, watch out that you are not consumed by one another." (εἰ δὲ ἀλλήλους δάκνετε καὶ κατεσθίετε, βλέπετε μὴ ὑπ' ἀλλήλων ἀναλωθῆτε.)

As we just discussed above, Paul here begins to give more nuance to the idea of "loving each other." He gives three actions that describe the opposite of love, actions that we might assume the Galatians are participating in. More specifically, he describes two actions, "biting and consuming" that they appear to be guilty of and one action that will result from the first two. The three actions he describes come from the world of eating. They are all also present tense verbs denoting continual action: "If you continually..." While each of these words can describe actions beyond the context of eating, the use of three semantically similar verbs suggests a concept sealed to that particular imagery. In the context of strong legalism saturating the culture of this community, Paul says "When you take bites out of each other and keep gnawing on each other, you end up devouring each other." The point seems to be two-fold: 1) the repeated hard that they are doing to each other is reciprocally damaging and 2) the result will be the non-existence of the entire community. In other words, they may think they are damaging a part of the group when they attack that part in some way, but they are actually doing damage to the whole. Eventually, this damage will destroy the entire community.

Here, these bites and gnawings are left a little ambiguous. The terms themselves may suggest some sort of "fraud" but that does not appear to fit the context very well. The terms in verse 26 may give us a hint. "Let us not become conceited, provoking one another, envying one another." Also, Paul makes several lists similar to the one who makes in 5.19-21. This list has an usually large reference to ideas related to causing division. This idea makes sense since Paul is essentially saying "don't do things that cause divisions" here even with the word picture. As readers, though, we will continue to hold those ideas in ambiguity as we wait for the author to define them more clearly.

# Galatians 5.16-26[153]

**Interpretive Translation:**

So, what do you need to do? You need to live life as if you were walking around in a conversation with the Spirit. This is how you will grow into the image of Christ.[154] Don't try to follow God through the strength of human drives, impulses, systems and instincts. The natural human way of obeying God works against the Spirit's way and the Spirit's way works against the human way. They are diametrically opposed to each other, polar opposites, not compatible. Pursuing godliness through human faculties will always leave you disappointed.[155] On the other hand, if you walk around in a conversation with the Spirit[156] listening to him as he directs your steps, you will discover that "rule following" and "trying your best" no longer have anything to do with your spiritual life. You don't obey God that way anymore. When you try to live a Christian life through self-discipline or willpower you might be surprised at what "moral deeds"

---

[153] As I approach this text some thoughts from previous material. 1) the inheritance is the Holy Spirit. 2) future is optative and subjunctive present time not just future time. "the do not wish to inherit the kingdom of God" or "they might not inherit the kingdom of God" or "They do not inherit the kingdom of God in this case." It could also get its aspect from the previous participle which is present tense. Future relates to intent. Even in English, there is no real future only intent as seen in the auxiliary word formation from "will" (wish/want). "I intend to" Future signifies intent (wish/desire) 3) the language of walking comes up frequently: the circumcision party "toddles and stumbles" in the gospel. Paul refers to law (those that are written into the universe) as the "ordered steps." Here he says "walk in the Spirit" which he parallels to "being ordered by the Spirit" which he parallels to "living by the Spirit" and "following the ordered steps of the Spirit." These different but similar ideas form a thread in the text that allows us as the readers to sense the semantic concepts he is speaking about.

[154] This sentence is not in the Greek text, but it's implied when compared to the parallel texts in chapters 4.1-7 and 3.1-5. (In addition to the other "walk in the Spirit" texts throughout this paragraph.)

[155] Lit: "so that you do not do the things you desire." "Desire" being a syn for "ἐπιθυμία" desire, lust, drive, etc. i.e. if you live by the desires/passion/drives of the natural man you will not actually get what you desire/are passionate for.

[156] Using this to show the clear parallel to 5.16.

appear in your life. You will find yourself living in the sexual immorality that the law itself repudiates. Not only that, but you will eventually reach a level of sexual perversion that even disgusts *everyone*, even the pagans. You will even find yourselves participating in idol worship by having sex with pagan temple prostitutes as you try to procure the favor of the gods through erotic idolatry. It gets worse. If this promiscuity isn't bad enough, you will start creating divisions between one Christian and another. You won't even be nice to each other! You will debate subtle, legalistic nuances of moral restrictions. You will resent the freedom other people have because they believe in a radical level of grace. This of course will lead you to angry, judgmental finger-wagging and a "we are better than you" attitude. You will divide up into groups based on your "rules," "convictions" and "doctrinal purity" even though none of this come from the Bible. At best, they come from unessential and debatable Scriptural subtleties. At worst, they come from ideas invented by religious zealots obsessed with trying to impress God with their upstanding morality. They think their actions can make them more or less holy before an infinitely holy God and then, as a result, more pure than those who have such loose, anything-goes standards. What's next? These holier-than-thou legalists will eventually find themselves in the grip of a repulsive evil they would've never imagined. Like the Israelites when they tried to follow God's commandments, they may even end up in a drunken orgy with the priests and priestesses of foreign deities.[157] (Yeah, trying to follow the law didn't work out for them either!) What they thought led to a life pleasing to God turned into quicksand beneath their feet leaving them captured in worse wickedness than they ever imagined possible. The natural, legalistic way of following God always leaves us struggling against an un-defeatable foe. The harder we struggle the deeper we go into the darkness. As I've been trying to tell you, godliness doesn't work that way. When a person tries to practice godliness this way, they are rejecting the inheritance God promised—the leading, direction, intervention and reign of his Spirit.

---

[157] Notice that I have strongly emphasized the context of the immediate text and the entire epistle to bring out the emphasis that these negative qualities are all related to legalistic moralism.

Compare that to the supernatural fruit the Spirit produces when we trust *him* to make us godly. His life will flow into and out of us producing an intrinsic affection for God and others that moves us to sacrifice whatever comforts necessary to help our friends (and even our enemies) find true happiness. We will also be filled with this happiness ourselves, a complete happiness that is not impacted by mood or circumstances. God's own sense of calm and confidence will begin to be reflected in our emotions stilling all worry, stress and anxiety. If God is in control of every moment, mechanism and molecule in the universe and he loves us perfectly, what do we have to worry about anyway? The Spirit will also give us his viewpoint on *time*. He is never in a hurry. He is never late. He is always on time.

When we trust him, the Spirit gives us so much love, happiness, peace and patience that we can't help but be generous; selfless; consistent; authentic; stable, not moody, fickle, capricious or affected by impulses or personality quirks. He causes us to be humble, empathetic, kind and gentle in every way—word choice, tone, facial expressions.[158] No set of rules could ever produce[159] *this kind of life.*[160] Of course, those who are one with Christ (and by being one with him, share in his life) have died to the human way of becoming like Christ. When we were crucified with Christ we became dead to the interests, faculties and instincts of our natural self.[161] We died to our own source of spiritual life so that we can live out of the provision of Christ's life. If you live through the Spirit of Christ, walking around in an intimate conversation with him, you will find yourself going where the Spirit leads without even trying.

---

[158] You may notice that this list includes more descriptions than English translations. This is to bring out the nuances included in each single concept.

[159] or "is according to" this kind of life.

[160] See commentary below. This potential translation fits the context better that "no law is against these things."

[161] There is a clear parallel to Galatians 2:19-20, "Though the law we died to the law and live by God. I am crucified with Christ, but I still live. Only now, I no longer live my life. I find life by trusting in another person to live it for me. Christ lives my life." This is also in parallel to 6.15 "I am crucified to this universe, i.e. age" where Paul brings to a climax the thesis he suggested in 1.4: Christ delivers us from the standing evil ruling system, i.e. the law.

You won't need to try and follow rules written in a book.[162] Instead, you will walk beside the Spirit of Christ, hand in hand, and go where he goes.

This way of life, the Spirit way, has no similarities to the legalistic mindset of the false, world-based gospels some people in the church are following. Their air of superiority creates an epidemic of resentment as they call out others for their sinful practices. Why do they think they have the right to single others out? They possess the kind of baseless, spiritual arrogance that always emerges out of a pharisaical, moral performance mindset.[163]

**Summary Commentary:**

Paul, building off the platform of the previous paragraphs, namely his guidance that the Spirit goes to work in us as we wait on him to produce the "hope for righteousness" and love for others, moves into a description of the ethical system that arises from a life led by and empowered by the Spirit. This life contrasts the life "of the law." The life of the law, which he here also calls a life of the flesh as he did in Galatians 3.1-4, produces the opposite effect as compared to what one intends, a life that is significantly contrary to the law and destructive to the community. The person who lives by the Spirit experiences the Spirit's production or produce. A life characterized by kindness and service to others generally. He gives a list of the characterizations of the fruit of the Spirit to clarify the details of what it means to "love each other" as he stated in the previous section.

Not only does Paul clarify what it means to love each other in this text, but he also clarifies where this life arises. The Spirit produces this life in the person who walks in the Spirit, is led by the Spirit, wants to

---

[162] The term "stoicheo" suggests that the outcome of walking with the Spirit is intended to contrast the rule-following system of the law code. See commentary below.

[163] Lit. "Those who are led by the Spirit will not be conceited, calling people out and thereby creating divisions."

receive the Spirit, lives from the Spirit and walks in the same path of the Spirit, i.e. goes where He leads.

**Galatians 5.16** "But I say, walk by the Spirit, and you will not gratify the desires of the flesh." (Λέγω δέ, πνεύματι περιπατεῖτε καὶ ἐπιθυμίαν σαρκὸς οὐ μὴ τελέσητε.)

Paul builds off the previous concept from the preceding paragraphs. In either 4.12 or 5.13, Paul shifts into what we might call a study of the "ethical" mechanism of the gospel. (4.12-5.12 may be a text that transitions from orthodoxy to orthopraxy; it may serve as the "part 2" of the text of the peak transition between what preceded and what follows; it may also simply be "what do you do when you believe the gospel: you still don't do the law -characterized by circumcision- you, instead, walk in the Spirit -which he characterizes in many ways. The theme of this section might be how does one get Christ to "do you any good" or have any effect.)

Paul uses many markers to suggest a new section here. Many have been discussed in the previous sections. Here is a quick re-summarization: 1) he uses "Now I say" which is a somewhat elevated speech pattern suggesting a likely transition. 2) he uses "walk in the Spirit" here and then repeats a similar phrase in both 5.18 and 5.25. 3) In 5.26 he repeats a similar set of guidelines as he stated in 5.15 -different lexemes but parallel semantically and grammatically. 4) "The works of the flesh" text and the "fruit of the Spirit" text stand in a parallel position creating cohesion between 19-23 at least. 5) Verse 24 may be parallel to 5.16b-17 via the lexeme "sarx". 6) Verses 5.26-6.2 have many lexical parallels. All of this suggests that Galatians 5.15 (or 16) through Galatians 5.25 is a section of text.

The main idea in this section comes from the parallelisms around the terms walk, lead, inherit (see below), live, and step. This text is about "The outcome the Spirit produces when a person walks in the Spirit." We might also add "And the outcome the natural man produces when a person lives in that system." Paul expands on the likely thesis of

5.1-5.12: We wait expectantly on the desire of righteousness from the Spirit through faith; only faith, once it is activated, produces anything good and it does so through love.

Notice Paul uses walking, running, stepping and standing language often throughout Galatians. His purpose in going to the Jerusalem council was to make sure he did not "run" meaninglessly. His rebuke to the cohort from James and Peter too was that they stumbled like a toddler in their faith in the gospel. In Galatians 4 Paul calls the law the "basic steps" of the universe. In 5.17 he says the Galatians had previously been running well. He speaks to "standing firm" in their freedom in 5.1. In 5.4 the Galatians are falling, not standing in it, out of grace. Here, in 5.16-25, he uses the same cluster of language: walk, be led, and step. This cluster helps us sense Paul's mental picture and determine the overall context of the book. How do we refrain from stumbling in the gospel and, instead run well by standing firm in our freedom and his grace and walk in the Spirit? The picture he paints relates to walking.

The term "walk" is a present tense imperative verb from the Greek word *peripateo* (περιπατέω). As a present tense verb, it means to live like this or practice it all the time. The term itself can simply mean to walk but often includes the nuance "to walk around with" or to stroll. Some lexicons refer to strolling through a marketplace or also show that the term was used to describe how one might learn from a philosopher, listening to him while they walked around together. It is also similar to the Hebrew term (and form) used when the Bible says Adam and Even heard the sound of God "walking around in the garden" and then later used to describe Noah and Enoch as those who "walked around" with God. The term can also simply mean "to go" or to live. So here it means either to walk around with, stroll around with the Spirit or to live "by," in the power of the Spirit.

Paul, in 5.25, suggests he means both when he says "Those who live by the Spirit, should step with the Spirit." He appears to connect both ideas -living through the power of the Spirit and walking around with the Spirit- into one overarching concept. In the concept of the book,

Paul has described our relationship with the Spirit as the intimacy of a father and a son and even, by implication, the marital relationship (in the reflection on Abraham and Sarah having Isaac). The Spirit has been sent into our hearts speaking out passionately. So, when we read here that we should walk around with the Spirit we potentially should see a connection between the Spirit speaking inside of us, as he stated previously, and this activity. A Greek reader most likely would have had the philosopher and cohort concept in mind when they read this text. The Jewish reader may have had the rabbi and disciple structure in mind.

Paul might also intend us to read 1.11-17 in a similar light, as a sort of real-life example. As opposed to going to Jerusalem to learn from the Apostles and in contrast to how he learned rabbinical Judaism, Paul learned the gospel through revelation from Jesus as he walked around in the desert. Then, eventually, he went to Jerusalem as the result of a revelation. As we said in the commentary on this text his use of the same term, translated revelation in both cases, to describe his experience suggests that he might be referring to the Spirit of Jesus speaking to him. He was "walking in the Spirit."

By using the present tense Paul says that a person must continually walk around with the Spirit and in his power. This construction also suggested a conditional state for the next statement where he basically says "while you are walking with the spirit you will not gratify the flesh." The verb translated in the ESV is a future tense verb. The future tense should not typically be thought of as suggesting an action in future time but suggesting a potential or desired action instead of a certain one. Most grammarians suggest that it is to be translated as subjunctive or optative based on context. Here literally that might be: I direct you to continually walk around with the Spirit. While you do this you have the potential or desire to not complete the desires of the flesh. (We will look at some of the other concepts in this verse below and suggest further nuance to our understanding.) The term "and" in this context most likely means "then" so Paul describes a result of obeying this command. The time of the verb is more likely gained from the main verb in this conditional statement than from the future tense. The action of the "gratification" is either a potential action or a desired action instead of a factual action. (Factual action being something that has happened or is happening versus may or may not happen depending on the practice of the condition.)

The term translated "gratify" in the ESV and "fulfill" in other translations comes from the root *teleō* (τελέω). It typically means *to cause something to happen for some result, to obey as a means of fulfilling the purpose of a rule or standard, or to bring an activity to a successful finish.* We may put these options simply as to fulfill, obey or finish. This is the same root Paul uses in Galatians 3.3 where he describes the opposite of a believer's "beginning" in the Spirit: "Do you become **mature** through human faculties." There the meaning appears to be related to what we typically refer to as sanctification or growing into maturity as believers. This fits that context as it stands in contrast to the James cohort that stumbled like an immature toddler in the gospel. While Paul uses a slightly different form in that text this semantic concept most likely should influence our thinking here too. The object of this verb is *epithumia*, "desires" or "lusts" of the flesh. So, with that in mind, it probably means something like "fulfill" but with a nuance related to completing or growing/advancing in doing them. In other words, it most likely does not simply mean "to do" or "to obey."

The term flesh means more than "sinful" as we often think, or "sinful desires." Paul describes the flesh more along the lines of the body including the organs that think, feel, learn, choose, desire, etc. In Ephesians 2 he describes the flesh as the body and the mind. In many texts, as in Galatians 3:1-4, the flesh is the operating aspect of the human as they "try to mature spiritually" or that which "does the law." In Romans, he uses it in parallel to *anthropos*, or humanity. In many ways, Paul's conception of the flesh reflects a very similar understanding of the individual as what we might consider in modernity; it is very empirical and naturalistic. The flesh is the body, its organs and their processes. This includes the brain with its multitude of systems like the thinking system, language system, limbic system, etc. We are not suggesting that this is a supernatural understanding of the physical brain that would have otherwise been unavailable to Paul, though this is not conceptually impossible. We are suggesting a theologically and exegetically derived concept for the human condition that more closely resembles a modern understanding than what we might intuitively expect.

The object that we referred to above, translated desires in the ESV, means basically "strong desire or want." As the "desires" and wants of the human body and brain, we might think of concepts like "drives and impulses" and even "instincts." In some cases it is used to describe one who is thirsty, desiring or wanting water. Psychologists often describe the human as a "biochemical reward motivation system." In overly simplistic terms, the body rewards us for behaviors that should be repeated with chemicals that make us feel good. So our wants, desires, drives, etc operate out of this system. Some even suggest that every thought we have or decision we make, even though we may perceive it as being "rational," actually comes from these deep impulses. By combining concepts of physical desires (like hunger, thirst, survival, sleep, comfort, and sexual release) with desires we might consider more "psychological," Paul describes the human condition similarly. The most important takeaway from this broader understanding of the flesh and its "drives" is that this concept describes more than raw animistic urges. It describes our thinking, our choosing, our will or intent to do, etc. When a person seeks to obey a command of Scripture, the *flesh* has been activated and is being activated. In many ways, the flesh and its wants simply refer to me, and all that I am, apart from the Spirit, all that I was born with and all that I have learned from others: me, my will, my ability to think and decipher, my ability to operate out of discipline and responsibility. The opposite of that is the gift of the Spirit, the Spirit having been given into our inner man with his thoughts, emotions, desires and power.

We might translate this sentence more interpretively as, "This is what I am trying to tell you: when you walk around in a conversation with the Spirit and live out of the strength he gives you then you are less likely to find yourself increasing and expanding in behaviors that grow out of the instincts, impulses and thought patterns that comes from your sin-infected bodies, brains, and biochemical systems."

While this verse has a matching bracket in verse 25 providing an end for this section, it also has a likely parallel in verse 18 where it says, "If you are led by the Spirit, you are not under the law." (There are four parallel statements in this paragraph giving the unit a clear structure: 1) walk in the Spirit and do not mature by the flesh; 2) be led by the Spirit; you are not under the law; 3) those who practice such things [works of the flesh] may not be experiencing the inheritance of the kingdom; 4) If you live by the Spirit, you will step in the footprints of the Spirit.) We will look at the verse in more detail below. Here Paul implies that to be maturing and advancing in the instincts of the flesh or natural human systems is the same as or similar to trying to live by a law system. We typically think of living in the flesh as living under the influence of the base desires of our bodies. Paul defines living in the flesh as the same condition as trying to live by the law. He may also intend a similar meaning for the parallel phrase "those who practice these things will not inherit the kingdom of God." We will show how that is the case below and also wrestle with these potentially confusing words. Note here that Paul may intend for us to understand "advancing in the desires of the flesh" (5.16) as a parallel idea with a similar meaning to "the committed and ritual practice of these things" (5.21) which are the works that come out of the flesh system. With all this in mind, Paul describes this life that is not "out of Christ" as being under the law and therefore a pursuit of spiritual growth and advancement through human systems and skills and one that leads to the habitual practice of disdained actions. This also helps us understand what Paul meant by "fulfill the desires of the flesh." He refers to a person growing in their practice of these instincts and drives. As we will see, practice relates to the kind of participation a person might display in a religion or witchcraft. It implies a commitment and a ritualistic regularly repeated set of actions and habits. This coordinates with what we have already seen about the term flesh. It is a system (like the law) not much different than the law system. Or we could say that the flesh's approach to moral behavior and improvement (exactly what is denoted by Paul here) is a kind of religious system and that this system is synonymous in many ways with the law system of rabbinical Judaism.

**Galatians 5.17** "For the desires of the flesh are against the Spirit, and the desires of the Spirit are against the flesh, for these are opposed to each other, to keep you from doing the things you want to do." ( ἡ γὰρ σὰρξ ἐπιθυμεῖ κατὰ τοῦ πνεύματος, τὸ δὲ πνεῦμα κατὰ τῆς σαρκός, ταῦτα γὰρ ἀλλήλοις ἀντίκειται, ἵνα μὴ ἃ ἐὰν θέλητε ταῦτα ποιῆτε. )

Paul continues explaining the concept he introduced in the previous verse. This verse explains why a person who walks in the Spirit does not advance in practicing the instincts of the flesh and why someone who practices within the system of human nature and ability does not advance in the supernatural outworking of the Spirit. As we have already seen in the previous verse Paul is casting these two entities as two different systems: Spirit and Flesh/Law. He says that both of these systems have "desires" or drives, instincts, etc, but that they are contrary to each other. Specifically, he says that they are *opposed* to each other. The word translated opposed can mean those who are set against each other or in opposition to each other, literally "to stand against." The idea is that they are binary opposites, not compatible. One set of concepts is allergic to the other set of concepts. They are diametrically opposed, mutually exclusive. The two systems cannot coexist. You cannot take a little from one system and a little from another. In many ways, he is stating the same concept he stated at the end of chapter 4 when he said "children of the free woman (Spirit) cannot coexist with children of the slave woman (law/flesh)." New wine cannot be put into old wineskins.

The ramification of this conflict is that a person does the things they do not want. Paul probably suggests here that those who want to do the law (or live by their natural faculties, skills and disciplines) end up doing the opposite. In the list he gives below, he specifically includes terminology that suggests specifically that the flesh produces actions that are contrary to the law amongst other problematic behaviors. The term "to want" is a synonym of "desire" so that Paul connects "wants of the flesh" with "things you want." This then describes the condition not of the non-believer per se or of all believers either. It describes the life of the believer who lives by the strength, faculties and abilities of the natural man.

**Galatians 5.18** "But if you are led by the Spirit, you are not under the law. " ( εἰ δὲ πνεύματι ἄγεσθε, οὐκ ἐστὲ ὑπὸ νόμον.)

Paul contrasts the condition he just described. If you are under law (and living based on the flesh) you will do the things you ironically do not want to do. If you are led by the Spirit conversely, you are not under a law system and therefore not bound to this same expectation: doing things you do not want. Paul suggests that to be under law necessarily means to be under this cursed situation. Paul uses the terminology "under law" to describe those who seek to be justified (and then receive the work of the Spirit) by doing good works or "by the flesh." These are, he says, like a person underneath supervisors and managers, or in other words, like little children under strict supervision. This is what it means to be under law. To be in the Spirit (or in faith) means the Spirit is inside of us desiring, speaking, leading, etc., moving us into our full identity as sons of God and masters over the entire property, or, to put it another way, co-regents with the king as he "rules" in us and through us. (Paul uses this analogy to connect many "kingdom of God" concepts. He will use that same concept again in a parallel text.) "Under the law," then, should remind us of the contrast he made to being one with Christ by faith in the promise so that we receive the inheritance, i.e. the Spirit based on our position in Christ and not our performance. In other words, even by saying "under law" he echos all that he said there and shows that this text is an echo, too, of those concepts, concepts he initially developed in Galatians 3.1-4 (and even 2.20). This, then, explains that, and that explains this. (As we have seen and will see, there are other parallels too that connect this text to that one.)

So, when we read "be led" by the Spirit, it is in parallel with "Walk around with the Spirit" and the description of us receiving our inheritance of the Spirit, him "being sent into our hearts crying Abba." We could even include his statements about the Spirit "maturing" us (3.3) defining our spiritual experiences (3.4), who God supplies to us and the one who works supernaturally in us (3.5), and the "blessing" of Abraham with its many connotations (3.14). This seems to be the main idea in Galatians: experience the work of the Spirit through faith. He defines in more detail what that faith looks like and what that experience looks like throughout (expanding from 3.1-5). Here it means to be "led by the Spirit." As we walk around with the Spirit, we listen to him, hear him, and go where he leads us and gives us the strength to go. No more. No less. We respond to the instincts, impulses and drives the Spirit gives us in the context of faith and relationship, a relationship characterized by parent/child (4.1-7) and husband/wife relationships (4.21-31).

Possibly the picture of the philosopher, teacher or rabbi mentioned above comes into play here too. Paul will use the term "stoicho" (step with) in verse 25 which means to follow in the path of someone. This term fits the concept of following the pedagogy of a rabbi or philosopher as well. Another possible meaning relates to one meaning from BDAG, "to make use of time for specific purpose, send, observe." We can see how this might relate to "walk around with" the Spirit. "Celebrate with the Spirit" or "Spend time observing" the Holy Spirit. The term can even mean "to go" so that here it simply might mean "go" with the Spirit, another term that connects to the idea of "walk." Paul most likely had a combination in mind of walking around with (intimacy) and following the leadership of the Spirit (led by) as he walks with you.

A possible helpful way to read this might be: If you follow the Holy Spirit around through your life, going where he leads you, you can not also be under the rule of any law system that creates the dynamic where you do the things you don't want to do.

**Galatians 5.19-21a** "Now the works of the flesh are evident: sexual immorality, impurity, sensuality, idolatry, sorcery, enmity, strife, jealousy, fits of anger, rivalries, dissensions, divisions, envy, drunkenness, orgies, and things like these." (φανερὰ δέ ἐστιν τὰ ἔργα τῆς σαρκός, ἅτινά ἐστιν πορνεία, ἀκαθαρσία, ἀσέλγεια, εἰδωλολατρία, φαρμακεία, ἔχθραι, ἔρις, ζῆλος, θυμοί, ἐριθεῖαι, διχοστασίαι, αἱρέσεις, φθόνοι, μέθαι, κῶμοι καὶ τὰ ὅμοια τούτοις)

Because of the nature of these verses, we will work through them as a unit. What Paul suggests as he begins this thought is that these works "manifest" out of living by the natural man. He also suggests that they are rather obvious and instinctual. No one is surprised by such a list. We might even say, based on the term Paul used, that these are public or community standards. These are values that everyone holds or behaviors that everyone would not want others to do. He could also mean, instead of the options explained above, that these behaviors are external behaviors observable by others. Based on context, the first idea seems to be most accurate, that these works "appear" or become apparent as one grows or advances by the natural faculties. He says, the works that come out of the flesh show up and then describes them. They are:

Section One: Sexual Issues

*porneia* - This term has a broad range of meaning. It can mean generally anything that is against the Torah, especially the moral code. It can specifically mean for a person to have sex with a person who is not married to them. It can refer to the female side of sexual sin. The man commits adultery when he has sex with a person who is married to another man. The woman commits *porneia* when she has sex with someone when she is married to another man. It can refer to prostitution generally and specifically to prostitution associated with religious rituals related to false deities. It can also simply mean sexual practices not accepted by the culture where it is used. (Something like our term taboo.) How then does Paul use it here? Generally we might say he means "immoral sexual intercourse" in the most general sense but the next two terms most likely help us narrow down the intended meaning a bit more.

*akatharsia* - This term refers specifically to ritual impurity as it relates to the levitical code. A person was considered unclean (and therefore could not approach the presence of God in the tabernacle) when they were in conflict with the levitical code. This included someone who just has just had a baby, was on their period and other issues not related to morality. In other words, Biblically, uncleanness and immorality or "sinful" are not the same or even similar ideas. In this context, it most likely helps us define *porneia* and, in the case, it would mean sexual intercourse that is forbidden in the law. The Law forbids adultery, incest, beastiality, and male homosexuality. (Compare 2 Corinthians 12:21) If this meaning is correct, we should notice the irony. In the Law one could not go into the presence of God when they were unclean. In the gospel, the presence of God comes into a person and makes them no longer unclean.

*aselgeia* - Some texts translate this as sensuality. It can mean debauchery in general but typically refers to sexual immorality. According to Lightfoot it means "open and reckless content of propriety" (or properness). The idea may, in this context, refer to a lack of self-constrain sexually so that the guilty party participates in sexual activity that is considered socially unacceptable. What we might see between these two terms (uncleanness above and sensuality here) is an explanation of use of porneia above more specifically as sexual intercourse that is both forbidden in the law of Moses and also by cultural standards. These two standards form a matrix that raises the standard for those who walk in the Spirit. (However, we should still remember that this is a result of walking according to natural means, being perfect by the flesh, not a moral law to be obeyed or a behavior to be avoided.

*eidololatria* - Specifically means idol worship. No doubt Paul wants us to think broadly in those terms here. It is also possible that he intends for us to read something like "sex as a part of idol worship." In a context dominated by descriptions of sexual sin the more specific meaning is most likely emphasized as idolatry and sex with temple prostitutes and priests/priestess went hand in hand in this culture.

*pharmakeia* - Here, Paul refers to witchcraft, making magical potions and casting spells. With the proximity to idol worship and the conceptual relation, Paul continues to build, within this context, one thought on another. This magic was often in relations to idol worship (binding of the false deities to some action) so Paul may intend that we read this term in relationship to idol worship and possibly even in relationship to sexual practices related to idol worship and potions or spells. We might read it as: forbidden sex, unlawful sex, socially frowned upon sex, sex in idol worship, idol worship in general and using of spells and potions.

The five terms above all come from the Law of Moses and point back to it. This appears to be intentional. Paul's purpose may be 1) to show that a person who tries to do the law (advancing through the natural human systems) will end up breaking the law egregiously (contextually, it is implied that these are the things that a person does not want to do but does) and/or 2) to set the stage for the next section of the list where he mainly speaks to issues of division and disunity in the church. By setting the stage this way he gains agreement from the Jewish reader, "yes those things are bad" and then begins adding to the list issues that they may tolerate. In other words, his point may be to show his audience that the tolerated issues of disunity are just as bad and contrary to the work of the Spirit as the transgressions regulated by the law of Moses. The law-obsessed reader would amen the first part of the list loudly only to find themselves in front of the prophet hearing the rebuke, "You are the man."

Section Two: Divisive Issue

*echthrai* - Here, as we just described, he shifts to a cluster of words related to disunity among the church. Much like he used a very general term there *porneia*, he uses a very general term here to begin this shift, translated "divisions" in the ESV. This is a good translation. It can mean something like hostility or generally acting unfriendly and hostile. It is probably helpful to think about the idea of unfriendliness in this context versus the stronger term hostility. The contrast in the list about the fruit of the Spirit suggests that all unfriendliness arises out of the flesh and kindness and friendliness arise out of the Spirit. We might also generalize the term as "divisive behavior." With this in mind, we will give short definitions to the terms below. They each present a way in which we cause disunity in the church.

*eris* - arguing over nuances that create factions and discord

*zelos* - envious resentment

*thumoi* - angry outbursts; not controlling one's temper

*erithemai* - (notice that the root is eris from above) selfish ambition or self-serving actions.

*dichostasiai* - divisive attitudes

*haireseis* - divisive doctrinal positions

*phthonoi* - a comparison that leads to disdain towards others


Section Three: Pagan Parties

The list concludes with a cluster related to the first cluster.

*methai* - drunkenness

*komoi* - wild drunken parties that were often a part of idol worship and included sexual debauchery.

He ends the list by saying "and things like these." This serves to enforce the idea that Paul is not giving an exhaustive list but sharing general concepts. He also uses very similar terminology in this verse "things like these" as he used in verse 17, "things…these things" suggesting that this list is in reference to that concept.

Overall what appears to be happening with the arrangement of this list is as follows: At first we read about five issues that are clearly restricted in the law or considered taboo in society. Sexual immorality is a vague term here but is potentially intended to make us think of all sexual-oriented directions in the Torah. Impurity actually means "unclean" and most likely refers to any practice that might make someone ritually unclean according to the Torah; in this specific context "unclean" may mean sexual practices against the prohibitions listed in the Torah. "Sensuality" refers to behaviors that would be repudiated by a person's community. Idolatry would clearly be against God's law. Witchcraft was also forbidden in the Torah. With these obvious admonitions, Paul made sure to get this readers saying amen and nodding in agreement. Then, he describes attributes that he has repeatedly ascribed to the law way of thinking. (We have a tendency to think of these as different categories of behavior, but the Jewish mindset may have seen sexual promiscuity, paganism and idolatry as different aspects of the same abhorrent behavior.) The next eight descriptions present some sort of divisive, abusive or otherwise unloving behavior that manifests out of the law/works/flesh way of living. It's as if Paul says, you know these first things are bad, but these unloving attitudes that your self-dependency creates are just as bad.

The last two restrictions further the strategy connecting unloving attitudes and action to activities the law-abiding Christians in Galatia would spurn. They both describe the manifestations of self-dependency in relationship to participating in pagan worship festivals (think party in our time) characterized by drunkenness and sexually-oriented cultic practices. This appears to be Paul's trump card. It's basically the worst thing Paul can come up with. It's most likely a reference to Numbers 25, a pivotal point in the life of Israel where they participated in sexually charged pagan worship with Moabite temple prostitutes.

**Galatians 5.21b** "I warn you, as I warned you before, that those who do such things will not inherit the kingdom of God." (ἃ προλέγω ὑμῖν, καθὼς προεῖπον ὅτι οἱ τὰ τοιαῦτα πράσσοντες βασιλείαν θεοῦ οὐ κληρονομήσουσιν. )

As Paul ends the subsection about the works of the flesh and begins the section regarding the fruit of the Spirit, he makes a comment that needs to be read carefully. After writing an entire epistle about justification and sanctification coming through faith in the promise of the Spirit, he makes what may appear to be a surprising statement: those who practice the immoral actions he just enumerated will not inherit the kingdom of God. What does he mean? Does he mean they will lose their justification? Does he mean they were never truly justified? Does he mean something else? Something more in line with the message he has taught during the rest of the book?

Consider the structural elements of this sentence. He repeats the lexemes he used at the beginning of this section, *lego*, I say, suggesting that something about this sentence may be parallel with the first sentence: Now I say, walk around with the Spirit and you potentially will not advance through the instincts and impulses of the flesh. Another aspect to this text suggests that these two sentences night be parallel. In Galatians, when Paul speaks of "inheritance," he specifically refers to the Holy Spirit. Practically we could say that Paul says here: those who practice these things do not receive the Spirit. So, with this parallel and the inner-textual connection back to inheritance as the Holy Spirit we might suggest that Paul here refers to the same issue or topic he refers to in 5.16, 5.18 and 5.25, walking in the Spirit, being led by the Spirit, living by the Spirit and stepping behind the Spirit. Structurally this means that "In the Spirit" language occurs at the beginning of the section (v.16) proceeds and closes the list of works of the flesh (v.18), precedes the fruit of the Spirit list (v.18) and ends the section (v.25). One further element suggests a parallelism between these four sentences. Grammatically they are all conditional statements formed in four distinct ways (using four different classes of conditional construction). So as we read this sentence, we should read it in light of the other "in the Spirit" phrases. Paul expresses, with new nuance, the same basic concept in each instance.

With this in mind lets work through the text. The ESV begins the sentence as "I warn you…" while in the Greek text it actually begins with a relative pronoun "which things." The relative pronoun refers to the list of things (including "things like these"). So the sentence should more properly begin "which things I previously said to you just as said them before." This means that the content of Paul's words (or possibly warning) most likely included the list of the things that precedes this clause not the statement about those who practice these things that follows. According to most lexicons the term "prolego" that is used here, first in the present tense and second in the aorist tense, means to say before or earlier. According to Louw Nida it can also mean "to warn." Paul says here then either that he is predicting these things (and predicted them before) or he is warning them (and has warned them before). Both make sense in the context. Paul earlier in this letter used a similar construction to refer to a repetition in the letter. "But even if we or an angel from heaven should preach to you a gospel contrary to the one we preached to you, let him be accursed. As we have said before, so now I say again: If anyone is preaching to you a gospel contrary to the one you received, let him be accursed." -Galatians 1.8–9 ESV This usage might suggest the nuance of "warning" but more specifically refers to the fact that Paul is repeating himself. Most lexicons though suggest that the concept of warning is not a part of the word, that it only attracts this nuance through context. The word means either simply to say earlier, previously or to predict. Whether or not a reader understands this word as "prediction," "say previously" or "warn," it probably relates to how he or she reads the entire clause. As we have seen it may not read as it is often understood, as a warning per se. It may read as a predictive description. For these reasons I would probably read the text as, "I am predicting these things just like I predicted them before." To me this fits the interpretation of "inherit the kingdom of God" more accurately, is closer to the lexical meaning of the word and makes more sense grammatically. Assuming this is the right way to read *prolego*, what is Paul predicting? He predicts the outcome of "advancing through the instincts of the natural faculties (flesh)." The next clause, read in context to the book of Galatians, will add strength to this reading.

"that those who do such things will not inherit the kingdom of God" - As translated here it appears that this is the content of Paul's warning or prediction. He warned or predicted *that* these practicers would not experience this inheritance. Another option could be that it explains *why* Paul predicted that these works would come out of human based living. The Greek term "hoti" can mean either. "I suggested that these things would arise out the flesh *because* those who practice these kinds of things do not inherit the kingdom." This fits better when we read the text with the relative pronoun that begins the sentence, "which things I predict."

The term translated "do" is the Greek word *prasso*. It means to do or to practice in this context. Related to the latter idea it is also used to describe the practice of witchcraft, Judaism, religion and other similar concepts. This suggests that it means "to practice rituals as a part of a commitment to a religion or belief system." So, when Paul refers to those who practice these behaviors, he may infer that they are practicing ritualistically out of a commitment to a belief system, the system he has rebutted throughout the epistle, the other gospel, the law, the flesh system. The term occurs in the present tense so that we should read the action of the verb as continual, repeated action. We might overstate it as: those who continually practice these things (as a part of their ritualistic commitment) are those who do not inherit.

As we have seen the next clause relates to other phrases and sentences in this section. We have referred to this collection of sentences as "in the Spirit" statements. Paul clearly connects the idea of "inheritance" to the Spirit in Galatians 3.5-14 where he shows that the promise, the inheritance and giving the Spirit all refer to the same experience (see especially 3.14). Then, in Galatians 4.1-6, he elaborates on the idea more, showing that because we are one with Christ our identity with God is as Christ and the Spirit of the Son is being poured into us based on this until and identity. Thus, we continue in faith in the work of Christ on the cross for our redemption and in his resurrection for the pouring out of the Spirit, apart from the works of the flesh, natural faculties and human abilities. The Spirit, who the Father supplied to us and through whom he worked supernaturally in us (Galatians 3.1-4) by responding to the message of the gospel with faith, has been sent into our hearts by the Father (notice the similar language between Galatians

3.1-4 and Galatians 4.6). In us, in our inner man, he is speaking. When he speaks he does so with emotion and passion, "crying" in the text. He speaks *in us* locationally and speaks *to God* for us directionally. (Though this is not to suggest that he does not speak to us. The bigger point is that he is speaking and that speaking feels at least at times similar to a cry.) He hints at the work of the Spirit again when he says in 5.5 that our faith turns into action as we wait on the Spirit to give us the desire or expectation of righteousness that comes through faith (versus efforts based on the natural, human faculties and abilities). He also characterizes this experience in relation to our hearts being filled with love that makes our faith "operational." (5.6) It is out of this experience of the Spirit that he then describes our ultimate ethic, to love others. He then goes on to develop what that looks like including the text at hand. We will see in the next verse that within this experience the Spirit produces love in many different facets and several desirable emotions like peace and happiness. To summarize, this cluster of ideas suggests that when Paul says "inherit" the kingdom of God he means to receive or experience (maybe stand in?) this experience of the Spirit, one characterized by supernatural power, the intimacy of a child and their "Abba" (and possibly the marital relationship between Abraham and Sarah that produces Isaac), waiting on a heart change where we begin to desire and expect righteousness from Him and many emotions: affection, happiness, peace, etc. The inheritance of the kingdom of God equals the inheritance of the Spirit of God.

We see for the first time in Galatians Paul speaking to the kingdom of God, a topic that occurred often in the synoptic Gospels (especially Matthew) but less so in Paul. It may be that Paul includes this reference to make sure his readers know that as he refers to "life in the Spirit" he is on the same topic as other writers when they speak to the kingdom of God. As a parallel to "be led by the Spirit" we see Paul forming a theology of the kingdom of God as "being under the rule of God through the Spirit of the Son." It may also support this link that "inherit" and "law" share a same lexeme,"nomos" meaning law specifically. So, in connection to "if you are led by the Spirit you are not under the law (nomos). Paul says, "If someone practices these things they do not inherit (nomos) the kingdom of God."

This is not too dissimilar to what he says in Romans 14.16, "The kingdom of God is not a matter of religious rules like eating and drinking but of receiving righteousness, peace and happiness from the Holy Spirit." Also Colossians 1.12, "The Father…has qualified you to share in the inheritance of the saints in light. He has delivered us from the domain of darkness and transferred us to the kingdom of his beloved Son." Notice that he links "inheritance of light" with the kingdom which he contrasts to the "domain of darkness." The phrase "delivered us out of the domain of darkness" is semantically equivalent to Galatians 1.4b "who…to deliver us from the present (the one with dominion) evil age." This helps us see that Paul is not teaching about these ideas only in Galatians, ideas related to experiencing the Spirit and the kingdom, he connects the ideas frequently.

An expanded look at Colossians 1 helps us see these connections:

"And so, from the day we heard, we have not ceased to pray for you, asking that you may be filled with the knowledge of his will in all spiritual wisdom and understanding, so as to walk in a manner worthy of the Lord, fully pleasing to him: bearing fruit in every good work and increasing in the knowledge of God; being strengthened with all power, according to his glorious might, for all endurance and patience with joy; giving thanks to the Father, who has qualified you to share in the inheritance of the saints in light. He has delivered us from the domain of darkness and transferred us to the kingdom of his beloved Son, in whom we have redemption, the forgiveness of sins." -Colossians 1.9–14 ESV

This text parallels a similar one in Ephesians:

"In him we have redemption through his blood, the forgiveness of our trespasses, according to the riches of his grace, which he lavished upon us, in all wisdom and insight making known to us the mystery of his will, according to his purpose, which he set forth in Christ as a plan for the fullness of time, to unite all things in him, things in heaven and things on earth. In him we have obtained an inheritance, having been predestined according to the purpose of him who works all things according to the counsel of his will, so that we who were the first to hope in Christ might be to the praise of his glory. In him you also, when you heard the word of truth, the gospel of your salvation, and believed in him, were sealed with the promised Holy Spirit, who is the guarantee of our inheritance until we acquire possession of it, to the praise of his glory. For this reason, because I have heard of your faith in the Lord Jesus and your love toward all the saints, I do not cease to give thanks for you, remembering you in my prayers, that the God of our Lord Jesus Christ, the Father of glory, may give you the Spirit of wisdom and of revelation in the knowledge of him, having the eyes of your hearts enlightened, that you may know what is the hope to which he has called you, what are the riches of his glorious inheritance in the saints, and what is the immeasurable greatness of his power toward us who believe, according to the working of his great might that he worked in Christ when he raised him from the dead and seated him at his right hand in the heavenly places, far above all rule and authority and power and dominion, and above every name that is named, not only in this age but also in the one to come. And he put all things under his feet and gave him as head over all things to the church, which is his body, the fullness of him who fills all in all." -Ephesians 1.7–23 ESV

In both texts, he refers to our inheritance. It is an inheritance of light and glory (God's revealed presence) and God's power, resurrection power. This same power also operates in, through and from Christ from his position of authority over all things (kingdom). From his throne (kingdom) he is filling all things, or expressing rule and dominion over all things via his church. Notice in Ephesians too that we experience this inheritance as we receive the Spirit's wisdom, revelation and knowing of the person of God. (Similar to Galatians where Paul operates under "revelation" in chapter one as an example of how we live in intimacy with the Spirit.) Through this experience of the Spirit, in Ephesians, he is uniting all things in him, or bringing all things under his headship and lordship, i.e. rule and kingdom. Like in Galatians, Paul wants the Christians in Ephesus to experience the Spirit, "the inheritance of glory," (See 1 Corinthians 2.8 - God gives us his glory.) or, as he describes it in Ephesians 1.22-23 Summarization: Christ filling (saturating, taking dominion over) all things. God connects the inheritance to Christ's rule and filling of the church and all things, to the power of the resurrection, the shared glory of God (shared to us), the Spirit giving us wisdom, knowledge and revelation and our hearts being given "light."

In Ephesians 3.14-19 he returns to the same ideas (this text is parallel to Ephesians1, especially 1.15-23). He wants the Ephesians to have riches of glory and strength and power from the the Spirit so that "you may be filled with all the fullness of God." (God's presence and dominion saturating us through and through.) Then again in Ephesians 4.9-16, Paul describes Jesus being enthroned as king so he can "fill all things" and operate as the head of the church from where he supplies the needs the church. (The term he uses for supply in verse 16 is the same term he uses in Galatians 3.3 where he "supplies" the Spirit.)

In Colossians, he connects several ideas and characteristics to the "Inheritance."

- Comes from being filled with knowledge, wisdom and understanding from the Spirit. (1.9)
- Purpose is "walking in a manner worthy of the Lord, fully pleasing to him, bearing fruit, increasing in intimacy with God." (1.10)
- Receiving strength and power equal to his power and glory. (1.11)
- The result of this strength is "all obedience, patience and happiness." (1.11) (Similar to the fruit of the Spirit.)
- Deliverance from the domain of darkness (1.13)
- Transference into the kingdom of his beloved Son (1.13)
- The mystery hidden for ages (1.27)
- Christ in you, the hope of glory (the riches of glory that the mystery is about) (1.27)
- "That we may present everyone matures in Christ." (1.28) Same word for mature we have seen in Galatians (root: teleo)

Paul then consistently refers to the inheritance as the Spirit's power and revelation and how Christ exercises dominion, i.e. the kingdom of God.

These ideas, inheritance and kingdom, are intentionally together. They both suggest a meaning of the rule of the Spirit. He rules, reveals, fills and empowers as we walk, hear, and step with him.

The phrase "They will not inherit the kingdom of God," when considered in context with the book of Galatians and Paul's theological development of these terms most likely does not mean the same thing as "salvation" or justification. It refers to the experience that Paul wants the "saved" Galatians to receive by faith from the Spirit, an experience that defines (or should define) what it means for them to mature as Christians. The next question relates to order. What is the cause and what is the effect? As written in most English translations it suggests that behavior (not doing the list that precedes this verse) is the cause and the effect is inheriting the kingdom. "Those who do these things will not inherit the kingdom of God." It's the use of the future tense that confuses. When we read the future tense we read the first clause (When someone practices these things) as the condition for an outcome that is certain or factual in the future if that concision is met. The future in Greek does not actually refer, typically, to future time. The tense often does signify mainly temporal information. Many grammarians suggest that the future tense in Greek should be understood in the same way as the subjunctive or optative. (See commentary on 5.16) With this in mind we could either read this verse as future time "they will not inherit," subjunctive "they potentially do not inherit," or optative "they wish not to inherit." To understand this grammatical concept it may be helpful to think about English. Most linguistics do not consider the future tense in English to actually be future time. This is why we create the English future with the auxiliary "will" as in "I will leave tomorrow." The verb will, when it is used alone means "to desire, choose, want to;" so when we say "I will leave," we are saying "I want to leave." Our future tense also has an optative meaning more than a future time meaning. This may be because future time events are not certain from our point of view; we can only express potential realities (subjunctive) and intended or desired realities (optative).

A similar phrase occurs in Ephesians 5.5, "Everyone that who is sexually immoral or impure, or who is covetous (that is an idolater) has no inheritance in the kingdom of God." In this case Paul makes a similar statement but he uses the present tense verb, in this case *exo* in Greek, with the term inheritance in a noun form. So we might say that Paul says a person is characterized by these things "is not -at the same time- holding on to the inheritance of the kingdom." It is helpful here, as above, to remember what Paul meant by inheritance in Ephesians: living in intimacy with the Spirit so that you experience his power. (It could also be that Paul intends for us to read "has no inheritance" in conjunction or in parallel with "be filled with the Spirit" -Ephesians 5:18) In this text then we have a potentially clarifying version of the same theological idea. Those who are doing these things (the same type of things as he lists in Galatians 5) are not holding onto the inheritance (or holding the inheritance close), the Spirit. This verse suggest that the optative or subjunctive interpretation of "inherit" is likely correct.[164]

With all of this in mind we should translate this sentence as, "I am predicting this and did predict it because those who systematically practice these type of lifestyles do not simultaneously hold the reigning God, the Spirit of Jesus, near at all times. As I said above, the two approaches are not compatible."

**Galatians 5.22-23a** "But the fruit of the Spirit is love, joy, peace, patience, kindness, goodness, faithfulness, gentleness, self-control; " (ὁ δὲ καρπὸς τοῦ πνεύματός ἐστιν ἀγάπη χαρὰ εἰρήνη, μακροθυμία χρηστότης ἀγαθωσύνη, πίστις πραΰτης ἐγκράτεια· )

---

[164] 1 Corinthians 6:9-11 uses the same back language "the unrighteous will not inherit the kingdom of God" using the future tense. If the the future temporal element is not intended it may also be either optative or subjunctive. "The unrighteous may not or do not intend to inherit (take into their possession) the kingdom of God." Also, Paul may be writing here about one's positional righteousness when he says "unrighteous." He may mean unjustified. The lists that follows may characterize a person's life but God does not consider the believer those things. Instead they are declared holy and righteous. (Aorist passive verbs are used here and that is significant. They are not righteous and holy; they are give holiness and righteousness.) In other words, this paragraph is about a different perspective on "inheriting the kingdom" or experiencing the Spirit. In the most simple terms, he most likely is saying that those who are not justified do not experience the Spirit. Because he is speaking only of a theoretical reality he uses the future tense as a subjunctive mood.

Further supporting the thesis about the phrase "they will not inherit the kingdom of God" actually meaning that these practitioners of the works of the flesh do not possess or experience the rule of the Spirit as they are practicing these actions is the fact the contrast of this idea (noted by the conduction but; de in Greek) is the Spirit bearing fruit. Possessing the inheritance (the Spirit) and the Spirit bearing fruit forms the center of this section and with that may be the central idea. If this is the case, Paul defines this "thesis" with the other "in the Spirit" phrases throughout. Notice also the contrast between the fruit of the Spirit and works of the flesh. The Spirit creates the attitudes and actions below like a fruit, from his life as it were. Similar maybe to how Sarah produced Isaac (the heir, or "inheritor") and then how we experience the production of fruit, supernaturally. While a literary connection to John 15 is unlikely the same concepts are described here. Through faith and intimacy with God through the Spirit fruit is produced or rather, what is emphasized here, the Spirit produces fruit. The natural man as a comparison (Paul intends this comparison to have a semantic value here) "works" or labors and then ends up with undesirable actions. We might also read this sentence in light of "if we live by the Spirit." This is Paul's description of what it means (at least partially) to live by the Spirit. The Spirit, as life, is producing fruit in us.

The fruit of the Spirit:

Love - *agapē* - we studied this term above as we first encountered it in 5.4. Generally it means affection towards someone that leads to devotion then acts on their behalf. Here it is significant that Paul begins with love. Within the material at the beginning of chapter 5 focusing on freedom and the reality that faith, not following the law, is what means something with Christ, Paul says that faith works or becomes operative (meaning it operates actively) through love. Or, faith in the gospel creates love that creates loving action. Then Paul describes the outworking ethic of the gospel as "loving your neighbor." So, when we get right at the center of this text about walking in the Spirit and right at the beginning of the list we find "love" again showing that this text reverse engineers a bit how the gospel through faith creates love in our hearts that leads to service for others. This list in many ways is an expansion of that simple primary ideal: love. 5.13-the end of Galatians describes the kind of love the Spirit produces in us as we walk around with him, being led by him, and follow in his steps.

Joy - *chara* - A feeling of happiness.

Peace - *eirēnē* - lack of anxiety and inner turmoil; tranquil a state of tranquility, harmony, well-being; not at war.

Patience - *makrothymia* - a state of emotional calm in the face of provocation or misfortune without complaint or irritation

Kindness - *chrēstotēs* - to do something beneficial for someone out of kindness; generous, helpfulness, goodness toward another, SPICQ: If Pauline *chrestotes* emphasizes goodness, mildness, and generosity above all else, it retains the nobility given the word by his contemporaries, which distinguishes it from *praytes*. HERE: kindness of generosity, maybe "generous kindness" or kind generous. There is also "mildness" in the idea as in quiet and humble posture and presentation. In the second century, the spectacle of Christian agape was so stunning for pagans—"Vides, inquiunt, ut invicem se diligant" ("Behold, how [Vol. 3, p. 516] they love one another!")—that according to Tertullian, they called Christians not *christiani* but *chrestiani*, "made up of mildness or kindness."

Goodness - *agathōsynē* - goodness but also generous giving; Either a positive moral quality: goodness or maybe integrity or generosity. Most likely generosity is in mind in context and connection to previous word.

Faithfulness - *pistis* - faith or faithfulness (integrity, with character and dependability). Context suggests faith.

Gentleness - *prautēs* - gentle, meek, mild attitude, BDAG: the quality of not being overly impressed by a sense of one's self-importance, gentleness, humility, courtesy, considerateness, meekness SPICQ: calmness, mules are "tamed" not angry, aggressive, wild, caustic in attitude or disposition, calm, composed, quiet, meek, gracious, humble, etc soothed and soothing. Contrast a wild animal with a domesticated one. Non-condemning, attacking, judging, even "lenient" serenity in a person.

Self-Control - *egkrateia* - to exercise complete control over one's desires and actions. BDAG: restraint of one's emotions, impulses, or desires, self-control. Literally "in power" or in control. Has urges and desires but controls them. The desires do not have their way with you; over power you. They are overpowered. A stronger power overcomes their power. What an athlete does to be a good athlete submits to "all *egkrataie*" Disciplined. Not given over to one's natural impulses of stomach, sex, tongue etc. Lead others after you "lead" yourself. "Empowered" (literally) It is as if the dualistic thoughts of the Greeks separate the mind from the natural impulses so that this idea suggests in their paradigm for your mind to be in control of your body and its desires, cravings, instincts, etc. Description of Joseph when he met his brothers in Egypt - he wept privately then he "gained control of himself" and went out to them. HERE: "natural desires are under control" but by the Spirit not the self. *Under restraint. Not impulsive.*

As a person lives in faith in the work of Christ to provide the Spirit to them fully and without restraint and then walks around with him, He produces these things, these fruit, into their lives. Affection, Kindness, Happiness, Tranquility, Benevolent actions, Generous, Faithful, Gentle, Gracious, Under His Control, and the end of Anxiety. Devotionally we should remember that these are what the Spirit does and so what God does and how God is.

**Galatians 5.23b** "against such things there is no law." (κατὰ τῶν τοιούτων οὐκ ἔστιν νόμος. )

Paul ends his list with a statement potentially meant to echo "Those who are led by the Spirit are not under the law." He is about to write other ideas in the following two verses that also echo the first stanza of this section. Woodenly Paul says "Into these things or against these not is law." By using law without the article he most likely refers to the law as a system, the same system he refers to in the phrase under the law and "maturing through the flesh." Law based religion or rule based religion is not into these things or against these things. The idea most English translations convey in this sentence is that the law is not against doing these things or there is not a law anywhere against doing these things. It very well could mean just that. It could also mean that "law" is not in alignment with these things. In other words, as above with the desires of the flesh, <u>the law is not compatible with these things.</u> The issue that causes the ambiguity is the preposition *kata* (translated against in the ESV). It can mean against, but it can also mean "as, with or like." (It is used to translate the preposition k$^e$ in Hebrew.) In this case it might mean "Law systems are not like these things" or "in alignment with these things."

Both meanings have contextual reasons in their favor. In favor of the first option (There is not a law anywhere against these types of behaviors) is the fact that the *kata* earlier in the text where the Spirit and the flesh are opposed (*kata*) to each other. Though this could be an intentional contrast. Also, Paul has somewhat shifted his tone regarding the law in this section and the one preceding it. This would add another layer on top of that. (More so if he is referring to the Mosaic law but he could also refer here to "law systems" in general as explained previously.) In favor of the second is the context of the book: Law systems are not aligned with producing this kind of behavior. If this is parallel to the verses above that would seem to be the meaning. "If you are led by the Spirit, you are not under the law…law systems are not in alignment with this life anyway." Paul will say next "and those who belong to Christ have crucified the flesh system." It may make more sense for him to say prior to this statement about the natural system (flesh) that the law system (which he connects to the law) is not "with" the fruits of the Spirit. In other words, the law system does not produce this kind of life. A slight majority of the evidence suggests this reading.

**Galatians 5.24** "And those who belong to Christ Jesus have crucified the flesh with its passions and desires." ( οἱ δὲ τοῦ Χριστοῦ ['Ιησοῦ] τὴν σάρκα ἐσταύρωσαν σὺν τοῖς παθήμασιν καὶ ταῖς ἐπιθυμίαις.)

As we read this text we should remember that it is connected to the previous phrase: law style approaches to God are not compatible with the Spirit's fruit bearing and to the first verses of this section where Paul says basically: do not seek to grow through the faculties of the natural man or via the law because these systems are contrary to the Spirit system. Here, with the designation "those of Christ" Paul likely connects the ideas of this section back to Galatians 3.26-28 where he describes the identity of those who have faith: they are in Christ, one with Christ, joint-heirs with Christ, "of Christ." This suggests that Paul is here not speaking of an action to be taken (however lightly we should think about action) but a positional identity. Those who are in unity with Christ, those who belong to Him and are being created by him as the phrase "of Christ" may suggest, he is their source, they are crucified with him, Paul has stated, and here reminds us that means the flesh system is dead regarding them. They have crucified, past tense, the flesh. This is not an action to strive after it is an action, the death of the flesh, that has been accomplished just like our justification. By faith you are in Christ. Those in Christ were crucified spiritually when he was crucified. In them, what was murdered and what is now dead is the flesh system, the natural system and the law system. What does this mean? It means for the believer this system has been disempowered already. Remembering that the flesh is equated with law (above and in 3.1-4), Paul repeatedly describes these two systems (law and flesh) not actually as two but as one. Elsewhere Paul says that we are dead to the law (Galatians 2:19). Here he says the flesh is dead to us. The connection to Galatians 2.20 also helps us further define what flesh is. There Paul says "I am crucified" and here the flesh is crucified. This suggests the flesh is me, "I" but not just simply my physical self. My physical body was not crucified with Christ but something about my immaterial self did die when he died. We know that Paul at times does see the human as a physical being which has organs that produce emotions, desires, will, intelligence, etc. Here he emphasis subtly the nonphysical aspect of the flesh, the entity and faculties that this physical body creates. This is important because we might be tempted to read Paul's writing in a very dualistic, gnostic way. The physical is bad. The spiritual is good. Paul is careful to connect the flesh not just to the physical body but to the immaterial "soul" that describes that which the body does. It is similar to the mind/body considerations philosophers make today. Paul seems here to suggest an understanding of the human as body and mind: two entities that are also one. The soul (mind, immaterial self) appears to be a way to describe the immaterial (to the human eye) processes that the body and its organs do. So, as we think about the flesh, we should not just think of the body and its desires and emotions but the body, its organs, the processes that those organs create which Paul calls here "feelings and drives." Paul had written at the beginning of chapter 3 "Have you actually experienced nothing?" referring to the experiences of the Spirit. Here the root for "experience" is *pathos*, the same root that is used here. This may be an intentional contrast (as we have seen there are other connections to 2.20-3.4). The Galatians had, in the beginning of their faith, experienced some affections and emotions that arise from the Spirit. Paul challenged their abandonment of "faith" as an abandonment of the Spirit using their ecstatic experiences as a part of his argument. "You did not experience nothing." Now here, he says the flesh system, "I" also experiences feelings and desires.

In stating that the flesh is dead via crucifixion he is also contrasting the flesh's ability to produce anything with the Spirit's. The Spirit produces fruit through its life. The flesh, as a dead entity, produces death. As we will see next, he follows up this thought with a contrasting statement about life in the Spirit. Some, those who walk in the Spirit, "are made alive by the Spirit." Conceptually, he basically repeats 2.19-20 "For I died to the law through the law so that I might live by God. I am crucified in Christ. Now, I myself no longer live. Now, Christ lives in me. But, the life I currently live in the flesh, I live by faith in the Son of God."

**Galatians 5.25** "If we live by the Spirit, let us also keep in step with the Spirit." (Εἰ ζῶμεν πνεύματι, πνεύματι καὶ στοιχῶμεν.)

We have crucified our flesh. How then do we live if our natural system is dead? If the human, natural system that could be a source of religious and moral growth and motivation is no longer in charge how do we live? Galatians 2.19-20 says we live by God and then explains that as "Christ lives our lives as we have faith in him." (Which he explains as "wanting him to do something.") Here, in the same context conceptually, he says we "live by the Spirit." This connection has a big impact on how we read this letter. It defines "We live by the Spirit" as the Spirit (of Christ and God) living in and through us. It affirms that when Paul says we have crucified the flesh he means the same thing as "I" being crucified (poor grammar intended), and as dying to the law. We affirm what we have suggested elsewhere, these concepts, the law, the flesh, and "I" are all the same system. This also suggests a more detailed explanation to what Paul means when he says "the life I now live (I do not live it) I live by faith in the Son." He means to walk around with the Spirit, to let the Spirit lead us and take us along, to receive the inheritance (like a gift), to take the passive position of letting the Spirit bear fruit in our lives as opposed to us working out of our natural will, discipline, emotions, etc., to walk in the path of the Spirit. It also has the reverse effect. These descriptions should be seen within the context of "faith instead of doing." Walk around with the Spirit would then mean "walk around listening to the Spirit and trusting him to do the work." "Being led by" would mean "trusting the Spirit to direct us and carry us along" (possible meaning of "ago" used here. Receiving the inheritance would become a word picture of our posture of "receivers of a gift" and suggest the passivity of accepting that gift, the inheritance. Living in the Spirit would be living out based on what he lives in us, trusting him to live out in us what is required. The choice is to either live by the Spirit or live by (look for life and fruit/production from) the flesh. Faith is that choice. Do you look to or seek "life" from the Spirit or the flesh? Do you seek fruit, life, "growth towards maturity" from the Spirit or the flesh that performs the law? (Sin ruled flesh attempts to do law-code, live by rules and regulations, which brings condemnation as sinner, transgressor which brings death.) Paul limits "faith" to the side of the Spirit and uses "work" on the side of the Law and Flesh but ultimately faith is the beginning point of each system. One has faith that *this way* will provide the desired outcome. The faith system though, stays within the parameters of faith to define its system. It looks only to God, to Christ, to the Spirit for maturity and righteousness never to the human and its abilities. (Remember he has contextually defined faith as "wanting or seeking something from someone" in Galatians 2.15-6 and as "expectantly waiting on" that thing from the Spirit in Galatians 5.2-4. With this in mind, faith means to want someone to do something, to seek them to do something, to wait for them to do something that you believe they will do AND it means -related to waiting- that you will not do the thing yourself. Contextually it is also the opposite of working and doing or rule following. It is the opposite of what the human can do with all its drives, emotions, thinking, etc. The ultimate meaning of faith becomes "sourcing" where do you source your righteousness from? Your life from? God or the natural faculties.)

The effect of the condition "If we live by the Spirit" is "we potentially may step with the Spirit." The ESV translates this as a command. It actually is not an imperative verb. It is a subjunctive verb. (The grammar here suggests a subjunctive reading of the parallel passages that use the future tense: "inherit [future tense] the kingdom of God.] This is a promise made to those who "live by the Spirit" as opposed to those who "live by the flesh." The promise is that they will "step" in the Spirit. The term comes from the military and often means "to march." This can suggest the idea of following orders, walking in a line, walking behind a person, walking in the footsteps or tracks of a person. This becomes, in some contexts, to conduct oneself and to imitate. Paul uses this root when he describes the "basic steps of the world" which in that context could mean elementary, basic ideas, the basic rules a person must obey (something like natural law), the basic elements that make up the universe (think earth, fire, wind and water) or the spiritual entities that many in this world believed were behind those elements. Because he uses this terminology in that context to refer to the law he most likely is referring to something like "the basic rules of the universe." We said above that this may have been a way for him to show that the law is not just the law written in the Torah but also includes the intrinsic rules and moral codes followed by all men, that "approach to successfully being moral," the following rules approach, even the most basic ones. This is important because here he suggests that when we live by the Spirit, the outcome we can expect is one where we follow in the steps of the Spirit (Same root as "basic rules," *stoicheo.*)

This line is clearly connected to the idea of "walking in the Spirit." The connection further affirms that walking around in the Spirit is how we live by the Spirit and that when we do so we will find ourselves "following the Spirit," i.e. living out what he is living out. The picture, when connected to the context, may suggest something similar to a child dancing on the feet of their father more than trying to imitate their father. Ultimately though the picture is that when you simply walk around with the Spirit, talking with him, listening to him, etc, you will find yourself going along with him too. He is living his life in you and your life, for you, and therefore bearing his fruit, the fruit he creates himself, his own actions, attitudes, emotions, thoughts etc, in you. We experience this as we "expectantly wait on him" to produce it and as we "want him and him alone" to produce it, as we source it from him and not our selves in any way.

**Galatians 5.26** "Let us not become conceited, provoking one another, envying one another." (μὴ γινώμεθα κενόδοξοι, ἀλλήλους προκαλούμενοι, ἀλλήλοις φθονοῦντες.)

As Paul transitioned into this section on "walking in the Spirit" he said, "But if you bite and devour one another, watch out that you are not consumed by one another." Verse 26 is parallel to this verse. Both are to describe what it means "to love your neighbor as yourself" which he suggests is what will define a person's life when the Spirit is living it. Here he again uses a subjunctive mood describing this potential life. "We may not in this case be conceited." The term translated conceited (kenodoxos) means to have a high but baseless opinion about oneself, arrogance and vanity. Then he gives two characteristics of being this inflated using two present tense particles which means they represent ongoing action. These participles likely describe outcomes of the arrogant and vain mindset. This causes those in the group to "call out" each other another (provoking each other) and to resent each other. The baseless arrogance (probably based on religious and moral performance considering the context) is the cause for the behavior suggesting the provocation through calling out is potentially something similar to our version of "calling someone out" or pointing someone out or singling someone out. The resentment that then arises between the members of the group may then be based on this singling out and/or the possible benefits the person gets who meets the religious standard of the group. Paul describes here a situation where some, by following a list of rules, start to think highly of themselves, though they have no reason to. Then they start to accuse those who do not see *their* standard of being moral inferior and they begin to resent each other and not like each other as a result. Ultimately the result is division and discord. Remembering the parallel text. With these actions, they are biting and chewing on each other, i.e fighting with each other over rule following and doctrine, and will eventually destroy the entire organization. Paul will show another way to deal with spiritual weakness in the next paragraph. Instead of superiority he recommends the posture of a servant.

# Galatians 6.1-5

**Interpretive Translation:**

My dear family, when a person, is addicted to any of these offensive or divisive behaviors[165], those of you who walk with the Spirit[166] and live out of his strength should carefully and gently[167] support this person until they become whole and walk in the Spirit themselves. While you walk along aside this person, helping them mend their faith, keep yourselves focused on the gospel and this will not turn into testing season for you. Help each other carry life's loads. This is all it takes to live out Christ's law: Love others as yourself. Here's why: when someone has a high estimation of himself even though that person actually doesn't come close to the standard God expects, that person tricks themselves into their false arrogant conclusions. Each person, in this case, sees their human works as the standard[168] which causes them to be impressed with themselves alone and not focus on helping others. With this mindset a person is left to bear the load all alone and alone the load feels so much heavier than when they are carried together.

**Summary Commentary:**

---

[165] Trying to reflect the ambiguity of *paraptomi*. It can mean "offense" generally or often an offense between two people. In this context, it may be connected to the divisive behaviors just described but that is not certain.

[166] "The Spiritual" in this context has just been described in the previous three chapters.

[167] The term of course means restore. It is used to restore a bone and to mend cloth or nets. The idea is to return to a previous whole state. The picture of careful mending and resetting a bone seems gentle.

[168] "To test" can be to regard something worthwhile (LN). The idea seems to be that they "approve" of their works when they shouldn't. (Note the use of "works" which has typically been negative in Galatians and is most contextually connected to "works of the flesh.")

As Paul closes out the section on walking in the Spirit he emphasizes the work of the Spirit in us towards others. The Spirit moves us away from divisiveness and offensive behavior. In this, the fruit he bears is ultimately an expansion on the command "love your neighbor" that Paul referred to earlier in this section. Remember he shifted in 5.3 towards faith activating through love. He described that process as waiting on the Spirit to give you the hope of righteousness (or desire of righteousness). He calls this entire process "of faith." In other words, this is what it looks like to live out of faith. Out of that he reminds the reader that this is what freedom is really for. "Use it this way" or make it useful in this way not as path back into natural, human-faculty based religion. He then defines that this will show up as love for others. Then in the text that immediately precedes this one he shows that walking in the Spirit will end selfish and divisive behavior and produce, the Spirit will then produce, a life characterized by love, reconciliation, kindness, benevolence, gentleness, happiness, patience and peace towards others. Now, in this text Paul describes what this love looks like concretely.

This text is organized into three parts. Part 1 (A1) is 6.1-2a. Part 2 (B), the center of a *chiasm* forming the text, 6.2b, and then Part 3 (A2). We see the parallel nature between A1 and A2 by two elements: 1) the repeat of the "bearing" language at the end, 2) two conditional clauses begin each sections and 3) The "bear" language in both cases is preceded with a semantic reference to "testing."

Ultimately, Paul explains in this text that a person who is spiritual, ie. walks in the Spirit, will help another believer when they are addicted to some wrong. This will be done in a way that reflects the fruit, bearing of the Spirit he has just described. We see this connection through his use specifically of the term *prautes* which means gentleness (see more commentary on *prautes* above). This gentleness should characterize the efforts of restoring a person. The second half of this paragraph suggests that a person who thinks they are something is a person who thinks their own work to be "approved;" they think their lives are the standard and they boast in themselves alone and bear their burdens alone. In the last version of "bear burdens" Paul shifts to a different word for "burden" from a general concept to a specific term that means something like "ship cargo." His point is that a person who bears his burden alone bears a burden impossible to carry.

**Galatians 6.1** "Brothers, if anyone is caught in any transgression, you who are spiritual should restore him in a spirit of gentleness. Keep watch on yourself, lest you too be tempted." (Ἀδελφοί, ἐὰν καὶ προλημφθῇ ἄνθρωπος ἔν τινι παραπτώματι, ὑμεῖς οἱ πνευματικοὶ καταρτίζετε τὸν τοιοῦτον ἐν πνεύματι πραΰτητος, σκοπῶν σεαυτὸν μὴ καὶ σὺ πειρασθῇς.)

Paul makes a clear shift in this verse using the term "brothers" to show a new section. This may show that this text has a connection structurally to 5.11, the last time Paul has used the term. He clearly wants the reader to make a connection between this paragraph and the 5.13-15; this connection suggests that the section shift begins in 5.11 making 5.11-15 the parallel section.[169] We see several connections between the two paragraphs but the main one is "Fulfill the law with this one thing: Love your neighbor as yourself." And then here in this section he centers the entire text around "Fulfill the law of Christ."

He goes on to describe the responsibilities of one who is "spiritual." He has clearly described the spiritual above: those who walk in the Spirit, are led by the Spirit, who receive the inheritance (the Spirit), and those who, since they live by the Spirit, follow in his path. We have seen that the spiritual ones experience the bearing of fruit from the Spirit and that fruit is characterized ultimately by treating others with love. Here, Paul gets more specific: he directs them to "restore" those who are caught in any kind of transgression.

---

[169] This would also make "I wish those who unsettle you to emasculate themselves" in parallel to "if you bit and devour each other be careful that you are not consumed by each other" which makes sense. This also fits since "for you were called" is typically relative to a previous clause. The idea suggested by this structure is that 1) Paul moves out of this topic about circumcision by stating "why do I still preach it?" He then rebukes unloving actions (devouring) followed by a shift towards the Galatians need to respond to the devouring with love. He ultimately says, those who live under the law are not fulfilling the law because they are not living in love.

"Caught" comes from a word that means either "to get involved in" from one aspect to "captured or imprisoned" on the other extreme. Here it could be either. Someone involved in an offensive behavior or someone addicted to an offensive behavior. The element that may suggest the latter is the requirement to "restore" the person which may suggest a stronger captivity to the action than simply "involved in" though we should not use this suggestion as a way to weigh how we might serve each other.

The behavior this person is addicted to is either 1) sin (or error, mistake[170]), 2) apostasy (it used the same root as "to fall away" Paul used in 5.3 "to fall away from grace," or 3) offense against another person. Contextually it seems either apostasy or offense against a person fits best. Paul is probably either challenging the spiritual to restore those who are not believing the gospel (apostasy) or those who are causing the division. Admittedly, these two descriptions are relevant to the same group. The false teachers, those who taught and practiced law, clearly did not live by grace (faith in the Spirit). Their lives, as law based lives, ended up being defined by offensive and divisive behaviors. Generally, the closer context would determine we read this as "offensive against others" but the parallel helps us see that Paul connects here this offensive behavior to those who do not live in faith in the Spirit.

Whether Paul wants us to read this as moral failure generally, a behavior that leads to offense or abandoning the gospel, the response the spiritual person has is "to restore." The term restore means to make whole. It was used to describe the mending process one might use for a net, a cloth or an injury, including resetting a bone. This describes a process (it is a present tense verb: continual action) wherein a person regularly and repeatedly takes the necessary steps to help someone return to a place of "wholeness." That wholeness may be in relation to the offensive or immoral behavior (they are returned to the body in peace) or in relation to returning to faith in the gospel. Paul says to do

---

[170] Used to described a costly military decision that caused loss in battle.

this habitually or receptively. It suggests the same regular maintenance one might think of when a fisherman mends his nets weekly or even in our time, the regular work necessary to give someone physical therapy. Paul uses the term prautes to describe how the spiritual are to approach this therapy. This term serves two purposes: 1) to connect this action back to the fruit of the Spirit showing us that a) this is love (see above) and b) this is what the Spirit does in us when we walk in the Spirit and 2) it, more obviously, shows what our approach to restoration should (or will look like) when we are spiritual. It is kind, gracious, gentle, slow, compassionate and loving. The importance of using this kind of word here is that it helps us see what the loving action looks like. One might, if simply "love" was used, think of the love one shows when they tell a person hard truths in a firm and potentially aggressive way. Paul uses the term *prautes* to help us understand what love looks like when it is from the Spirit -it is not harsh or aggressive.

When a person walks in the Spirit, the Spirit bears his life, his fruit into them. That fruit is characterized by gentle love. When that love is applied in situations when another Christian is struggling with a moral issue or a doctrinal issue, one that causes division especially, the "spiritual person" mends and restores the person slowly, gently and patiently. (We would add all of the descriptions of the fruit of the Spirit here.)

During this process a person should also continually watch or guard themselves. This verb (keep watch) is a present participle. It tells the reader how they are to "restore" others or how that process should be characterized. It could even be translated "When you are guarding yourselves mend others" or more traditionally, "Mend others while also guarding yourselves." The parallel text, 5.11-4, ends with the phrase "watch yourself" using a different word, *blepo* versus *skopo*, but both have a similar meaning. So, in 5.14 Paul says watch out that you do not consume each other and here he says, while you are watching yourselves, mend each other." It is this "mending" intention or philosophy, that happens as one watches out for destructive behavior, that protects a person from being tested. If you focus on restoring and mending others then even as you "Watch out for yourself" you will not be tested in this way. In other words, you will not be tested or shown to bite and devour others.

Paul uses the terminology "testing" (*peiradzo*) here and a synonym in 6.4 (*dokimadzo*). He previously used the idea of testing when describing the experience the Galatians had when they took care of Paul during his ailment. His condition was a "trial" or testing for them. This may suggest that Paul's condition was similar to the *paraptome* above, the offensive or moral issue or, and more likely, Paul here connects the "mending" the spiritual will do to the "physical mending" they contributed to him. In his case, as they loved him by serving him during his physical ailment they experienced a trial, test or difficult experience (*peiradzo*). In the case here, they will love their brothers by serving them during a spiritual ailment and then not experience, because of the work of restoration, a trial, test or difficult experience. Most likely here, Paul means "testing" in the sense of temptation. The temptation or allurement is described in the second half of this paragraph.

**Galatians 6.2** "Bear one another's burdens, and so fulfill the law of Christ." (Ἀλλήλων τὰ βάρη βαστάζετε καὶ οὕτως ἀναπληρώσετε τὸν νόμον τοῦ Χριστοῦ.)

At the end of part 2 of this section Paul describes the process from the previous verse. Here he gives the command to bear the burdens of other believers. This statement echos what Paul said in 5.10 where Paul says that those who are causing division and troubling the Galatians through their false, anti-gospel doctrine, will bear judgment. Those who "mend" others will bear the burdens of others and in so doing will not even face the same trials much less the negative outcome of "judgment." (See 5.10-11)

The verb bear is present tense imperative verb. Paul here says, then, to always over and over bear, help carry, the difficulties of others. The term burden means simply difficulty. It is often used to describe the difficult part of a job: the labor intensive part. Always help each other with the difficult parts Paul says.

From "Brothers" to "Bear each other's burdens" forms part one of this section. The phrase "And so fulfill the law of Christ" occurs in the center right between part one and part two. Its position tells that this paragraph is about "fulfilling the law of Christ." Also, it is linked structurally to "fulfill the law: love you neighbor" (5.14) showing what Paul means by the law of Christ. Putting the connections together we learn: 1) Loving a neighbor (another believer mainly) fulfills the Mosaic Law ironically more than trying to obey that very list of rules; 2) the law of Christ is "to love your neighbor" and 3) this loving action is a part of the fruit that the Spirit bears in the life of the one who walks with the Spirit. This layering suggests that those who try to do the law do not actually do it. Those who walk in the Spirit fulfill the law of Christ and in so doing fulfill the essence of the Mosaic law too. By trying, through human faculties, to perform righteousness and the law a person fails to meet the standard. By instead, in faith, living in intimacy with the Spirit waiting on him to create righteousness in a person the law is met and superseded.

**Galatians 6.3** "For if anyone thinks he is something, when he is nothing, he deceives himself." (εἰ γὰρ δοκεῖ τις εἶναί τι μηδὲν ὤν, φρεναπατᾷ ἑαυτόν.)

Paul continues here to explain why someone should live out what he has just described. Grammatically the "for" (gar) explains "Bear" in the previous verse. Semantically we could say it explains all of 5.1-2. The first justification Paul gives for practicing the mending behavior is that a person who "evaluates himself to be something while actually being nothing deceives himself." This conditional clause could refer to a person who does not practice the restoration ministry prescribed above. This person evaluates themselves highly though they are not actually anything. This may suggest a person who sees themselves as meeting the standard of God's law because of their religious works even though this doesn't actually make them better before God or compared to others. The term is connected structurally, semantically and lexically to *kendoxos* above (conceited in 5.25) which means "to think highly of oneself with no reasons, i.e. vainly." The person here does the same. They think highly of themselves ("to be something") but their estimation is vain. This suggests that Paul is contrasting the behavior of one who lives in the Spirit, love, bearing each others burdens, etc., with those who live by the flesh: conceited, thinking themselves something while actually being nothing. This inner-textual (or intextual) link helps us read these verses more accurately. They are focused on the same conceited, divisive legalistic approach Paul has spend pages rebuking. They are, he shows clearly by making this connection, the same as the conceited in 5.25, those who mature through the flesh in 5.16, those who bite and devour in 5.15; those who unsettle the Galatians and persecute Paul in 5.11-12; those who trouble the Galatians in 5.10; those who hinder the Galatians from progressing in the gospel in 5.7 and probably personified by "Hagar and Ishmael" at the end of chapter 4. This person tricks himself. The term "deceive" was repeated from 5.10 "to take another view" from the gospel. These are giving themselves another false view. (Notice also the lexical and semantic parallels to chapter 2.1-10. "Those who were thought be something.")

**Galatians 6.4** "But let each one test his own work, and then his reason to boast will be in himself alone and not in his neighbor." (τὸ δὲ ἔργον ἑαυτοῦ δοκιμαζέτω ἕκαστος, καὶ τότε εἰς ἑαυτὸν μόνον τὸ καύχημα ἕξει καὶ οὐκ εἰς τὸν ἕτερον·)

This sentence literally says "But the works of him he boasts in each person." The "of him" tells us that Paul is still referring to the same person. He deceives himself thinking he is something being nothing and he "tests" his works. The term "test" is lexically parallel to "evaluates" (thinks in ESV) from verse 3 and semantically parallel to "tests" or "trial" (tempted in ESV) in verse 1b. Here it most likely means to test and then to "approve" his works. Another potentially fitting meaning is "to find worthwhile." Basically, he evaluates himself as something in the previous verse is repeated here as "approves his own works." This person assesses himself as good enough or even as the standard of holiness. This leads to this person having pride and boasting in himself only and not in others. Note the parallel between this verse and the "conceit" in 5.25. A flesh built person has pride in their own works, vain empty, reasonless pride and not in others. They do not approach those "captured by an offense" with an intend to mend with gentleness and graciousness. They bite and chew and provoke "calling them out." (Consider the use of the term works here again. Throughout Galatians -as opposed to some other epistles- works is considered as a negative and structurally refers to works that come from human faculties.)

Paul will use this same term in his last paragraph to clarify what he means by "another. Neighbor in ESV but more literally "another." Here he does not boast in "another" but himself.""But far be it from me to boast except in the cross of our Lord Jesus Christ" (Galatians 6.14 ESV) The legalists, in contrast, seem to boast in themselves because of the religious performance of the Galatians.

The other parallel may suggest that Paul says "these approve of their own works" and those who walk in the Spirit mending others with the spirit of gentleness need no test nor will experience one. The tests -to approve or not to approve- are over.

**Galatians 6.5** "For each will have to bear his own load." (ἕκαστος γὰρ τὸ ἴδιον φορτίον βαστάσει.)

At the conclusion of this paragraph Paul repeats a similar phrase he used to end part 1 (5.1-2a). He says "For each will have to bear his own load." Again, it is "each of these" contextually. Each of these, those who are conceited and use their own works as the standard by which they boast in themselves and do not serve others, these have to bear their own burdens. Paul switches the term for burden to "cargo load" suggesting he wants us to see this life as one that has to carry more by trying to carry all alone.

# Galatians 6.6-10

**Interpretive Translation:**

Those who follow the teacher's ideas[171] should stay connected and committed to helping each other in every way. Do not allow yourself to be tricked or misled into false conclusions. God can't be outwitted or tricked himself. No matter what you think or do this will always be true: the type of seed a person plants into the soil determines the type of fruit they will harvest. When someone plants seeds that come from natural, human faculties the harvest will be the best a human can produce, but that will still ultimately be a harvest that rots and decays. On the other hand, when someone plants seeds that come from the Spirit they will harvest the best the Spirit can produce, a harvest that is connected to never-ending, supernatural life.[172] Just like the farmer must patiently wait on the harvest, we should not stop waiting on the Spirit to produce good fruit.[173] We will reap this fruit when its harvest season arrives as long as we do not give up too soon.[174] So then, as we begin to experience the fruit of this harvest,[175] we should help everyone in beneficial and meaningful ways prioritizing the community that believes the gospel of faith.[176]

---

[171] Lit. "Let them fellowship and partner, those who are taught the system by the teacher in all good things." Those who share are the ones who have been taught and not the teacher. (could be "let them share, those who are taught the system, with the teacher all good things.")

[172] Versus "an age of evil dominion" instead of "ages of the dominion of life." (cf. 1.3)

[173] Lit: "The good producing, we must not stop waiting for."

[174] Sounds similar to "wait on the hope of righteousness in the Spirit" from Galatians 5.3.

[175] In context "as we have season" refers to the time of harvest. "As we have possessed harvest time," i.e. reap the fruit of the harvest.

[176] Paul says "*oikos* of faith." In 2.15-19 he discussed "re-*oikosing*" the law system. So here, he most likely refers to those who believe and live by the real gospel, the system of faith.

**Summary Commentary:**

Paul has spent most of chapter five and the first paragraph of chapter six showing the reader the life they should expect when they live by faith. This life is one by the Spirit as we wait on the desire for righteousness from him. This righteousness, Paul says, is ultimately defined as love for others. In its simplest form, the fruit of the Spirit is love. Paul gives a tangible description of what this love looks like in 5.1-5. We bear each other's burdens. A life of helping others flows out of "walking with the Spirit."

With this in mind we have the context for the paragraph at hand: walking in the Spirit creates love for others in our hearts. So, when we read the command to "share" in all good things we are not surprised. We will see in a more detailed analysis below that Paul most likely expects any who are adherents to his teaching remaining in Galatia to fellowship and partner together. His focus continues to be on how they help each other. Some commentaries suggest this text is a turn towards a request from Paul for financial support. They may very well be; Paul does so elsewhere notably in 2 Corinthians. Context suggests Paul continues in this text with the same theme in the previous section: helping each other. (See more below.) Paul warns the Galatians against deception. The false teachers in the previous section were deceived over evaluating their own works and thereby thinking they were good enough. Paul is warning against this same deception. In some ways one could say the book of Galatians could be titled: do not be deceived. Those who believe and teach a false gospel are in Galatia attempting to deceive them. The result of this deception is God being mocked. Paul says that a person makes a mockery of God when they are deceived in the ways those are described as being deceived in the previous paragraph.

The principle that overcomes or trumps the error that mocks God is the idea that the type of seed a person plants into the soil determines the type of fruit that will be harvested. Paul, in the rest of the paragraph explains how this idea relates to "walking in the Spirit." He says that a person can sow seed from the Spirit or the flesh. The flesh, the natural man's seed produces death, decay and rottenness. It is human, what else should be expected? The Spirit's seed produces eternal life, the life that is eternal in quality. This analogy describes walking in the Spirit to be a matter of faith. The seed one plants reveals the fruit they want and the source they look to for that fruit.

Paul goes on to explain the main reason he uses the seed analogy. (Note the connection to the fruit of the Spirit above.) It represents the process he has described earlier. The seed goes into the ground (faith) and then the farmer waits on it to produce. The focus in the next two sentences is on waiting: not giving up on the Spirit. Every seed has a process of planting, growth, blossoming, etc. The seed has a season too. It will produce during its unique harvest time. We just have to wait on it, him. As we wait on him the harvest season will arrive ("opportunity" in ESV) and when it does, when the fruit of the Spirit is ready, we will work the good, the beneficial for everyone, but especially those who are in the household of faith. This last reference, the household of faith, is in parallel to "those who are taught the message by the teacher" in verse 6.6 above. This helps us define both Paul's meaning there and here. The household of faith is the part of the audience that still adheres to Paul's gospel message.

**Galatians 6.6** "Let the one who is taught the word share all good things with the one who teaches." (Κοινωνείτω δὲ ὁ κατηχούμενος τὸν λόγον τῷ κατηχοῦντι ἐν πᾶσιν ἀγαθοῖς.)

The subject of this verse is "the one who was taught." The term *katēcheō* typically refers to the adherent to a detailed system of teaching. The same root describes the teacher. These are the ones taught the system by the system's teacher. This may be a way for Paul to refer to the adherents of his message. The present tense verb form suggests this concept as well. This was a practice the followers regularly participated in. He is stating this concept as a principle instead of a personal request. The principle is that all the adherents of a "teaching" should take care of each other. What have the teacher's followers been taught- "the word." As modern readers we immediately read "the word" as Scripture. Paul typically used the term "writings" when referring to "Scripture." In this context it most likely means something like theology, doctrine, philosophy, ideas, etc. Verse 10 parallels this sentence and describes this same group of people as "the household of faith" or those in the community who live by faith instead of law. These adherents to a specific philosopher's ideas should "share all good things." The term translated share comes from *koinōneō* meaning to share in things, goods, community etc. as well as to socialize and connect. It can also mean "to partner in a joint cause." To simplify, they should share all good things, socialize in good ways or partner together for good purposes. The only other time Paul uses this root in Galatians is in chapter 2 where he says Peter, James and John "gave him the right hand of *koinoneia*." In this context the term suggests partnership and alignment. Paul uses many of the same words in both 2.1-14 and this text which implies that Paul is ultimately suggesting that all of his followers do exactly the same thing he and the Jerusalem leaders did in chapter two. They welcomed each other as being a part of the same group and teaching the same message. (Paul could be saying here that those who heard his teaching previously, the Galatians, should offer him the same *koinoneai*.)

The term translated in the ESV as "goodness" in 5.22, *agathōsynē*, may give us a hint to Paul's exact point. In the verse at hand the term *agathōsynē* is behind the English gloss "good things." This is likely an intentional connection to "agathōsynē" above in the description of the fruit of the Spirit. As we saw above, it suggests doing good, helpful, tangibly beneficial actions for others. In this context we might suggest that "all good things" means to help each other in tangibly beneficial ways like acts of service and taking care of each others' needs. (This same phenomenon happens in the previous paragraph where Paul uses another reference in the fruit of the Spirit description, *prautes*, to define "bearing each other's burdens," i.e. loving each other.) In verses 9 and 10 Paul appears to give us parallel ideas: v.9 "produce the good" and "working the good." Both terms lean toward taking action that brings beneficial results: action, serving, helping etc.

Literally the verse says, "Let them share, the ones who are taught the logos by the teacher, in all good things." A possible translation that reflects the meaning of the text could be: Those who follow the teacher's ideas should stay connected and committed to helping each other in every way.

**Galatians 6.7** "Do not be deceived: God is not mocked, for whatever one sows, that will he also reap." (Μὴ πλανᾶσθε, θεὸς οὐ μυκτηρίζεται. ὃ γὰρ ἐὰν σπείρῃ ἄνθρωπος, τοῦτο καὶ θερίσει·)

Remembering that Paul had just recently discussed those who have been deceived (using a different root in this case) Paul warns the Galatians to not be deceived. Galatians 6.3 says, "When someone has a high estimation of himself even though that person actually doesn't come close to the standard God expects, that person tricks themselves into their false arrogant conclusions." (My translation) In the previous text, Paul links those who are conceited with no valid reason (5.25), those who think they are something while being nothing, and those who are deceived. The wording Paul uses here suggests a link to that same group, their thinking, doctrine and the selfish behavior that comes out of it. Paul in some ways says here "Do not think like those who are troubling you with a false gospel." These connections help us understand what Paul meant when he wrote next "God is not mocked." This could be understood as a command like "let them share" in 6.6. Here it could be "let him not be mocked" which means in its deep structure "do not mock God." The term "mock" is a present passive verb regardless meaning that the actor in this sentence is not God but someone else and that the action described is continual action. So "Stop mocking God" could be a way to understand the sentence or "God is never mocked" if the indicative is to be read instead of the imperative.

The term mocked, "myktērizō," means to turn up the nose at someone or something or treat them with contempt. Other ways to read it include: to ridicule, to sneer. This is what the Pharisees and other rulers of Jerusalem did to Jesus when they thought his teaching was absurd or laughable. In this case, the term followed a formula: Jesus said X. The Pharisees heard Y. They responded with *mykterizo*; they thought his teaching was proven ridiculous. In each case though they had not understood what was really going on. Time or a more accurate understanding of reality would reveal his teaching was not ridiculous. Do not be deceived by the false teachings. Do not think God ridiculous in your deception. Paul may here connect this statement to the word picture he is about to describe. The mockery associated with God in this text may be related to one's expectation that a seed of one type not produce another type (which is absurd), or it might be connected to waiting for the seed to bear fruit. In the latter example we might imagine Paul addressing someone who mocks the promise Paul has implied. If you wait on the Spirit he will give you righteousness. If their response is mockery, "where is it?" his answer is "just wait."

As we suggested above this can be taken as a command "do not ridicule God" (as a result of being deceived like those in the previous section) or as a promise "God will not ultimately be ridiculed." The context suggests an imperative based on the preceding imperatives and those in parallel texts below. Ridicule becomes a sort of designation of not having faith and not waiting on God: to not have faith is part and parcel with ridicule and laughing at God. (Not much different than what Ishmael did to Isaac.)

"for whatever one sows, that will he also reap." - Literally this clause is "what, if a man might sow, this also he will reap." "What" is the direct object of the verb sow. We might also translate it "if a man sows whatever, this he will also reap." This could have been a common phrase in the culture. The meaning is clear. The thing a man sows he also reaps. Or the type of seed a man sows he reaps the same type of thing. It important to point out that Paul gives this sowing and reaping analogy after describing the produce of the Spirit, the fruit of the Spirit above. He is in the same mental picture. Next, he will elaborate on how he connects the two ideas together.

**Galatians 6.8** "For the one who sows to his own flesh will from the flesh reap corruption, but the one who sows to the Spirit will from the Spirit reap eternal life." (ὅτι ὁ σπείρων εἰς τὴν σάρκα ἑαυτοῦ ἐκ τῆς σαρκὸς θερίσει φθοράν, ὁ δὲ σπείρων εἰς τὸ πνεῦμα ἐκ τοῦ πνεύματος θερίσει ζωὴν αἰώνιον)

This verse includes two parallel sentences that occur in the middle and at the peak of this section. They explain the idea above. "A person reaps the same kind as they sow." We might read "for" as "for example." In the first sentence the sower plants "with his flesh." If the previous sentence sets the stage for the entire word picture. The flesh, or natural human aspects of the person, is the "seed" the sower plants. The action of the planting is a continual action. The sower continually plants these seeds. One might see this as an analogy for "seeking the life in the seed" or "seeking righteousness in the faculties and abilities of the natural man." In other words, faith in the flesh. What does the sower get from these seeds? He gets flesh back, or, we might say, the best the natural man can produce. Paul then describes the flesh this sower reaps as "corruption" using a word that can mean decay, rottenness and death. No doubt two word-plays are occurring. The moment a living thing is harvested from the ground it begins to die, which is then seen in its rottenness and decay. Actual physical flesh is the same. The moment it stops receiving life (i.e. oxygen, breath, "spirit") it begins to die and move towards the same decay. Paul uses this physical outcome as a picture of the kind of produce the "human nature" can produce. This term is also used in Genesis to describe the condition of humanity are the fall: human nature was perverted and "filled with iniquity." Paul's logic seems to be that human nature, disconnected from the life of God, cannot be expected to produce life. Death produces death. There may also be a connection back to "envious" in the list of works of the flesh above. The two terms are phonetically almost the same. (*phthora* and *phthonos*) This connection suggests that Paul wants us to read this sentence in light of this list. This decay can be found in the list and the list can be characterized by decay. It is also in contrast to the eternal life that characterizes the fruit of the Spirit in the next clause too. Paul here intends for us to contrast again the fruit of the Spirit and the work of the flesh: they both produce the lists above and those lists are here described as death and life respectively.

The next sentence contrasts with the first. The one who continually sows the seed with the Spirit, i.e. the working of the Spirit, the life of the Spirit, out of the Spirit will reap life. This life is divine, supernatural life as designated by the descriptor eternal. Paul may intend a contrast to the "dominating evil age" that Christ delivers us from in Galatians 1.4. (Both use the same root: *aionos*.) While the connection is weak in some ways, the fact that Paul might end the book by answering a question he implied in its beginning should not surprise the reader. Instead of the dominating evil era, rule, we have life from the Spirit that is of the eternal era.

Most importantly, the connections in this text to the previous section(s) suggest that Paul is not referring in this section to making donations to his ministry. He is continuing along the same thought process he began in chapter five and further describing the nature of waking in the Spirit. In this case, he uses the terminology "sowing with the Spirit."

We will remember here too that the law and flesh produce death. The problem Paul says with the law is that it cannot produce life. He says this in parallel with texts referring to the inheritance, the promise, and the Spirit. The Spirit then, is the "life producer" that contrasts the law and the flesh that cannot produce life.

**Galatians 6.9** "And let us not grow weary of doing good, for in due season we will reap, if we do not give up." (τὸ δὲ καλὸν ποιοῦντες μὴ ἐγκακῶμεν, καιρῷ γὰρ ἰδίῳ θερίσομεν μὴ ἐκλυόμενοι.)

Paul continues the sowing/harvesting word picture. The ESV translates *poieo* ("to do, make, produce") as "do" here but in context, it most likely refers to "produce." (Same term used when Paul says earlier "if a law could have been written that could produce life.") The topic then is to "produce good." The good most likely refers to the fruit of the Spirit above. It is in parallel to *agathos* (seen again in the next clause) and through that connection most likely means the good the Spirit produces. We should not "grow weary" or, a better translation might be "not stop waiting" or "not give up" on the production of good. Poieo (to do, produce) is a present particle. The subject of this particle may be undefined meaning that we are waiting not on ourselves to produce good but on another. This clause could be translated as "Do not stop waiting on the one who produces good." Contextually, this fits better than most English translations that suggest the sower is to not stop doing good themselves. The word picture of the sower waiting on harvest sets the context too. Another literal translation of the text could be "We do not do bad when he does good." While this is not a good translation it does help us see the contrasting roots between the two phases. We do not "lose enthusiasm," i.e. quit waiting -which comes from the root "to do bad" -*kakos*. The Spirit does "good," *kalos*. This may explain why Paul uses *kalos* here instead of *agathos* which he uses below.

Why do we not stop waiting for the good to be produced? Because "in due season" we will harvest. In due season means "in its time" or "in the seed's time." Every type of seed has a time it should be planted, a time it needs to grow until maturity and bear ripe fruit and then a time it needs to be harvested. When Paul says "in its time," he is referring to its harvest season. We will eventually have a harvest, during the harvest season if we "do not give up." Most translators see this term, *ekluo*, as parallel with, egkakeō, which we translated as "do not stop waiting" and the ESV translated as "do not grow weary" (means "lose enthusiasm"). No doubt Paul intended this parallelism. The term in the second phrase, *ekluo*, may add the sense of "lose strength" or give out. In both cases, the admonition relates to quitting. Do not quit waiting.

We could summarize this text as, "Do not stop waiting on the one who produces good (the fruit of the Spirit). We will have a harvest of this good fruit when harvest time occurs as long as we simply do not get too exhausted to wait."

**Galatians 6.10** "So then, as we have opportunity, let us do good to everyone, and especially to those who are of the household of faith." (Αρα οὖν ὡς καιρὸν ἔχομεν, ἐργαζώμεθα τὸ ἀγαθὸν πρὸς πάντας, μάλιστα δὲ πρὸς τοὺς οἰκείους τῆς πίστεως.)

As we move into this final sentence remember that it is parallel to this first sentence "Share good with those who were taught by the teacher," i.e. share good with fellow adherents to the teacher's doctrine. It is also parallel to "producing good" in verse 9. Paul says here, "so then" suggesting a conclusion to the paragraph, "as we have opportunity." Opportunity is the same word as "season" in the previous sentence (kairos). This suggests that Paul is referring to the harvest in this text too. In these words, he is not saying that this command should be followed when an opportunity arises but when the fruit of Spirit is produced or experienced. This is a different way of saying what he said in Galatians 5.3 "Wait on the desire for righteous by the Spirit." So, the moment we are looking for is not opportune based on external circumstances or situations but on the internal work of the Spirit. "As you experience the season of harvesting the fruit of the Spirit, we must work good." This is the first time Paul has stated explicitly that a person should "work" in the epistle. He spends the entire letter describing how works should truly operate. They arise out of the production of the Spirit at the right time. We simply wait on them. Again, he uses the term agathos, as he did in verse 6, to describe working or acting in such a way that is helpful. He may also intend to connect his phrase "faith works" from Galatians 5.4 to this paragraph. There "faith works" (*energon*) because of love (as love fills the heart) as a result of a person's waiting on the Spirit to enflame love in us. Here, we work as a result of waiting for the fruits of the Spirit -love, goodness, etc.- to be produced in us. When it is we work good -that which is helpful and beneficial- towards everyone. Again, by making the connection back to the list of descriptions of the fruits of the Spirit, Paul infers that he does not only mean "good" but all the characteristics of the fruits of the Spirit in service to others. The preposition "pros" in the phrase "for all" could mean here "in addition to all." So that we are working not only the good -as Paul noted above in verse 6- but "in addition to all the fruits of the Spirit."

Paul adds a final note that reflects the sentiment he shared at the beginning of the paragraph. We should work "good" and all the fruits of the Spirit mostly toward the household of faith. This is a way for Paul to describe those who follow the gospel of faith he has repeatedly explained and defended here. Paul's unique admonition is to act graciously to those who are true believers.

# Galatians 6.11-16

**Interpretive Translation:**

Now look at this! I am writing this part with my own hand. That's why it has such large letters. (I wouldn't be able to do this if you hadn't helped me during my visit!) Let me summarize what has been said. If someone pressures you to practice circumcision, it is because they are obsessed[177] with looking good when it comes to human morality and religion.[178] They only care about avoiding the attacking persecution and offensive message that comes from an authentic understanding of the meaning of Christ's death on the cross. This is obvious when you look at their lives. They themselves do not practice many of the rules and regulations written in the Torah, but they are obsessed with making sure you practice circumcision so that they can they can tell everyone in Jerusalem about your human religious zeal and look good in front of their legalistic friends.

With me, it will never be this way. I don't want to brag about anything I do or you do to anyone. I only brag about the very message they are afraid of being associated with: the message about our Lord Jesus Christ's death on the cross. I only want him to look good even if it makes me and our religion look bad. When he died on the cross I also died to the natural human universe of law; and obedience and this system, this universe is dead to me. I no longer live in a world where I am required to obey the rules and regulations of the Torah or those written into the fabric of nature. Now, as I said earlier, circumcision means nothing. Uncircumcision is nothing. The only thing that matters now is the new system, the new creation. This is a creation that the Spirit is forming through faith as we wait on Him to create it in us and through us just like the seeds create supernatural life as we wait on them. You will experience peace and a supernatural desire for righteousness as you live in this new system, walking along the path

---

[177] Lit "they continually desire"

[178] "with flesh" could also be "with others."

with the Spirit. You will be the true Israel of God, the true seed. As for the rest of you. Leave me alone and stop bothering me. I myself already bear physical wounds as a result of serving Jesus. These wounds mark me as a slave of Christ. Let the free favor that our Lord Jesus Christ gives fill your heart and dominate your thinking, dear family. Let it be.

**Summary Commentary:** Paul ends his letter by returning to many elements of the material from previous texts. Mainly, he echoes what was said in 2.1-14 and then again in 5.1-14. His conclusion serves to identify his chief ideas. Here those ideas are that circumcision or any law following stands in contrast to the message of the cross and ultimately such disassociation as its goal. The cross says the law is not good enough and that we need his death. The law says you can be good enough. Paul summarizes a key takeaway of the book by returning to our joint crucifixion with Christ. Previously he has said that we are dead to the law and that we crucify our natural way of thinking and being godly (the flesh). Here he refers to these same concepts as the "cosmos." This reference refers to the system, the natural, created system that he has identified with the law, both those written in the Torah and those written into the fabric of the universe. (See commentary on Galatians 4.6ff). He is dead to this system because he died with Christ. In its place a new creation, a new system exists. In this system following the law or not following the law means nothing. It is nothing. The only thing that matters in this new system is this new creation. This text parallels what he said in Galatians 5.3-4, but instead of "new creation" he says that it is faith that activates through love that operates effectually in this new system. This statement is explained when he describes this operating process as "waiting on the Spirit for the hope of righteousness in faith." In other words, this love, this hope is given to whoever lives by faith and waits on the Spirit to produce it or create it. We would say, in this light, that we wait on the new creation of the Spirit in the world, in us and through us, a creation that arises out of love for others. The Spirit is the creative force and love is the creation in the new system. Paul returns to both mercy, perhaps as a reference to Galatians 5.3, and peace, as a reference to the fruit of the Spirit, as he finishes his remarks. Those who walk in the Spirit, who step in the path based on this new standard, system or dominion (rule in ESV), experience mercy and peace. These are not only the seed, as we saw in chapters 3 and 4, they are the true Israel of God, the new Israel.

**Galatians 6.11** "See with what large letters I am writing to you with my own hand." (Ἴδετε πηλίκοις ὑμῖν γράμμασιν ἔγραψα τῇ ἐμῇ χειρί)

Paul begins a new paragraph with "See" and he also shows this text serves as a unique semantic peak by adding the phrasing "I write this part with my own hand." The reference to large letters may connect back to his physical ailment in chapter 4 where he seems to refer to experiencing an eye issue. This serves to remind the Galatians of their love for him one more time suggesting that he would not be able to write at all if it was not for their service and love. It is as if to say "Look at me, I am writing and you made it possible." This is another sentimental allure Paul hints at as he woos the Galatians back to the gospel. This may also serve as an inner-textual link to that narrative to help us see that this section ends that section (and then the entire book).

**Galatians 6.12** "It is those who want to make a good showing in the flesh who would force you to be circumcised, and only in order that they may not be persecuted for the cross of Christ." (Ὅσοι θέλουσιν εὐπροσωπῆσαι ἐν σαρκί, οὗτοι ἀναγκάζουσιν ὑμᾶς περιτέμνεσθαι, μόνον ἵνα τῷ σταυρῷ τοῦ Χριστοῦ μὴ διώκωνται.)

Paul will describe "those who want" in the next two verses. Here they want to make a good showing, or to put it more simply, they want to look good "in the flesh" or in the human, natural religious system and moral performance structures. They are showing off based on those who adhere to the practice of circumcision. In a link back to Galatians 2.4, Paul says they compel or require the Galatians to practice circumcision. Here as there, the present tense suggests an ongoing practice versus the event that a person experiences suggesting a prohibition against the religious practice with nothing being inferred about the surgery as a medical procedure. Paul had said that Titus was not compelled or required to be circumcised when he appeared before the Jerusalem council. This link infers a connection. It potentially suggests that while Titus was not required to be circumcised by this group something changed and now they were requiring people to be circumcised out of fear of persecution. They did not want to be persecuted for the cross while Paul, in 5.6 *was* persecuted. The message of the cross suggests the end of circumcision and the law. In so doing, it offended those who maintained the need to keep practicing the law.

**Galatians 6.13** "For even those who are circumcised do not themselves keep the law, but they desire to have you circumcised that they may boast in your flesh." (οὐδὲ γὰρ οἱ περιτεμνόμενοι αὐτοὶ νόμον φυλάσσουσιν ἀλλὰ θέλουσιν ὑμᾶς περιτέμνεσθαι, ἵνα ἐν τῇ ὑμετέρᾳ σαρκὶ καυχήσωνται.)

Before returning to a description of what they "want" and bracketing the first stanza, Paul describes this group as "those who are practicing circumcision." He also says that though they practice circumcision and compel the Galatians to do the same, they themselves do not observe the law. Even with this being the case, they "want" the Galatians to be circumcised. Above they wanted to look good or show off. Here they want the Galatians to practice circumcision so they can brag. Some thought they were something when they were nothing above (6.4). This same boastful spirit characterizes the false teachers. They want to brag about the religious zealousness of the Galatians.

Paul, on the other hand, has no desire to brag about himself or others when it comes to human religious performance.

**Galatians 6.14** "But far be it from me to boast except in the cross of our Lord Jesus Christ, by which the world has been crucified to me, and I to the world." (Ἐμοὶ δὲ μὴ γένοιτο καυχᾶσθαι εἰ μὴ ἐν τῷ σταυρῷ τοῦ κυρίου ἡμῶν Ἰησοῦ Χριστοῦ, δι' οὗ ἐμοὶ κόσμος ἐσταύρωται κἀγὼ κόσμῳ.)

"Let it never be so with me" to brag Paul says in essence declaring a wish, or a desire. He will say in the next clause that he will brag in the cross alone but this suggests that he will not brag in anything else especially the types of supposed successes the false teachers are bragging about: religious and moral performance, being good. He will never brag "except" (in Greek if not in) about the cross of Christ. This sentence parallels the Galatians making a show "only so that about the cross of Christ they would not be attacked." The cross defined Paul's message and he proclaimed it proudly (the term brag originally meant "to cry out loudly and publicly"). The Galatians allowed fear of persecution and ostracization to make them shift from the gospel of the cross to legalism. Peter had done the same stumbling over the gospel out of fear of the circumcision party. Paul did not shift. When Paul described the fear of the false teachers he said they were afraid of being persecuted because of the "cross of Christ." Here he says he is proud of the cross of our Lord Jesus Christ. He uses three extra designations to describe Christ in this case giving a subtle rebuke to those who fear suggesting that they do not know Jesus beyond his designation as "Messiah."

The reason he brags about the cross alone is because of what it accomplished. Here he echos Galatians 2.20 and 5.24. In those cases, it is either plainly stated or suggested strongly that the flesh and law are crucified through our joint crucifixion with Christ. Here it is the "kosmos" that is crucified. Paul is dead to the cosmos and the cosmos is dead to him. He says in other words that this system, the universe if you will, that operates by law and by flesh, that labels actions sin or not sin (c.f. 2.15-18) has no impact or power in his life. He is dead to that structure. This is similar to what he said when he wrote: "If I reestablish the administration I disempowered (The law that defined me as a transgressor), I mark myself as a transgressor. (My translation)." In this same text, he goes on to say that he died to the law, to this system through the rules of this system via the substitutionary death of Christ.

**Galatians 6.15** "For neither circumcision counts for anything, nor uncircumcision, but a new creation." (οὔτε γὰρ περιτομή τί ἐστιν οὔτε ἀκροβυστία ἀλλὰ καινὴ κτίσις)

As if to say "in this system" (as opposed to the one I am dead to) different things matter, different things count. In the old system, circumcision (or not) matters in some way. In this system, it is not anything. This is basically a quote of the last sentence in Galatians 5.5-6 "For through the Spirit, by faith, we ourselves eagerly wait for the hope of righteousness. For in Christ Jesus neither circumcision nor uncircumcision counts for anything, but only faith working through love." Where he says in that text "only faith working through love" here he says "a new creation." When we look back at the original reference we see that Paul ultimately defined how the life of faith "operates." Faith operates through love. He then goes onto describe that in much more detail throughout the rest of the book. In that same text, "faith operating through love" is a summarization of the clause that had gone before it: we wait expectantly on the hope (desire) of righteousness by the Spirit through faith. In other words, in this original verse, Paul says that a life of faith turns into an operating or producing life as the Spirit creates love in the believer's heart. Our posture then is to wait on the Spirit to create this love, this righteousness. So, when Paul says here that a new creation is the only "thing" in this new system he is referring to the work of the Spirit that we wait on as believers. This language also connects to the fruit-bearing language of the "fruit of the Spirit" text in chapter 5 and the "sow with the Spirit" language of the previous text. Text. *Creation* is a near synonym of *produce*. The Spirit bears fruit that is eternal life, supernatural life. In the old paradigm, people performed, produced and were responsible for creating. In this paradigm the Spirit performs, produces and creates not a fleshly, dying, decaying, rotting works but fruit characterized by God's life force. In the new system, the new universe, the Spirit is creating something new in us and through us, the kingdom of God, the domain created through love, God's reconciling love wherein he reconciles all things and all people to himself. Ephesians 2.10 says we are created by Christ Jesus and 2.15 says that he "created in himself" (in Christ) "one new man," the new man being that which is reconciled and unified to Jesus. Ephesians 4.23 says we are made new in the spirit of our minds and put on this new man which is created in the likeness of God himself. Here, at the end of Galatians and the start of Ephesians, Paul emphasizes the work of the Spirit as the work of new creation, a theme that he will elaborate on more fully in the letter to the Ephesians.

**Galatians 6.16** "And as for all who walk by this rule, peace and mercy be upon them, and upon the Israel of God." (καὶ ὅσοι τῷ κανόνι τούτῳ στοιχήσουσιν, εἰρήνη ἐπ' αὐτοὺς καὶ ἔλεος καὶ ἐπὶ τὸν Ἰσραὴλ τοῦ θεοῦ.)

In many ways, this begins a common salutation for Paul to the "brothers." "Peace and Mercy" Distinctive to this sentence though is Paul's designation of peace and mercy to be directed towards "as many as step by this rule." He uses the same term as he used in Galatians 5.25 when he said "If we live by the Spirit, we should also walk in his path." (My translation). As we saw in the study of that text *stoicheo* means to walk in line, walk behind, to march to orders, or to walk in the footprints or path of another. Paul uses the same root here to make sure we connect the ideas here, new creation, different "cosmos" to that line of thinking. He could have said, "Those who practice what I said in Galatians 5 will have peace and mercy" and the meaning would have been the same. He adds here the new term "kanon" saying that the peace and mercy are for those who walk according to this canon. This could simply refer to "this book" i.e. the message of this book. It could also refer to "this standard" meaning the standard that he has set up. It could also refer to the system of the new creation, the new cosmos, the universe. Kanon is parallel phonetically to "new" *kaineh*. Both may be parallel to kosmos. Most likely these three terms together give us the best sense of the word canon in this context. It refers to "the new system" of the gospel, the new "rule."

He also designates this group as the "Israel of God." Paul similarly develops the idea of Israel in Romans 9-11. In the context of Galatians perhaps Paul is connecting the idea of "the seed of Abraham," of which people are joined by faith so that by that faith they are "the seed of

Abraham," to Israel and giving one last inference to a key theological message. Regardless, he clearly describes those who live by faith in the cross as true Israel providing an implied rebuke to those who live by the law and practice circumcision.

**Galatians 6.17** "From now on let no one cause me trouble, for I bear on my body the marks of Jesus." (Τοῦ λοιποῦ κόπους μοι μηδεὶς παρεχέτω· ἐγὼ γὰρ τὰ στίγματα τοῦ Ἰησοῦ ἐν τῷ σώματί μου βαστάζω.)

Using language that echoes 5.7 "those who hindered you" (same root), Paul designates them outside of peace and mercy. He says, "From the rest, let no one cause me trouble (hinder me)." And then describes himself as bearing the "marks" or "slavery-tatoo" of Christ. This could refer to scars on his body from being beaten for the faith. Paul may intend these scars to serve as a tattoo marking as a servant of Christ. In the same way, he was proud of the cross, he was proud of his identity as a servant of Christ, even if it meant beating. Within context, Paul might be suggesting that the scars on his body serve as a sign of how great a love the Spirit works into the believer: one that serves others even through persecution. (Note again the parallel to Paul's statement about being persecuted in 5.7-10.) Even as he ends his letter he hints at the power of his love for the Galatians and his life, his love, as a proof of the power of the gospel.

**Galatians 6.18** "The grace of our Lord Jesus Christ be with your spirit, brothers. Amen.
 (Η χάρις τοῦ κυρίου ἡμῶν Ἰησοῦ Χριστοῦ μετὰ τοῦ πνεύματος ὑμῶν, ἀδελφοί· ἀμήν.)

In his last sentence, he returns to grace and subtly refers to the new creation from verse 15. "The grace of our Lord Jesus Christ be with your spirit." The spirit refers potentially to the aspect of a person that is the new creation, bonded with Jesus. His prayer then is that his grace fill the spirits and influence the thinking of the Galatians.

# Bibliography

Bauer, W., Danker, F. W. (2000). A Greek-English Lexicon of the New Testament and Other Early Christian Literature, 3rd ed. (BDAG). University of Chicago Press.

Calvin, J. (1854). Calvin's Commentary on Galatians. Calvin Translation Society.

de Boer, M. C. (2011). Galatians: A Commentary (The New Testament Library). N/A.

Desilva, D. (2018). The Letter of Galatians. Wm. B. Eerdmans Publishing.

Dunn, J. (1993). Epistle to the Galatians. Baker Publishing Group.

Keller, T. (2013). Galatians for you. The Good Book Company.

Louw, J. P., Nida, E. A. (1996). Greek-English Lexicon of the New Testament Based on Semantic Domains. United Bible Societies.

Luther, M. (2006). Commentary on the Epistle to the Galatians. Kregel Publication.

Nyland, A. (2010). Galatians: The Source New Testament With Extensive Notes on Greek Word Meaning. Smith and Stirling Publishing.

Robertson, A. T. (2006). Grammar of the Greek New Testament in the Light of Historical Research. Faithlife.

Sailhamer, J. H. (1992). The Pentateuch as Narrative: A Biblical-Theological Commentary. Zondervan.

Sailhamer, J. H. (1994). NIV Compact Bible Commentary. Zondervan.

Sailhamer, J. H. (2009). The Meaning of the Pentateuch: Revelation, Composition and Interpretation. IVP Academic.

Schreiner, T. R. (2010). Exegetical Commentary on the New Testament: Galatians. Zondervan.

Silva, M. (2014). New International Dictionary of New Testament Theology and Exegesis Set (NIDNTTE). Zondervan.

Spicq, C. (1994). Theological Lexicon of the New Testament. Hendrickson.

von Siebenthal, H. (2019). Ancient Greek Grammar for the Study of the New Testament. Peter Lang Publishing.

Printed in Great Britain
by Amazon